PEACEFUL FAMILIES

Peaceful Families

AMERICAN MUSLIM EFFORTS
AGAINST DOMESTIC VIOLENCE

JULIANE HAMMER

PRINCETON UNIVERSITY PRESS

PRINCETON & OXFORD

Published by Princeton University Press
41 William Street, Princeton, New Jersey 08540
6 Oxford Street, Woodstock, Oxfordshire OX20 1TR

press.princeton.edu

Library of Congress Control Number 2018964758
ISBN 978-0-691-19087-7

British Library Cataloging-in-Publication Data is available

Editorial: Fred Appel and Thalia Leaf
Production Editorial: Jill Harris
Jacket Design: Layla Mac Rory
Production: Erin Suydam
Publicity: Nathalie Levine and Kathryn Stevens

This book has been composed in Arno

Printed on acid-free paper. ∞

Printed in the United States of America

10 9 8 7 6 5 4 3 2 1

CONTENTS

ACKNOWLEDGMENTS

THIS BOOK HAS BEEN hard to research and harder to write. It would have been impossible without the enthusiasm and support of the many Muslim advocates and service providers who agreed to share their experiences and tell their stories, and who asked me probing and incisive questions in response to mine. I cannot name them but I hope they know that I am in awe of their courage and determination.

I have been blessed with a family that supports my work and makes my life beautiful. To my partner, Cemil, who is in competition with me over who writes the best acknowledgment: You have been there every step of the way; you have listened and read, commented and mirrored, admired and confirmed, and you have shared my outrage at the pain human beings inflict on each other every day. You are my rock in a world that scares me a little bit more every day—with you I will survive or go down fighting for what is just and beautiful. To Leyla, whose brilliant mind, sparkling wit, and generous love have fueled me in the darkest of times. And to Mehtap, whose heart is so big and whose courage to stand up for what is right seems endless, I think of you when I lose heart. Thank you, for another "Go, Mama, Go" poster for this book and for the one where every letter of my name is an amazing attribute: Joyful, Unstoppable, Loving, Intelligent, Amazing, Never Give Up, Excellent. My daughters are the reason for this work: I want the world to be a better place for them, a place that nurtures them to be their best selves and a place that is safer than it was for me. Recent political developments have both increased my worry for them and demonstrated what is possible when people unite for justice.

In the past few years I have lost several elders: my Papa, Bernhard Hammer, who instilled a love of books, languages, and learning in me; Onkel Hermi, Hermann Hammer, who shared stories and followed my academic career with pride; and 'Ammu Jamil Shami, whose presence was always warm and full of heart and whose absence from the world is deeply felt. The loss of Fatima

Mernissi and Saba Mahmood, two giants in feminist Muslim women studies, has reminded me that life is fragile and that every day matters.

I am grateful for the support and friendship of several women who make the world livable: Saadia Yacoob is always there when I need encouragement and reminds me of the beauty of God's love. Kecia Ali has been on my side, luckily, since we first met, and I have admired her work and her courage for even longer. Aysha Hidayatullah allows me to doubt and to question and cares enough to check in on me when things are the worst. Homayra Ziad has been there for my tirades and with unfailing grace reminds me of what matters. Alison Kysia is the critical and supportive friend every scholar wishes for and this book would not have happened without her. Amal Eqeiq sends me her poetry on postcards from the world and za'tar to remind me of Palestine. Megan Goodwin is often the audience I write for in my head and unfailingly and critically encourages me to dig deeper and try harder in the face of obstacles. Shannon Schorey has convinced me, for now, that theory lives in all kinds of places and that I have it in me. You all are proof that community is what we make it.

I think of sisterhood and lifting each other up in sharing in the struggle in and beyond the academy: Su'ad Abdul Khabeer, Donna Auston, Sylvia Chan-Malik, Rosemary Corbett, Sarah Eltantawi, Zareena Grewal, Shehnaz Haqqani, Sajida Jalalzai, Anne Joh, Sadaf Knight, Debra Majeed, Jerusha Rhodes, Shabana Mir, Fatima Seedat, Sa'diyya Shaikh, Laury Silvers, Riem Spielhaus, Najeeba Syeed, Farah Zeb, and many others.

I acknowledge my indebtedness to the work of Amina Wadud and Ziba Mir-Hosseini in this and my other academic and religious endeavors.

I am grateful for the friendship, occasional snark, and constant intellectual challenges that come from Michael Muhammad Knight—he has changed the way I think about our field and my place in it. Zaid Adhami reminds me that there are good men in the world and that honest debate can be at the core of ethical academic engagement. Carl Ernst, Omid Safi, Kambiz GhaneaBassiri, Edward Curtis, Zaheer Ali, and Mohammad Khalil have provided encouragement along the way and I am grateful for their presence in the field.

I am blessed to have had students who have become colleagues and friends over the years: Ilyse Morgenstein-Fuerst, Kathy Foody, Shailey Patel, Atiya Husain, Katie Merriman, Micah Hughes, Samah Choudhury, Hina Muneeruddin, Alejandro Escalante, Barbara Sostaita, Becca Hendriksen, Israel Dominguez, and Samee Siddiqui. Micah was the only other person who voluntarily read the whole manuscript and provided helpful feedback even though I am his advisor. The decolonial solidarity crew is always on my mind in these difficult times: Imani Wadud, Caleb Moreno, Israel Durham, Amal Eqeiq, Saadia Yacoob, Zaid Adhami, and Jecca Namakkal.

It is customary to thank academic institutions for their support, and I acknowledge fellowship and leave support from George Mason University (GMU), the Institute for Arts and Humanities at the University of North Carolina (UNC) at Chapel Hill, and the UNC Provost's Office, as well as from the Institute for Policy and Understanding in Washington, D.C. It has been extraordinarily difficult to find funding for this project, and my efforts have taught me much about academic priorities, engaged scholarship, and the prevalence of discomfort in talking about domestic violence. The Institutional Review Boards at both GMU and UNC made things difficult but also reminded me of my ethical responsibility toward my interlocutors.

I am thankful to Fred Appel, my editor at Princeton University Press, for working with me for years on this project, for his patience, and for his meaningful and erudite feedback that made the final book better. The two anonymous reviewers of this book helped me see my project more clearly, and I thank them for their thoughtful and detailed and yet overwhelmingly positive comments.

To those who have been victims of domestic violence and to those who are fighting to end domestic abuse: I see you. This book is dedicated to those who continue the struggle and to those who had to rest for a while.

PEACEFUL FAMILIES

1

Shifting Landscapes
and a Missing Map

STUDYING MUSLIM EFFORTS
AGAINST DOMESTIC VIOLENCE

Violence is so ubiquitous and yet sometimes seems far away. Even after all this research I still have to remind myself that every second of my life, someone else's life is defined, limited, and destroyed by people and systems that assume the right to break and cut, to wound and scar, to wield the power over life and death of other human beings.

HOW OFTEN HAVE I SEEN WORDS from a poem by Warsan Shire on social media that talks about the poet touching a map of the world and asking where it hurts? The map answers, on behalf of the world, that it hurts everywhere, and the poem touches me every time.[1] There is so much pain and suffering around us; the whole world is hurting. Much of this human pain and suffering is caused by violence inflicted on some humans by other humans. Even when we think it is elsewhere and not in our lives, this violence is all around us: as state-sanctioned violence, as war, as armed conflict, as sexual assault, as child abuse, as gender-based violence, as racist hate crimes, as incarceration, as gun violence, and the list goes on. The horrors of wounds, blood, and scars are physical but pain comes in many forms, injuries can be nonphysical, and trauma inflicted goes beyond the body.

Why, then, do I write a book about violence? And how do I write such a book? The why is easier to explain: I am writing to stop the violence. I want all of it to end. Now. The how required me to start in a specific place, to think

1

about a specific aspect of the pervasive violence in our lives, and to find ways to go beyond it. My path to that goal has been to write this book about American Muslim efforts against domestic violence (DV). That there are people who, like me, want to end such violence gives me hope and it needs to be known.

Peaceful Families. House of Protection. Domestic Harmony. Healthy Families. House of Peace. These are concepts and indeed visions and goals to be found in the names of American Muslim organizations working against domestic violence in Muslim communities. Their central goal is simple: the eradication of domestic violence, a scourge that affects too many individuals, families, and communities in the United States and all over the world. Their work, however, is complicated, ongoing, and challenging. This book is about the people who carry out anti–domestic violence work in Muslim communities in the United States. It chronicles their efforts, their motivations, and their engagement with gender dynamics, textual interpretation, and religious authority.

It is also a book about domestic violence: about its victims and its perpetrators, about the structures, systems, and principles that allow domestic abuse to continue. It is the trauma and injury of the countless victims that makes the work of the advocates necessary and salient. I have ongoing concerns about erasing the victims and survivors from these pages by focusing on those who advocate for them and offer them support. However, the survivors and their stories are in every chapter and they are the reason this book came into being. I see and remember their pain and their suffering, and I deeply admire those who continue to work to end it. Thus this book on Muslim efforts against domestic violence is also a constant reminder of the existence of such violence in Muslim families and communities.

In what follows, I lay out the framework for the chapters of this book, including the sources and methods I employed in my study, the complex landscape of secondary literature on domestic violence, my arguments and theoretical contributions, the themes I trace throughout my research materials, and, finally, the structure of the book itself. I end with a short reflection on the politics of critique.

Mapping the Project

I was sitting in the back seat of her car when Karima, who was driving me back to the train station after an event at a Muslim community center, asked me how I had developed an academic interest in Muslim efforts against do-

mestic violence. I have been asked the same question by other Muslim advocates many times and still struggle with a short answer. I have not been the
victim or survivor of sustained abuse by an intimate partner, even though
there have been occasions in my life that would count as abusive and damag-
ing. I have only recently begun to piece together instances of abusive relationships that have surrounded me since childhood, but I never recognized or
named them as such before I began this research. If it was not an experience
of abuse or even the conscious witnessing of it, then what did inspire me to
write this book?

It was 2008 and I was reading essays in *Living Islam Out Loud* for my book
project on woman-led Friday prayer and Muslim women's activism. One essay
in the book stood out to me: Mohja Kahf writing about her jadedness in engaging in communal conversations about what Islam is, who has authority,
and how this Islam matters to her. She tells the story of her volunteer work
with a women's shelter and a battered Muslim woman for whom she was asked
to translate. The woman, severely physically and emotionally abused, was convinced that her abuse was in line with Islamic teachings and tried to find fault
with her own actions to justify it. Kahf experienced outrage, but instead of
further distancing herself from Islam and Muslims, she decided to engage:

> We are implicated for dropping out of the community and its discourses
> when we are alienated. For giving up on changing Islam. Like I had. For
> giving up on being part of the conversation, the Islam-talk.... Why I need
> this Islam-talk? Because it was the only talk that would get this battered
> woman out of her old worldview. She would not leave without Islam. She
> has to take her Islam with her to make a new life, a new way of thinking
> about life as a woman, alone in the world. I had to give her a jolt of Islam-
> CPR, and I needed it myself, too.[2]

In her quest for better answers, she encountered the works of Muslim women
scholars, like Amina Wadud, Asma Barlas, and Asifa Qureishi, scholars who
center their own exegetical and legal work on notions of gender justice, a
topic I will return to. She also engaged with more conservative scholars and
leaders and discovered that there was no support for domestic violence among
them either. I will return to this shortly as well. In that moment in 2008,
though, the idea for this research project and book was formed. First, I had to
find out more about domestic violence in Muslim communities. Then I realized that my contribution, as a religious studies scholar, would be to analyze
the religious frameworks and discourses surrounding domestic violence, and

from there it was a logical step to focus on those who produced and applied such frameworks in their efforts to end domestic violence.

The sources for this book are of several different kinds: interviews and participant observation notes from six years of ethnographic research and a wide array of textual materials collected since 2008. As in most of my projects, I combine analysis of ethnographic materials (which become texts through the research process) with the analysis of sources that are more commonly associated with the category text, many of which are categorized as primary texts in the humanities. They include books, articles, blog posts, social media conversations, YouTube videos, song lyrics, poetry, and magazine features to account for the breadth of conversations about domestic violence taking place in Muslim communities. Some are produced by victims and survivors, others by concerned community members, and a significant portion comes from religious scholars and leaders. Some of these textual materials date back to the 1990s while others were produced and included in the project in the last few months of writing in 2017. I began the ethnographic portion of the study in 2010, and in the six years that followed I conducted almost seventy interviews with advocates, activists, and service providers. I also attended over forty events, including DV awareness events in Muslim communities, social service provider conferences, cultural sensitivity training sessions for law enforcement, service providers, and lawyers, and strategic meetings of Muslim DV advocates.

From the outset, it was clear to me that I was not going to create a comprehensive map of Muslim efforts against domestic violence. I do not privilege ethnographic research over textual analysis (or vice versa), nor do I see them in competition with each other. There is an emerging picture in my analysis, and there are patterns, but most important, there are stories to be told and stories to be analyzed. My greatest regret is that only a fraction of the stories, people, ideas, and materials I encountered have made it into the book.

There is a second reason for the missing map alluded to in the title of this chapter: the landscape of Muslim efforts against domestic violence is constantly changing. There are many reasons for the relative instability of this landscape, including the toll that the work takes on those engaged in the field, leading to burnout and high turnover rates; the oscillating and challenging shifts in funding (and the lack thereof); the political landscape of anti-Muslim hostility and anti-feminist backlash; and the very nature of nonprofit organizations and movements.

This means that the people I interviewed may or may not still be in this line of work or activism. The organizations I worked with may have ceased to exist, they may continue to be actively engaged in these efforts, or they may have moved on to merge with larger organizations or have incorporated DV-focused programs into other social service frameworks.

Despite this shifting landscape, the scene or movement against DV among Muslims is small, small enough for people to know each other. It was thus important and necessary to obscure the identities of those I interviewed—because there are risks associated with involvement in anti-DV work that range from stigmatization in communities to threats of violence from perpetrators of DV. I employ several strategies to help ensure confidentiality. Some, like using pseudonyms for people, are common in ethnographic research and writing. Others, such as creating composite stories in some of the chapters, will garner more skepticism but are justified by the need for protection. Where that is the case, I have indicated it in the chapter. I also decided to not disclose which organizations I worked with because it is rather easy to identify individuals associated with certain organizations. There were many more organizations than I could directly research during the project. Where possible in terms of confidentiality, I acknowledge ideas and materials produced by specific organizations to give credit to them for their intellectual work.

In my six years of active ethnographic research, I encountered many people whom I consider heroes, women and men, who invest their lifetime, their energy, and their courage in this work. I entered their networks and circles as a Muslim insider, albeit as one who is easily identified as a Muslim feminist. As a white Muslim woman, as a convert, and as a Muslim woman who does not wear hijab, I am a very particular insider who is also a potential outsider in certain circles. Work against domestic violence, in Muslim communities even more so than in the mainstream, carries risks, and the people in the movement have many good reasons to be skeptical and to require effort to earn their trust. I built that trust over time and came to be recognized as someone who is deeply invested in anti-DV effort beyond writing a book or publishing an article. The advocates I encountered first offered help in accessing networks; they provided the names of others I should connect with and they vouched for me when I did so. This method of identifying research partners in Muslim communities and DV organizations also provided me with some sense of the networks that existed at the time of my encounters.

There is perhaps a question that needs to be answered about what I mean by American Muslim efforts against domestic violence. I had to formulate an answer to that question in order to tell people what my research was about and so that they could help me identify research partners. I focused my study on those individuals, organizations, and networks for whom being Muslim and employing a Muslim framework against DV was meaningful. This means that this specific aspect of their identity was, in their own estimation, significant for their work against DV. My study is limited to the United States, and within the United States, I recognize as an American Muslim (or Muslim American) each individual who lives and works in the United States and identifies as Muslim.

Domestic Violence as a Field of Study

While DV is often ignored or made invisible in public discourse, occasionally interrupted by campaigns to raise awareness of it, there is a sizable academic literature on the topic. The vast majority of publications, including many books and academic journal articles, are produced in fields such as social work, criminology, public health, and psychology. It is beyond the purview of this study to offer a survey of this literature. As part of my own project, I read several dozen of those books and articles to gain an understanding of the approaches, debates, and historical developments in the field. A number of them have been included in the bibliography. These sources address incidents of domestic violence, statistical distribution, analysis of intervention methods, descriptions of physical and psychological trauma, the effects of witnessing DV, the methods of service providers, the impact on service providers, the economic impact of DV, the role of legislation and the policing of DV, and cultural factors that impact incidents of DV, as well as the role of substance abuse, other forms of violent crime, and the challenging arena of producing reliable data on DV. There is also a growing awareness in the DV field of the need for more research on the relationship between domestic violence and other forms of societal violence including war, gun violence (which plays a significant role in DV murders), and sexual violence.

There is a second type of literature, not always academic but relevant to this chapter. Beginning in the 1970s and increasing in volume ever since, there is a body of literature that raises awareness of DV through the voices and stories of the victims. Included here are publications that intersect with another strand of materials: works that engage religious traditions and communities in the conversation about domestic violence. In chapter 7, I discuss some of those materials, including the *Journal of Religion and Abuse*, in more detail.

At the intersection of religion and domestic violence, there is a much smaller but growing literature on Muslims and domestic violence. I consulted a significant number of sources on domestic violence in Muslim-majority societies as well as in Muslim-minority communities, in the United States, but also in Europe and Australia. Many of these sources are also listed in the bibliography. Some of them, especially those providing statistical evidence for the rate of domestic violence in American Muslim communities, play an important role in Muslim awareness efforts and will be discussed further in later chapters. One of the challenges for researchers working on Muslims and DV in Muslim communities is the very category "Muslim." It intersects and is occasionally even conflated with other, ethnic categories, so that we see studies on Arab Americans, South Asian Americans, and others as overlapping with the religious category "Muslim." This in turn makes it possible to consider Muslims as a cultural rather than religious group and leads to a tension over cultural difference that I explore further in chapter 2. At times, there also is a clear reluctance to consider religion as a meaningful category of inquiry, either as a resource or as a problem. Addressing religion's relationship to DV is one important reason for writing this book.

Feminist Studies and Domestic Violence

There is an ongoing and at times raging debate about the relationship between feminist theory (and practice) on the one hand and addressing domestic violence in U.S. society on the other. Scholars have argued that it was the feminist movement that propelled domestic violence to the forefront of debates about families, women's rights, and state legislation regarding marriage and family. This process began in the 1960s but is far more complicated than a straightforward story of mainstreaming feminist critiques of patriarchal hierarchies and resulting abuse of patriarchal power. The work to create acknowledgment of DV followed by legal, social, and political remedies for the staggering presence of domestic abuse in the lives of American families has seen success, repeated backlash, and a meandering path in which accomplishments have become bargaining chips for political games on the federal and state levels; funding has been increased and then dried up, and the level of domestic abuse has not significantly changed.

Nevertheless, the secondary literature on domestic violence and work to end it is permeated by a foundational feminist critique of power hierarchies and notions of gender-based violence as the result of patriarchal structures, not only in families but also in society at large. The movement to end domestic violence has to be seen as part of a broader movement to end gender-based violence, including sexual assault, and to create a society in which all genders and sexual identities are protected from violence. This commitment to feminist notions of critique (and justice) has made scholarship on domestic violence one of the ideological battlegrounds for patriarchal and anti-feminist debates and initiatives. A political and ideological tension permeates academic fields of study as well as the anti-DV movement and the organizations and networks involved in the movement. One case in point is the ongoing debate about the Violence Against Women Act (first passed in 1994), which was preceded by heated debates that are renewed every time VAWA needs to be reauthorized by Congress.[3]

In addition, there is also the diversity of ideas and approaches within feminist theory as well as within the feminist movement to consider. This diversity is usually collapsed into sameness by its detractors but is significant for a more nuanced discussion, especially of intersectional feminist approaches.[4] It is perhaps confusing to also conclude that domestic violence is no longer a feminist issue only. As I will develop further, the project of creating and maintaining families free of intimate partner abuse can also be a patriarchal project and does not necessarily have to be linked to notions of gender-based violence, gender-based oppression, or gender-based discrimination.

A Note on Statistics

My survey reading of scholarship on domestic violence for this project has made me acutely aware of the prevalence of quantitative research in the field. It is indeed powerful to be able to say that one in three women has been a victim of physical abuse by an intimate partner in her lifetime. Fact sheets, produced by organizations like the National Coalition Against Domestic Violence (NCADV), a nonprofit organization that raises public awareness and works in public policy, attempt to generate a reaction when they list statistical evidence for the prevalence of DV and the devastation that it causes.[5] It is clear that statistical evidence can have a powerful impact in convincing scholars, activists, and especially lawmakers of the magnitude of the problem of domestic violence. This power of numbers has been recognized by organizations and advocates who utilize such statistics frequently in their public awareness work and to influence policy changes and decisions.

This focus on quantitative data, however, should not overshadow the fact that every single woman who is assaulted and abused is one woman too many. In addition, the statistical approach focuses on the victims rather than on the perpetrators: If one in three women experiences domestic violence, then how many men in our society are current or former perpetrators? How do statistics define and limit people to their status as victims of DV, and how do they obscure the complicated forms, stories, and trajectories of domestic abuse at its intersection with sexual assault and harassment as well as racist hate crimes and discrimination? Most importantly, though, how do we contend with the fact that the available data are always only a fraction of the actual incidents because there are many structural obstacles to reporting and thus documenting abuse?

Understanding Domestic Violence

After years of reading about and researching domestic violence I began to take for granted that everyone is familiar with the basic knowledge and frameworks employed to understand and address the issue. In conversations and presentations, however, it became clear that perpetual DV awareness campaigns, such as Domestic Violence Awareness Month every October, are necessary because specific communities and the general public lack awareness of the prevalence and dynamics of domestic abuse. In the appendix, I lay out some of the basic definitions and models that guide the work of advocates and service providers in the mainstream DV movement. This framing, especially the Power and Control Wheel, is important because of the way in which several chapters in this book discuss how Muslim anti-DV advocates position themselves vis-à-vis basic models for the causes and dynamics of domestic abuse and how they navigate the underlying assumptions and divergences between the "mainstream" and Muslim approaches.

Both the vast literature on domestic violence and the basic notions, definitions, and models undergirding advocacy and service work against domestic violence provided the foundation for my research in Muslim communities. However, I wanted to be careful to do more than analyze how Muslim efforts against domestic violence differ from those in the mainstream, thereby making the mainstream models normative and measuring Muslim efforts as divergent and/or derivative. Instead, I explore in this book how Muslim DV advocates themselves approach definitions of DV and models for understanding abusive family dynamics, thereby putting mainstream and Muslim models into conversation. I do not underestimate the power dynamic in that negotiation but instead recognize explicitly, here and elsewhere in the book, that at the intersection between Muslim community boundaries and mainstream funders as well as services, the mainstream has a powerful normative pull.

Ethics, Justice, and Patriarchy

In the very last paragraph above, it happened again: I described and then crossed the boundary between the inside and the outside: an invisible line that seems to separate Muslim communities, Muslim organizations, and Muslim advocates from the non-Muslim society surrounding them. This notion of boundaries is treacherous for it can mean that Muslims are not part of the American society they live among. That is not at all the impression I intend to give, and it does not hold as an empirical reality. Rather, Muslim work against domestic violence is embedded, indeed enmeshed, in larger societal structures and in mainstream DV work as well. There is, however, a dimension to Muslim anti-DV efforts that sets Muslims apart. I have already identified as my most important criterion for identifying research partners that I was interested specifically in explicitly Muslim efforts against DV. It is here that Islam as a religious tradition and as a framework reenters my considerations.

As I write this chapter at the very end of the book-writing process, I want to first present the central arguments in this book. I developed them through the research process, and the reader will have to go through the book to find support for them. They contribute to our understanding of the relationship between religious discourse and ethical practice; they establish a method for evaluating religious ethics in discourse and practice through a framework that foregrounds gender justice and employs Muslim feminist methodologies; and they develop the theoretical notion of protective patriarchy as it emerges in the context of Muslim efforts against domestic abuse.

An Ethic of Non-Abuse

In my years of working with Muslim advocates I often asked why they engage in this work. The same way they wanted to know what compelled me to write this book, I was interested in their motivations for dedicating much of their energy, passion, and time to this difficult work. I had approached the project with the assumption that Muslim advocates would point me to scriptural and exegetical resources in order to explain how Islam/the Qur'an is opposed to domestic abuse. And they often did point me to such resources, but the process whereby they constructed them as authoritative tools in their fight against DV seemed to never have started in the places where the texts dwell. Instead, they spoke of witnessing and/or experiencing abuse and instinctually recoiling from it as something deeply unethical and morally wrong. In other words, their own experiences and their affective responses to them lead to their activism. I eventually concluded that the activists possessed what I have come to call an *ethic of non-abuse*, which preceded their search for scriptural and thus divine support for their cause.

This ethic of non-abuse prioritizes change through praxis over change through discursive engagement. It is an ethic that is non-negotiable as a foundation, even though their notions of what constitutes non-abuse, which is more than the absence of violence, are more multivalent and complex.

My formulation of this ethic of non-abuse also comes from a longer trajectory in my own research practice. In much of my work on contemporary Muslim debates (and practices) regarding gender roles and gender justice, the greatest challenge has been to avoid the creation of a dichotomy between ideas of a "classical Islamic tradition" and its contemporary iterations. Similarly, there is an inherent tension in academic literature on American Muslims that tends to measure American Islam (if there is such a thing) against an assumed authentic Islam, typically in Muslim-majority societies. In both cases, what is practiced and discursively formulated in any given temporal or geographical context is measured against a preexisting model "Islam." It is also almost always found to be lacking in such comparisons.

This is especially true for projects that are characterized as reform oriented, which implies a movement for change. Such projects of change are predicated on a critique of the existing situation and explanations for the direction of desired change. The broadest and most powerful frame for considering such movements has been the debate about "Islam and modernity." It looms large in studies of Muslim reform movements and is deeply influenced by Eurocentric (and colonial) models of development and progress.

Simultaneously, the reference to a preexisting Islam, while itself a product of the nineteenth century,[6] has been used extensively as a tool in internal Muslim critique and rejection of reform projects as inauthentic, pro-colonial, and at times anti-Islam. This is especially evident in Muslim debates about gender equality and more specifically in feminist projects. Such projects, until now, have been analyzed in terms of their formulation of religious discourses that then were applied to specific contexts, in a linear flow from theory to practice, from discursive production to its application. And while practice and application have been recognized to have an impact on discursive formations, they have rarely been recognized as constitutive elements in a cycle where practice impacts discourse, which impacts practice.

In this book, I trace the practice of an ethic of non-abuse as the first entry point into this cycle, which then gets discursively supported in various ways. In other words, the religious framework, formulated through textual interpretation and negotiations of religious authority that I set out to study in this book, turned out to be secondary to anti–domestic violence *work*, that is, practice in the contexts I studied. The agents of this work, advocates, service providers, and even religious leaders, recognized the need for discursive religious support for their work *after* they committed themselves to addressing domestic violence in Muslim families. Often, the search for a stable Islamic framework was prompted by a deep cognitive dissonance between the activists' ethical frames and the disturbing realities of domestic violence.

In the process, the "Islamic tradition" or "Islam" is discursively constructed as relatively static and constant, which in turns renders Islam authoritative. Formulations such as "Islam says," "according to Islam," and "in Islam" serve to powerfully and authoritatively present the central ethic of non-abuse as preexisting and thus not up for negotiation. As I explore the specific context of anti-DV work in U.S. Muslim communities, I see broader implications for research on contemporary Muslim engagement with and construction of "tradition." Rather than advocating a deconstruction of tradition/Islam, I am interested in the continued production of the content of this tradition.

Gender Justice and Feminism

My scholarship and activism have long been concerned with gender justice. Not only have I studied Muslim women scholars and activists who may or may not self-identify as feminists,[7] but they share with me as a common goal their commitment to gender justice. Amina Wadud, one of the leading figures in this gender justice project, has formulated it as follows:

> The gender *jihad* is the struggle to establish gender justice in Muslim thought and praxis. At its simplest level, gender justice is gender mainstreaming— the inclusion of women in *all* aspects of Muslim practice, performance, policy construction, and in both political and religious leadership.[8]

Like Wadud and many others, including Asma Barlas, Kecia Ali, Aysha Hidayatullah, Ayesha Chaudhry, and Sa'diyya Shaikh,[9] I envision a world in which women do not experience gender-based violence in its many forms but are instead recognized as fully human. Or as a T-shirt my daughter likes to wear puts it: "Feminism is the radical notion that women are people." This commitment to a project to achieve gender justice and the more specific project to end domestic violence in Muslim families are intrinsically linked.

Several of the leading Muslim intellectuals and activists who have dedicated their lives to gender justice projects have also written about domestic violence and were, from the very beginning, my interlocutors and my community in this endeavor. I have developed my analysis in deep and sustained conversation with many of them and would insist on this book as a dynamic and dialogical project that aims to further conversation, deepen understanding, and, yes, change the world. These interlocutors, like Mohja Kahf, were influential in my decision to write this book. Their analysis of textual sources, most centrally the Qur'an, is significant for my analysis, even where I argue that in the realm of anti-DV work the ethic of non-abuse precedes the engagement with foundational Islamic texts. Where such textual engagement does appear, it is usually not foregrounding the work of "feminist" scholars, so I need to make sure to acknowledge the significance of feminist scholarship (and sisterhood) for my own work in this chapter. It will become clearer that such feminist scholarship and activism also run under the surface of Muslim DV work, albeit rarely directly acknowledged.

Here, I present foundational Muslim feminist analysis and (re)interpretation of a specific verse in the Qur'an, 4:34. The verse has been the subject of a substantial body of literature, especially produced by contemporary Muslim scholars and leaders, and it will reappear frequently in the pages of this book. I want to identify my own framework for addressing Qur'anic interpretation by placing my discussion of 4:34 in the context of Muslim women scholars and their struggle with arriving at a gender-just interpretation of the verse.

In Kecia Ali's translation, which retains the original Arabic terms to point to the difficulty of translation as a form of interpretation, it reads:

> Men are *qawwamun* (protectors/maintainers) in relation to women, according to what God has favored some over others and according to what they spend from their wealth. Righteous women are *qanitat* (obedient), guarding the unseen according to what God had guarded. Those (women) whose *nushuz* (disobedience) you fear, admonish them, and abandon them in their beds, and strike them. If they obey you, do not pursue a strategy against them. Indeed, God is Exalted, Great.[10]

Amina Wadud, in her groundbreaking reading of the Qur'an "from a woman's perspective," published in 1992, explained that the sequence she reads in the last part of the verse, from consultation between spouses in a situation of marital discord, to beds apart as a cooling off period for both spouses in marital discord, to the verb *daraba*, is a way to solve problems in a marriage. She struggles with the possibility of striking, hitting, or scourging a wife. She opts to emphasize that *daraba* can mean to strike but "does not necessarily indicate force or violence." Wadud then argues that, "in the light of the excessive violence

towards women indicated in the biographies of the Companions and by practices condemned in the Qur'an, this verse should be taken as prohibiting un-
checked violence against females. Thus, this is not permission but a severe
restriction of existing practices."[11]

In her 2006 book, *Inside the Gender Jihad*, she went several steps further
and declared: "Here I argue against any notion that it is acceptable for a man
to beat his wife. Any kind of strike, or any intention to apply the verse in that
manner, violate[s] other principles of the text itself—most notably 'justice'
and human dignity, as Allah has led humankind to understand today."[12] She
concludes that "saying 'no' to this verse" simply is an example of the trajectory of textual interpretation and represents the logical conclusion from the
Prophet's reported misgivings about the verse, to restricting its application in
fiqh (Islamic jurisprudence), to arguing over the possibility that *daraba* means
something other than "to strike" in the verse. She emphasizes that Muslims
need to acknowledge that "we intervene in the text."[13]

A special issue of *Comparative Islamic Studies* brought together four significant articles on Q 4:34.[14] The pieces by Kecia Ali, Karen Bauer, and Ayesha
Chaudhry chronicle the different approaches by historical and contemporary
exegetes and legal scholars and demonstrate both the relative unease in some
of the contemporary interpretations with what Chaudhry described as a
"problem of conscience and hermeneutics" in her piece. Laury Silvers's article, which has had a profound influence on my own struggles with the verse,
argues that Muslim readers of the Qur'an need to distinguish between onto-
logical commands and imperatives in the text and the need to take responsibility for one's actions as humans created by God. She writes: "I argue that all
the possible meanings of the verse indicate that the purpose of its existence is
to inspire the crisis of conscience that would lead us to prohibit beating.
Frankly, if the Prophet of God struggled over the matter, we should have the
humility to assume that we cannot do better. His example shows us that there
is no possible way to properly hit a woman."[15] Rather than saying no to the
Qur'an, Silvers reads the verse as requiring a conscientious choice to reject
any form of marital violence.

It was, however, Ayesha Chaudhry's 2014 book, *Domestic Violence and the
Islamic Tradition*, that provided the textual foundation for my own explorations in the American Muslim anti-DV movement. Chaudhry painstakingly
documents the exegetical engagement of Muslims with this Qur'anic verse
from the early period to today. She explores its circumstances of revelation and
its treatment as a source text for legal rulings on marital discipline. Chaudhry

demonstrates that premodern exegetes and legal scholars did not significantly differ in their understanding of 4:34, which they saw as part of the cosmological order God created and then explained through revelation. "In this framework, the disciplinary power of husbands was not only reasonable but moral, ethical, and just."[16] In contrast, modern exegetes as well as legal scholars have offered a wide variety of interpretations and readings of the verse that are in part possible through a rethinking of notions of justice and hierarchy, including in marriage, so that "it makes no sense for one spouse to have disciplinary privilege over the other, and it is never appropriate, ethical, moral, or just for a husband to hit his wife."[17] Chaudhry concludes that exegetes bring a specific set of expectations (she describes them as cosmologies) to the Qur'an and that these cosmologies are more important than the "actual words of the Qur'anic text."[18] In this way, she holds all interpreters of the Qur'an ethically accountable for their interpretations, especially of this verse.

Sa'diyya Shaikh's article on domestic violence in the Muslim community in South Africa, based on ethnographic research, became especially influential for my own thinking, and it added both a theoretical dimension and further urgency to my project. Shaikh articulates her "*tafsir* through praxis," an approach that foregrounds the practices of abused women in her study who live their interpretations of the Qur'an as embodied, rather than following or even themselves creating textual interpretations of the text. Shaikh describes women who experienced severe abuse and responded by refusing to accept that God would condone their suffering: "In their responses an image of God emerges as the witness-bearer of the oppressed, who will not accept the brutality and religious hypocrisy of the violent oppressor."[19]

Each of these scholars and their ideas have contributed to my own theoretical framework for researching Muslim efforts against domestic violence, and I count myself as part of a community of scholars committed to both gender justice and the critique of patriarchal systems that make gender-based violence possible. To me, my commitment to feminism is what Saba Mahmood has described as both a critique and a movement for change. While Mahmood is critical of some of the assumptions about freedom and agency that are necessary to diagnose the oppression of women by patriarchal hierarchies, she recognizes the interplay of feminist critique and feminist movements to change what some theoretical approaches critique as unjust.[20] The direct statement that patriarchal systems make gender-based violence possible is contentious, and I have wrestled with its implications throughout this project. In the end, I settled on weaving the notion of protective patriarchy through the book as a question rather than a pronouncement. I am critical of it while also recognizing that there are situations and projects in which protective patriarchy is both an ideological middle ground and an effective strategic tool.

Protective and Benevolent Patriarchy

In my research, I very rarely encountered anyone, men or women, who explicitly stated that domestic violence or even physical disciplining of a spouse was an ethical thing to do. So, does that mean that there is universal consensus on the ethic of non-abuse? If that were the case, we would not see the statistics, would not hear the stories of abuse, and would not need anti–domestic violence efforts at all. What I did realize is that ending domestic violence, unlike woman-led prayer, for example, is not an exclusively feminist issue and that, as will become clear in this book, not only is much of Muslim anti-DV work implicitly non-feminist, but advocates have also been reluctant to engage with feminist ideas. For me, the advocates' investment in a potentially hierarchical gender and family model and their insistence that hierarchy does not equal abuse have put into question my own normative feminist and religious commitments. I have wondered whether Muslim feminist scholars, including myself, need to rethink our value commitment in relation to sacred Islamic sources and seriously ask whether a commitment to gender equality and a particular idea of justice are, in fact, within the parameters of God's will and thus in line with human responsibility for achieving justice. What if human equality, including gender equality, is not God's intent? How do I account for the discrepancy between foundational texts, historical and contemporary communal practice, and utopian projects for the future? Aysha Hidayatullah has articulated the painful exploration of the "feminist edges of the Qur'an" in her book by the same title. She writes:

> I propose that scholars of feminist *tafsir* openly admit that it is our particular contemporary ideas about equality and justice that prompt us to see a dissonance between evidence for male-female mutuality and evidence for male-female hierarchy in the Qur'an—to admit that readings of the Qur'an that do not observe a dissonance between them or are unconcerned by them altogether are not necessarily defective readings of the Qur'an.[21]

I recognize protective patriarchy as both a reaction to feminist critiques of power hierarchies and the inherent potential for their abuse and as a potent tool in the fight against domestic violence. I thus analyze it in its different forms where it appeared in my research. I cautiously argue that embracing protective patriarchy may be an important strategic decision for anti-DV advocates that renders their efforts effective in Muslim communities, but I also worry about reenabling patriarchal structures that will inevitably lead to more potential for abuse of such power differentials.

The Bigger Picture: Gender, Authority, Religion, and Culture

In this book, with its urgency in addressing domestic violence, I have been worried about developing broader themes and conclusions from the very specific and focused work I did in my ethnographic and textual explorations. I continue to be concerned with the use of ethnographic fieldwork as well as the stories I encountered for some greater theoretical accomplishment. Domestic violence is not a case study or a means to a broader theoretical end. Rather, I find many of the debates and themes that have animated American Muslim discourses for at least the past few decades actualized in this book.

There is then a bigger picture that emerges from this book: debates about domestic violence and efforts to end it are part of a larger set of concerns about the relationship between gender roles, marriage, and sexuality on the one hand and questions of tradition, authority, and interpretation on the other. DV is an extreme example and it pushes these debates to their limits. In doing so, the fault lines and fissures of the central arguments come into sharp relief, because there is something at stake in arguing for or against marital hierarchies, for claiming that God has created men and women differently to live in complementarity and that marriage is half of a Muslim's religion.

Throughout the book, I trace notions of gender roles, equality, equity, hierarchy, and related questions of marriage to demonstrate how they function in DV work. I link them to debates about religious authority and the question of who has the authority to offer such interpretations. Because the concept of an ethic of non-abuse recognizes the interplay between discourse and practice as interdependent, interpretations do not assume privilege over practice, but as I demonstrate throughout, they carry weight in DV awareness work and they can produce or cement the authority of the Qur'an itself and of the Sunna, but they can also underscore or undermine the authority of scholars and activists.

One specific construct I encountered throughout the project was the insistence of advocates, scholars, and service providers that it is not only possible but indeed necessary to distinguish between what is religion and what is culture. This distinction, I argue in this book, is multivalent and gets deployed in a variety of ways. I attend to how and why it is deployed in most chapters in the book and thus pay particular attention to what might be at stake in separating one from the other. While I argue that this distinction is always a construction, it is one that can be powerful in the practical work of DV advocates and I do not deconstruct it to serve some kind of higher theoretical purpose. Instead, I subscribe to Gayatri Spivak's helpful concept of strategic essentialism, which she advocated in the 1980s as a way to unite disparate strands of the feminist movement.[22] Strategic essentialism makes it possible to identify the distinction between religion and culture as a powerful tool in the fight against domestic abuse, and advocates utilize it in creative and intentional ways as such.

As I identify my scholarship as informed by intersectional feminist analysis I need to recognize a major blind spot, or rather a silence, in my research results. There was no obvious mention in my interviews, observations, or readings of race. It is precisely the invisibility of race in communal conversations and my fieldwork that points to the size of the elephant in the room. This is less an issue of coding race as culture (see chapter 2) or even claiming that Islam as a tradition provides a communal umbrella that erases the issue of race. It is more about refusing to acknowledge that the racial/racist paradigm of the U.S. system and society permeates Muslim communities and works in tandem with older, and often colonial, structures of racial division and exclusion. While in other communal conversations race and racism, religious authority claims, and the fault lines of exclusion are beginning to be recognized, from Muslim participation in the Black Lives Matter movement to scholarship on the issue,[23] in DV work, analysis and critiques of race are continuously refused as a framework. No one ever mentioned or acknowledged racism *in* Muslim communities, even though several advocates openly acknowledged that they had experienced some of the rampant racism and anti-Muslim hostility in the mainstream DV movement.

This leads me to conclude that much more work is necessary to address this invisibility because making racism visible is the only way to dismantle it. The erasure of racial dynamics in DV work that focuses on gender delinks patriarchy from racism and it often forces us to choose between them: a deliberate political strategy to divide where united analysis and activisms would help recognize parallel and intersecting systems of hierarchy and oppression. It also contributes to the production of a notion of a Muslim mainstream, which is always a construction as much as it is an illusion, albeit a powerful one.[24] There is a link between the imagined mainstream and the Islamic tradition on the one hand, and the political search for and insistence on Muslim moderation on the other, as so powerfully analyzed by scholars of anti-Muslim hostility.[25] These broader structures and dynamics form the backdrop for this book, and I attend to them carefully where they appeared organically in the materials. Analysis of discourses and practices related to gender roles, authority, interpretation, and tradition, as well as religion and culture, has been central to much of my academic work in the past decade and this book is no exception. Indeed, initially I was tempted to build the very structure of the book around these themes. In the end, I decided on a very different way to organize the materials: around specific events, sources, and types of interactions I had with Muslim anti-DV advocates.

The Structure of the Book

I still wish I could have included more of the mountain of research materials in the book; told more stories; used even stronger words to get across the urgency of this project. I wish I had a way to share the faces, the emotions, the moments of despair, of anger, of realization, and of hope as I attended events and interviewed people. I do not have the capacity to share all of the above but I do share short excerpts from my research notes at the beginning of each chapter—to set the tone for the chapters and to connect the reader to the materials beyond possibly sterile academic language.

A note on writing in the first person throughout the book is in order: I employ the first-person singular pronoun "I" as an indicator of my feminist commitment to recognize my own positionality; I am open about my suspicion of the neat delineation between thoughts and feelings and, like many women, I have been trained to doubt my own arguments and employ particular phrases to limit my conclusions, to then be accused of not writing with enough authority. I share my arguments and analysis in this book, in the first-person singular, so that readers can decide for themselves whether they agree or disagree. I welcome the dialogue that such agreement and disagreement can produce and am confident about my arguments and analysis. My theorizing always comes from my source materials and continuously engages with existing scholarship, not in a derivative or supercessionist sense but in the spirit of academic exchange and, most importantly, with the express purpose of providing tools to make the world better.

This introductory chapter, in combination with the appendix ("Understanding Domestic Violence"), sets the stage for the other chapters of the book. The four core chapters of the book that focus on Muslim anti-DV work in and with American Muslim communities are bookended by chapters on public/media representations of domestic violence among Muslims in the beginning of the book (chapter 2) and Muslim negotiations with interfaith as well as mainstream and secular DV movements (chapter 7). Chapters 2 and 7 provide the bridges between "inside" and "outside" of Muslim DV work and discuss the constant flow between them.

In chapter 2, "Murder, Honor, and Culture," I analyze debates about Muslims and domestic violence in mainstream U.S. media outlets and other publications. I trace the attempts at self-representation by Muslims and at taking control of the narratives that surround reporting on DV incidents in Muslim communities. Central to discussions of Muslims and DV are the othering of Muslim communities through insisting on honor and honor killings as the only available frame and the simultaneous construction of Muslims as foreign to the United States through notions of culture that can include racialization as well as religious othering.

Chapter 3, "Need to Know," focuses on the multifaceted projects of Muslim advocates to educate Muslim communities about DV and offer Islam as a resource for ending abuse. The chapter presents how Muslim advocates develop their DV 101 model and what role the distinction between religion and culture plays in this model. I begin to explore the relationship between the ethic of non-abuse as rooted in practice and the development of textually based arguments against domestic violence. The chapter also offers further insights into the shifting landscape of Muslim efforts against DV through organizations.

In chapter 4, "Need to Teach," I focus on the interviews I conducted with Muslim advocates. I am interested in their motivations for dedicating themselves, for any length of time, to the work and for sharing their own analysis of the problem of domestic violence and their views on possible solutions. In the process, they have developed normative Islamic family models and ideas that further complicate the boundary between religion and culture.

Chapter 5, "To Lead and to Know," focuses on the training of Muslim community leaders as advocates against DV. The imam trainings and interviews with these leaders illustrate the tension between their claims to religious authority and their lack of knowledge about DV, which is borne out in their interactions with one another and with the (mostly female) leaders of the imam training sessions.

In chapter 6, "To Support and Defend," I move my attention to those in Muslim communities and organizations who provide direct services to Muslim victims of DV. I focus on the stories of several service providers to further my argument that these stories matter and need to be heard. I also sketch the landscape of Muslim DV services and offer some insights into the specific challenges this work entails.

Chapter 7, "Above and Beyond," links the work of Muslim advocates and service providers in Muslim communities and with Muslim clients to the broader DV movement, as well as analyzes their relationship with broader religious coalitions and organizations that have embraced an interfaith approach to DV. There are both similarities and differences in the ways in which religious communities have addressed DV and searched their traditions for resources to fight it. And the mainstream DV movement, which is very much part of American society, has proven to not be immune to the issues of othering, racializing, and marginalizing Muslims as both victims and advocates.

In the concluding chapter, "Looking Back and the Road Ahead," I describe an event at which the Muslim anti-DV movement was analyzed by its Muslim participants while pointing to larger frameworks of gender-based violence, anti-Muslim hostility, and racism. In addition to offering a conclusion to the book and the project, I allowed myself the freedom to develop further and deeper questions about my project and its reach. In what follows below, I move some of my concluding thoughts on the project to the beginning of the book.

A Reflection on Activism and Critique

That the personal is political is a given for me. That the academic—aka formalized knowledge production—is not only about power but also inherently political should be well established decades after Foucault's work on that topic in the 1970s and the still powerful critique of Orientalism as theorized by Edward Said.[26] Why then is there (still) so much investment in what is invariably described as either "objectivity" or "critical analysis"? As the humanities at least move away from objectivity as the term to describe the relationship of scholars to their research subjects, discourses on critique and analysis take their place. I am certainly not the first scholar to point out the investment in those terms, old and new, in white and male normativity that is made invisible as normative by claiming universality and, in religious studies in particular, detachment.

My scholarship is part of my activism, be it in the form of teaching, writing, or simply insisting on researching the agency, as well as the suffering, of the oppressed. Some of this book then is activism in the form of contributing to awareness, both of domestic violence as an issue and of the multifaceted efforts of American Muslims to end it. I have written about the policing of the boundary between detached scholarship, feminist normativity, and scholarly activism before and made clear that such writing is only necessary because some (too many) in the academy, in Islamic studies, and in religious studies— my academic disciplines—insist that activism somehow taints my scholarship. This book is part of my protest to resist such academic policing and a contribution to changing our conversations about the boundaries of our fields.[27]

The second axis of this reflection is my ongoing concern about the purpose of academic analysis and its relationship with critique as well as with deconstruction. I can say from the outset that I am not interested in deconstruction. The line between analysis and critique seems a little harder to pinpoint, and my own thinking on this line has been deeply influenced by a particular debate that dates back to 2012.

In November 2012, Lila Abu Lughod[28] and Maya Mikdashi, both Palestinian American scholars, published a fierce critique of the latest music video of a Palestinian hip-hop group, DAM. The song in question, "If I Could Go Back in Time," addressed the issue of honor killings in Palestine through a graphic video and lyrics that described the policing of women's bodies, patriarchal violence, and the dangers of a culture of silence.[29] In their article on the video, published on *Jadaliyya*, Abu Lughod and Mikdashi argued that DAM had fallen for an imperialist plot to blame such violence on Palestinian culture, thereby undermining Palestinian women's agency and activism.[30] DAM responded with an equally passionate rejection of that critique by pointing to the Palestinian women involved in making the video as well as the fact that their project in this song, calling out patriarchal violence against women, was an integral part of their political commitment to fighting the Israeli occupation of Palestine.[31] There was heated debate on the *Jadaliyya* website that only ended when Abu Lughod and Mikdashi published a follow-up letter to DAM, appealing to the value of solidarity during contentious debates.[32] What the debate brought into sharp relief was how complex the work of academics is whose work focuses on activism. This is not to say that academics cannot also be activists, but what happens to our locations in the academy when we critique activists (and artists) for their projects, their strategies, and, yes, their funding sources? Does global location matter in our intellectual projects? What purpose does our critical assessment of someone else's work serve?

It was in an article by Rochelle Terman that I found some of my own thoughts on this question, so central to my project, reflected and formulated as recognition of an impossible position that many of us in the study of Islam and gender have experienced. Terman moves from the "double bind between imperialism and gender injustice"[33] to the possibility of a double critique and from there to the need for responsible critique:

> In order to engage in the "productive undoing" of the double bind, I pro-
> pose we shift the paradigm of responsible critique from recruitability to
> one based on openness. A responsible critique is one that opens the wid-
> est analytic space in which a double critique can take place, qualifies the
> most voices, and allows for the greatest creativity in producing new politi-
> cal imaginaries. This applies to both feminists in the Muslim world who
> prioritize the critique of religious fundamentalism as well as academic
> postsecular feminists who prioritize the critique of liberal secular power.[34]

Where I engage in analysis as critique in this book, I do so with the deep-est respect for the advocates, leaders, and community members who carry out this work. When I first started this project, I was surprised by the willing-ness of many involved in fighting domestic violence in Muslim communities to acknowledge the issue and be the first to admit that silence was their great-est enemy. I was gifted a certain trust in my intentions when advocates real-ized that I self-identify as a member of the Muslim communities I study. Sometimes that trust was shaken when the same advocates found out about my feminist commitments and my earlier work on woman-led prayer.[35] Such moments in my fieldwork illustrated the tensions between feminist and non-feminist approaches to DV in Muslim communities, which will be further explored.

Overall I have encountered a range of responses to my interviews and, more recently, my writing on the project. One that I hoped would emerge was expressed gratitude for the opportunity to reflect on the goals, strategies, histories, and issues in Muslim DV work. I take great care to strike a balance between analysis, which often contains direct or indirect critique, and con-structive ways both to represent and to appreciate and honor the work of Muslim DV advocates. Based on the normative and activist commitments I have outlined and as long as those commitments and my positionality are

acknowledged in my writing, I see no reason to disguise my deep appreciation and the awe I feel in the face of the difficult work that they carry out on a
daily basis. My hope is that the analysis as well as the critique open up a productive space for conversation, reflection, and ultimately more tools for the
fight against domestic violence in Muslim communities and beyond.

2

Murder, Honor, and Culture

MEDIATIZED DEBATES ON MUSLIMS AND DOMESTIC VIOLENCE

I am afraid that the Muslim advocates would be reluctant to talk about domestic violence because they do not want to make Muslim communities look bad. Minority communities have to worry in different ways about "airing dirty laundry" in public. Islamophobia is so prevalent they might feel compelled to minimize the issue or they could refuse to talk to me.

THE NATIONAL STATISTICS on domestic violence, based on reported cases,[1] are staggering:

- A woman is more likely to be killed by a male partner (or former partner) than any other person.
- About 4,000 women die each year due to domestic violence.
- Of the total domestic violence homicides, about 75 percent of the victims were killed as they attempted to leave the relationship or after the relationship had ended.[2]

Such statistics are found in documents for service providers, informational materials, PowerPoint presentations, and academic research materials. They are repeated every year during Domestic Violence Awareness Month in October,[3] and they tell a powerful story of the most extreme and final form of the power and control wielded by perpetrators of domestic abuse. Domestic violence homicide is the ultimate expression of that control, the very control of the life and death of the victim.

There are no statistics to show how many of the victims of domestic violence homicides in the United States have been Muslim. If there were, would the discourses on American Muslim women murdered by male family members shift from insistence on the exceptionality of Muslims and the nature of such crimes as honor killings? Perhaps.

In this chapter, I reflect on three subtopics that are held together by their common connection to media representations and public perception. As reflected in the title of the chapter, they are murder, honor, and culture. *Murder* refers to examples of the representation of the murder of/by Muslims in the press at the time of the incidents; *honor* explores discourses on honor killings related to Muslims; and *culture* probes constructions of culture between religion and race, employed in analysis of and explanations for domestic violence murders in Muslim communities. I make no attempt to directly indict media producers as agents and blame them for the particular and often negative and stereotypical representations of American Muslims as other, inherently different and inherently foreign, not to mention suspicious and dangerous. Rather, I explore the connection between political goals and media production as they intersect with the lives of American Muslims and with the work of Muslim advocates against domestic violence.

In the chapter, I advance a set of related arguments:

- It is necessary and illuminating to analyze Muslim domestic violence murder cases within a framework of anti-Muslim hostility and propaganda prevalent in the U.S. media.
- American Muslim advocacy work against domestic violence takes place under the gaze of a pre- and misinformed American public and has to contend with the attitudes and expectations formed through media representations. The advocates are aware of that gaze, and this awareness in turn affects how they do their work and how they speak about it.
- Discourses on honor killings and domestic violence in Muslim communities are framed by theoretical as well as deeply political assumptions about the role of culture in domestic violence. Culture talk, in regard to Muslims, is so closely linked to religion (Islam) on one side and race (non-whiteness) on the other that easy slippage is common.
- The landscape of mediatized debates about domestic violence in Muslim communities is constituted by academic, public, and activist contributions that are all part of political discourse with direct impact on the lives of real people.

Taken together, these four arguments not only illustrate the complexity of discussing the murders of Muslim women in the United States but also provide an important part of the framing of American Muslim efforts against domestic violence as explored in later chapters by describing the public square in which Muslim advocates and service providers carry out their work.

Before turning to a particular domestic violence murder in 2009 and its aftermath, it is important to reflect on media representations of violence and murder and the complicity of spectators. In my recounting of the events in February 2009, I have chosen to minimize detailed descriptions of the ways in which the victim was killed, both in an attempt to avoid the sensationalism and thirst for gory detail that surround all reporting of physical violence in the media and because I believe that a focus on the mechanics of murder reduces the person killed to just the events of her death. That concern is only eclipsed by my fear of contributing to the industry of murder for entertainment. At the same time, it is vital to recognize the reality of domestic violence, of physical injury, of pain and terror, and the spiral of violence that sometimes ends in death.[4]

It is equally vexing for me to write about murder and violence in order to "reflect" on and develop an analysis of the ways in which domestic violence murders are discursively approached and received. It seems macabre at times to theorize death in this way, and I have never achieved any level of comfort with participating in this endeavor. My only argument for the significance and ethical acceptability of such a project is that awareness, public, communal, and academic, is an important tool for societal change and thus writing about these topics is important. I am encouraged by the words of Molly Dragiewicz:

> Unlike those who characterize "advocacy research" as political rather than scholarly, I recognize that all knowledge is political and either affirms or challenges existing hierarchies of power. Abdicating responsibility for the political implications of one's research does not eliminate those implications. To claim that all knowledge is political does not mean that all knowledge is relative or that all knowledges are equally valid.[5]

The Murder of Aasiya Zubair

On February 13, *Voz Is Neias?—The Voice of the Orthodox Jewish Community* ran the headline, "Orchard Park, NY—Police: Prominent NY Muslim Man Charged with Beheading His Wife," followed by this short article:

Orchard Park, NY—Orchard Park police are investigating a particularly gruesome killing, the beheading of a woman, after her husband—an influential member of the local Muslim community—reported her death to police Thursday.

Police identified the victim as Aasiya Z. Hassan, 37. Detectives have charged her husband, Muzzammil Hassan, 44, with second-degree murder. "He came to the police station at 6:20 p.m. [Thursday] and told us that she was dead," Orchard Park Police Chief Andrew Benz said late this morning. Muzzammil Hassan told police that his wife was at his business, Bridges TV, on Thorn Avenue in the village. Officers went to that location and discovered her body.

Muzzammil Hassan is the founder and chief executive officer of Bridges TV, which he launched in 2004, amid hopes that it would help portray Muslims in a more positive light. The killing apparently occurred some time late Thursday afternoon. Detectives still are looking for the murder weapon.

"Obviously, this is the worst form of domestic violence possible," Erie County District Attorney Frank A. Sedita III said today. Authorities say Aasiya Hassan recently had filed for divorce from her husband. "She had an order of protection that had him out of the home as of Friday the 6th [of February]," Benz said.

Muzzammil Hassan was arraigned before Village Justice Deborah Chimes and sent to the Erie County Holding Center.[6]

A day later, on February 14, a local newspaper, the *Buffalo News*, ran an article titled "Man Charged in Beheading of Wife." It was not the main headline as the western New York area was still reeling from a plane crash that had killed forty-nine people and the paper's main concern in the days following the crash on February 12 was to cover that event, investigations into its causes, and harrowing stories of the victims.

This article on the murder of Aasiya Zubair[7] provided fewer details than the one above and instead focused on reactions from friends and acquaintances who were in complete shock and disbelief. It also quoted Khalid Qazi, president of the Muslim Public Affairs Council (MPAC) of western New York: "'I cannot believe it—I know them both well,' he said Friday. 'I cannot get a handle on this.' It would be a mistake to link an act of domestic violence to the couple's religion, he added. 'There is no place for domestic violence in our religion—none,' Qazi said. 'Islam would 100 percent condemn it.'"[8]

As more details emerged, the story of the marriage and death of Aasiya Zubair took on a mediatized life of its own. Zubair had married Muzzammil Hassan in 2001. Hassan had come to the United States from Pakistan in 1984 and had been married twice before. Aasiya Zubair and her husband had two children, a six-year-old boy and a four-year-old girl, and also lived with two of Hassan's children from a previous marriage, Michael, who was seventeen at the time, and Sonia, who was eighteen. At least some family and community members were aware that Hassan had a history of family violence, which was the reason for divorce from his two previous wives. Zubair had lodged several complaints with the police over the years. She had acquired an order of protection on February 6 and she had filed for divorce.[9]

There was the oft-noted, if macabre irony that Hassan and Zubair had since 2004 worked on and for a Muslim TV channel, Bridges TV, which was formed with the express goal of countering negative stereotypes of Muslims and building bridges of communication between Muslims and non-Muslims in the United States. Even more macabre was the fact that Hassan committed the murder in the building that housed the TV station.

Honor Killing or DV Murder?

In the days following the murder, national news outlets reported on the events and began to debate much more than the details and facts of the case. The most relevant question now became how to evaluate what had occurred. The spectrum of answers to that question was a reflection of the larger politics of representation, of violence in Muslim communities, and against Muslim women. While the initial media coverage mentioned that both Hassan and Zubair were Pakistani Americans, and/or that they were Muslims, the ensuing debate, while more than two-sided, was divided between those who recognized the murder as a domestic violence fatality and those who insisted in increasingly shrill tones that the murder was an honor killing.

The latter were represented by well-known pundits in the world of anti-Muslim hostility and media production.[10] They included Daniel Pipes, who maintained a blog site for the case that was updated until July 2012 titled "Bridges TV, a Wife's Beheading, and Honor Murder."[11] In it, he collected news updates about the case but also shared articles and excerpts about honor violence and its characteristics, including references to Phyllis Chesler's article "Are Honor Killings Simply Domestic Violence?"[12]

The same Phyllis Chesler, described in a Fox News story on February 17 as "an author and professor of psychology," reportedly said: "The fierce and gruesome nature of this murder signals it's an honor killing ... what she did was worthy of capital punishment in his eyes."[13]

Right-wing pundit Pamela Geller posted on her blog a piece titled "Moderate Muslim Beheading in New York: 'Honor Killing.'" In the quotes around "honor killing" in the title, and throughout the blog post, she mocked the coverage of the murder as too politically correct and expressed disbelief that Hassan was "only" charged with second-degree murder. She also wrote: "The murderer 'wanted to improve the image of Muslims.' I wonder if he video-taped it—you know—jihad porn."[14]

The purported link between honor violence and Islam as well as Muslim "culture" plays a vital role in the continued production of anti-Muslim rhetoric and policymaking, especially in its connection to the equally purported oppression of Muslim women by their religion and their men. It is therefore not surprising that pundits would jump on the opportunity provided by the gruesome murder of Aasiya Zubair and then milk it for its publicity value as long as possible.

To represent the debate about honor killing versus domestic violence murder as clearly demarcated by anti-Muslim sentiments and politics on the one hand, and Muslim responses and attempts at representational damage control on the other, is temptingly easy but ultimately too simplistic to hold water. The *Buffalo News*, *New York Daily News*, and ABC News provided similar quotes attributed to Marcia Pappas, New York president of the National Organization for Women:[15] "This was apparently a terroristic version of an honor killing, a murder rooted in cultural notions about women's subordination to men ... too many Muslim men are using their religious beliefs to justify violence against women."[16] Pappas represented, more so than Phyllis Chesler, one face of mainstream American feminists, albeit the predominantly white middle-class kind so typical for first-wave feminism. A statement coming from someone as prominent in that movement as Pappas carried weight, including in U.S. policy circles; its significance in the making and unmaking of domestic violence–related policies and laws should not be underestimated.

It would be equally simplistic to assume that there are no Muslims who recognize the concepts of "honor violence" and "honor killings." Indeed, the media coverage included several people identified as Muslim who responded to the murder with a critique of what they saw as dangerous interpretations of Islam. One example is Nadia Shahram, who was mentioned in the same *Buffalo News* article as Marcia Pappas:

Nadia Shahram, a matrimonial lawyer in Williamsville, said that some Muslim men consider divorce a dishonor on their family. A teacher of family law and Islam at the University at Buffalo Law School, Shahram said that "fanatical" Muslims believe "honor killing" is justified for bringing dishonor on a family. While it has not been determined whether Aasiya Hassan's death had anything to do with fanatical beliefs, the community should address the attitudes that make divorce particularly difficult for many Muslim families, Shahram said. "I have not had one [case] where the husband wanted to settle outside of the court system," she said. In some interpretations, the Quran allows husbands to punish "disobedient" women, Shahram said, adding that this is a minority view.[17]

The February 17 Fox News piece quoting Phyllis Chesler also includes the opinion of Zuhdi Jasser, the founder and chairman of the American Islamic Forum for Democracy, who agreed with Chesler.

> "It certainly has all the markings of [an honor killing]," Jasser told FOXNews .com. "She expressed through the legal system that she was being abused, and at the moment she asked for divorce, she's not only murdered—she's decapitated.... The most dangerous aspect of this case is to simply say it's domestic violence," Jasser told FOXNews.com.

The din of "it was an honor killing," which I intentionally recounted here first, was matched but not drowned out by those voices who insisted that the murder of Aasiya Zubair had many widely recognized characteristics of a domestic violence murder. Zubair had experienced physical and psychological abuse in her marriage; she was separated from her husband; she had a restraining order; and she had filed for divorce. It is often at this stage that an abuser, who senses his loss of control over the victim, is most likely to attempt murder.

On February 19, 2009, Suzanne Tomkins, a professor at the University of Buffalo School of Law, wrote an opinion piece in the *Buffalo News* in which she argued that while religion and culture played an important role in explaining violence against women, they should not be used to diminish individual responsibility. She reported that since 1976, the U.S. Department of Justice has reported virtually unchanged rates of female homicide victims, 30 percent of whom had been killed by an intimate partner. She concluded by emphasizing that

> blaming acts of domestic violence on religion and culture, the economy, job stress, mental illness, post-traumatic stress syndrome experienced by returning veterans and other factors serves only to obfuscate and divert

from the real issue: Violence against women is happening at an alarming rate in our culture, and we have not yet committed the resources necessary to change this.[18]

Matt Gryta, in an article in the *Buffalo News* titled "Orchard Park Slaying Highlighted in Discussion of Domestic Violence," similarly linked the murder to broader issues of domestic violence in the United States and reported on a meeting of DV advocates and service providers in the same county where the murder had occurred.[19] In a "Focus: Domestic Violence" rubric piece, Sandra Tan and colleagues chronicled the history of domestic abuse Aasiya Zubair suffered leading up to her death. It described Hassan's controlling behavior, Aasiya's fear of him, her attempts to report physical violence to the police, friends and family who may have known about the abuse, and the façade of a stable marriage both Hassan and Zubair perpetuated to the outside world. It even related Hassan's stress about the failing TV station project and crumbling finances and his history of mental health issues. The article was framed by the assertion that Zubair had hesitated to expose her husband because she wanted to protect the reputation of the TV station, which represented her dream of a positive image of the Muslim community. " 'I think of Aasiya as a martyr,' said Faizan Haq, a local professor who helped launch Bridges TV. . . . 'She has given her life to protect the image of American Muslims. And as an American Muslim community, we owe it to her to not let this happen again.' "[20]

A nuanced Associated Press piece by Eric Gorski from February 21, 2009, directly acknowledged the challenges to Muslim representations and images in American public perception following the murder: "The killing and its aftermath raise hard questions for Muslims—about gender issues, about distinctions between cultural and religious practices, and about differing interpretations of Islamic texts regarding the treatment of women." Gorski listed several of the responses by Muslim leaders, organizations, and advocates and demonstrates the considerable spectrum of views and interpretations. The article concluded with a quote from Salma Abugideiri, of the Peaceful Families Project:

> Calling it an honor killing, it sort of takes it out of the mainstream conversation and makes it a conversation about those people from over there from those backward countries. . . . In fact, in this country and in mainstream society there are many cases where domestic violence escalates to the point where a woman is killed.[21]

The media coverage of the murder case eventually abated, but it was infused with new energy when Muzzammil Hassan went on trial for murder in January 2011, almost two years after the death of Aasiya Zubair. The reports about the trial reveled in another set of detailed descriptions about how Zubair was killed and further sensationalized the proceedings with claims that the trial had a "circus-like atmosphere and instant publicity."[22] There were bizarre turns in the trial as when Hassan decided to claim that he killed Zubair because *he* had battered spouse syndrome, saying that she had verbally abused him during their marriage. The prosecution's case rested on the accusation that Hassan killed his wife after repeatedly abusing her because she had filed for divorce and had left him. Hassan was found guilty of second-degree murder after the jury deliberated for less than an hour. On March 9, 2011, he was sentenced to twenty-five years to life in prison. The judge also issued a protection order for the two children of Aasiya Zubair.[23]

In a statement on February 12, 2011, right after Hassan's conviction, Remla Parthasarathy, on behalf of the Erie County Coalition against Family Violence, issued a statement, published in the *Buffalo News*, that reiterated the nature of the murder case as a domestic violence homicide:

> The community must understand that all domestic violence cases are serious and have the potential to end up as a homicide.... Every domestic violence case deserves a high degree of attention, and every victim deserves support. We hope the public realizes that this case is not exclusively a cultural issue or a problem within a specific community. Because of the ethnic origin of the defendant and victim, it would be easy to mistakenly dismiss this case as a "cultural concern." The reality is this is a domestic violence case, and the defendant manipulated his cultural norms to maintain his power and control over his spouse, as abusers in every culture do.[24]

On the same day, the *Buffalo News* also ran an article that chronicled the harrowing experience of the trial for Aasiya Zubair's family members and reflections of the jury members after the end of the trial.[25]

Since 2009, American Muslim community members and leaders have commemorated her death through different events, publications, and activities. It would be cynical to claim that American Muslim responses to the murder of Aasiya Zubair were primarily an attempt at reputational damage control. The shock and grief among many Muslims were real and cannot be expected to be reflected in media coverage in a meaningful way. In addition to mostly rejecting the language and claim of "honor violence," most of the public responses not only embraced the analysis of the killing as a DV murder but more importantly responded with both soul-searching self-reflection and explicit demands to Muslim communities.

Responding to Murder: American Muslim Leaders and Advocates

In what follows, I provide a glimpse of the many-fold responses and the many voices that participated in the simultaneously public and intra-Muslim conversation about the murder of Aasiya Zubair, which quickly became a broader conversation about domestic violence in Muslim families and communities. It is important to make explicit that Muslim community members, religious leaders, and DV workers are hyperaware that there is no such thing as an internal Muslim conversation that is not also taking place under the gaze of the broader American public. The increasing and intentional participation of American Muslims in media production as well as the rise of social media platforms as virtual spaces for communication and debate have offered Muslims better opportunities to communicate beyond localized communal spaces, but they have also added to the sense of being observed, if not outright surveilled, including by the U.S. government. This sense of heightened visibility, however, can also function as a tool to push conversations that are seen as necessary and important.[26]

There is a reason for beginning this chapter with a discussion of Aasiya Zubair's murder. I, like many other American Muslims, followed the news coverage and searched for more information and a better understanding of how such a terrible crime had occurred. By 2009, American Muslims had long developed the habit of, upon news of a crime or attack, hoping and praying that it did not involve any Muslims, fearing backlash and further heightened anti-Muslim sentiment and hate crimes. Hussein Rashid wrote on February 17, 2009:

> Immediately after the news broke, my first thought was crisis management. What does this event mean for the Muslim-American community? How will Muslims be perceived? As a Muslim, my first thought should have been to pray for the soul of the departed. Then I should have thought of the immediate concern, is there a family that needs to be cared for? What can we do to help?[27]

Ultimately, it was both the terrible nature of her murder and the reactions from Muslims, including an increased discussion of domestic violence as well as significantly improved networking between and visibility of Muslim DV organizations, that triggered the research contained in this book. It brought together my existing concern about domestic violence as a communal Muslim issue deeply interconnected with questions of gender justice and gender roles with textual explorations into the work of Muslim feminist scholar-activists and added an ethnographic dimension to the project. I started ethnographic work with Muslim organizations and advocates in October 2009, many of whom I became aware of through their public responses and efforts after Aasiya Zubair's death.

Rashid also wrote:

Horrible things are done to women every day, every minute, everywhere, by all kinds of people. It's not as though we are not aware of violence against women in the Muslim community. We are and we are trying to do something about it. But a moment like this shows how immediate the need is. The reality is that every community suffers from forms of domestic violence. It's not about religion; it's about power and control.[28]

At the forefront of the public Muslim response was the Peaceful Families Project (PFP), a Muslim DV organization founded in 1994 in northern Virginia. In a press release on February 14, 2009, PFP stated:

As the national Muslim organization in the United States solely devoted to ending domestic violence, we at PFP condemn, in the strongest terms possible, the horrific, brutal, and sadistic beheading of Aasiya Hassan. There is no justification for domestic violence of any kind, including psychological, verbal, physical, and sexual abuse. We have heard from numerous Muslim leaders, imams, activists, and families voicing their outrage against this calamity. We call upon Muslim families and leaders across the country to vocally address this tragedy in their communities by clarifying Islam's stance against domestic violence. We hope that every Muslim community will actively join us in working to end all forms of domestic violence in Muslim families by raising awareness and developing effective programming. We send our sincere prayers and heartfelt condolences to Aasiya Hassan's family and friends, and hope that the perpetrator of this monstrous crime will be brought to justice.[29]

Imam Mohamed Magid, the executive director of the All Dulles Area Muslim Society (ADAMS) Center in northern Virginia and then vice president of the Islamic Society of North America (ISNA), the largest Muslim community organization in the United States, issued a long statement, addressing the murder as a wake-up call to realize that violence against women is real and

that Muslims have an obligation to refute religious justifications and interpretations for domestic violence. He called on Muslim leaders and communities
to take domestic violence seriously as a communal issue and to both famil-
iarize themselves with organizations and services and work actively with DV
organizations to address the issue. The statement was both an assessment of
existing attitudes toward DV among Muslims and a manifesto for change. In
his concluding paragraph, Magid stated:

> Allah says in the Qur'an, "Behold, Luqman said to his son by way of in-
> struction ... O my son! Establish regular prayer, enjoin what is just, and
> forbid what is wrong; and bear with patient constancy whatever betide
> thee; for this is firmness (or purpose) in (the conduct of) affairs." (31:17).
> Let us pray that Allah will help us to stand for what is right and leave what
> is evil and to promote healthy marriages and peaceful family environments.
> Let us work together to prevent domestic violence and abuse and espe-
> cially, violence against women.[30]

These and other public statements and initiatives continued further into
the year 2009 and saw renewed vigor and effort through the trial and sentencing of Muzzammil Hassan in 2011. Asma T. Uddin, a Muslim lawyer, issued a
call to "move beyond the slogans" and demanded that "imams, leaders, and
spokespeople take the offensive, rather than merely the defensive," to address
domestic abuse in the Muslim community.[31] Wajahat Ali, playwright and
community advocate, was the point person for an initiative, in which "Muslim Americans call for swift action against domestic violence."[32] The statement called for sermons addressing domestic violence and utilizing existing
resources in the community better. It was endorsed by a significant number
of religious leaders as well as Muslim DV organizations and advocates listed
in the document. Shirin Sadeghi, after the sentencing of Hassan, wrote about
the murder case and warned that while many people had known about the
abuse, no one rose to the challenge to help and protect Zubair: "There are
millions of Aasiyas in the world. Look around you at the women in your life
and ask yourself if there is someone who could use your help, someone who
could die without you."[33]

An undated essay on Sound Vision by Abdul Malik Mujahid, titled "9 Things
You Can Do in Memory of Sister Aasiya Zubair," included the following ways
to respond:

- Organize DV awareness days in her memory.
- Check one's behavior for signs of domestic abuse.

- Raise awareness of DV in one's community.
- Demand Friday sermons on DV.
- Offer prayers for Aasiya Zubair and all victims of DV.
- Share DV resources with families and communities (in multiple languages).
- Explore volunteer opportunities at shelters and hotlines.[34]

Before returning to the vast literature and debate on honor killings and honor violence and how they relate to media, murder, and culture, I want to pause for a broader frame on the link between media and the phenomenon and production of anti-Muslim hostility, or what is more commonly called "Islamophobia."

On Gendered Anti-Muslim Hostility

There is now a vast literature, including an entire academic journal, dedicated to the study of Islamophobia. The term has become a convenient shorthand, and like every shorthand, it contains a problematic reductionism while proving a convenient label for a much more complex set of phenomena. Literally meaning "fear of Islam," Islamophobia is not an innate or natural fear of Islam or Muslims. Rather, it is an ideological construct produced and reproduced at the nexus of a number of political and intellectual currents that need to be taken into consideration and assessed critically in each instance or event of Islamophobic discourse and practice. I see it at the intersection of the following:

- Shifts in domestic politics in which Islam and Muslims become tools for renegotiating political allegiances, identities, and power structures.
- Imperial wars as extensions of colonial and neocolonial projects.
- Expressions of racism and bigotry in response to shifting demographic and political constellations.
- Negotiations of the nature and significance of feminism.
- Political exclusion and discrimination as part of shifting state powers and applications of liberal ideology.
- Civilizational discourses on the moral and cultural superiority of "western" powers, foremost among them the United States.

It can be frustrating to fragment and deconstruct the neat and all-encompassing framework used to discuss Islamophobia in current academic

analysis; and it is possible to argue that such fragmentation weakens the political power of the intellectual critique of Islamophobia. I insist that Islamophobia is not the product of a conspiracy against Islam and Muslims, originating
from one source that can conveniently be pinpointed and called out. Inspired
by the more helpful term *Islamfeindlichkeit* in my native German, I now use the
term "anti-Muslim hostility" for the majority of the phenomena listed above. I
have advocated for contextualized and nuanced analysis of specific incidents
in order to empower activist strategies and political interventions.[35]

Like all societal phenomena, anti-Muslim hostility is deeply gendered.
But how? There are several angles to this question that I address here. The
particular genderedness of anti-Muslim hostility can productively be explored
through a nuanced study of the ways in which Muslims are represented and
described in terms of gender identities and ascriptions. This genderedness is
most obvious in the binary representation of Muslim men as violent terrorists (both against "us" and Muslim women) and Muslim women as oppressed
and silenced (by Muslim men, Islam, and Muslim culture). Muslim men and
women in these representations (or stereotypes) are two sides of the same
coin: the violence of oppressive Muslim men is demonstrated in their treatment of their women, and the oppression of Muslim women is perpetrated
by violent Muslim men. No other factors or influences can be explored or
considered in such a neatly organized scenario.

There is an important connection between gender and sexuality, both in
how sexuality is mapped onto Muslim bodies and in how Muslim attitudes
to sexuality are used to define Muslims as other and as foreign to the United
States.[36] Concerns about sexual expression, repression, and control are, for
example, part and parcel of debates about Muslim women wearing headscarves or "the veil." The hijab will occasionally appear in my discussion as
an outward representation of Muslim women's identity. However, it is a tired
trope and one that has been discussed in academic literature in much detail
already.[37]

Muslim women are at the center of anti-Muslim discourses. This focus on
women clearly depends on their relationship to Muslim men; however, masculinity and the threat of dangerous Muslim men need further exploration
in our scholarship. Thinking about anti-Muslim hostility in gendered terms
and as a gendered construction is only a first step in this direction. Muslim
women occupy "center stage" in anti-Muslim discourse in two distinct and
contradicting ways: as objects of hate crimes and discrimination, Muslim
women have anti-Muslim hostility mapped onto them directly *and* as repre-

sentations of Muslims in American society; as objects of anti-Muslim discourse Muslim women are represented as victims of their religion, culture,
and Muslim men, therefore in need of saving, liberation, and intervention.
Women as producers of anti-Muslim discourse, both non-Muslim and Muslim, justify the second argument in the service of a range of political goals,
and their own gender matters for the effectiveness and impact of their arguments. A thorough analysis of gendered anti-Muslim hostility also needs to
take into consideration the problem of delineating the boundaries of what is
identified as anti-Muslim hostility as opposed to critical feminist discourse,
secular critique, and intra-Muslim reform.[38]

If we think of media as a diverse body of agents and organizations that
move in a triangle of influences, the points of which are media producers,
media consumers, and political actors, it becomes clear that a phenomenon
like anti-Muslim hostility needs to be traced throughout this triangle. This
task can be accomplished through an analysis of the ways in which concepts,
images, and representations are negotiated and debated through media. It is
vital, however, to also recognize the economic enterprise, or what scholars like
Carl Ernst and Nathan Lean have called the "Islamophobia industry." Several
reports, most notably "Fear Inc.," released in 2011 and 2015, followed the money
trails and political alliances of those who produced a significant body of anti-
Muslim rhetoric, political action, and media materials every year.[39]

Is it possible to analyze media representations and debates through the
(near) absence of particular associations and stereotypes? In what follows, I
do so in order to explore what constitutes the limits and boundaries of anti-
Muslim media representations and recognize the intersections of anti-Muslim
hostility with other forms of othering and exclusion. I introduce religion,
race, and culture, as well as gender, as categories for exploring the mediatized
existence of a murder case that occupied the United States much earlier than
the Aasiya Zubair murder, in 2002, not even a year after the attacks of September 11, 2001.

Mildred Muhammad:
The Muslim DV Murder That Was Not

I met Mildred Muhammad, the founder of an organization called After the
Trauma, which described its mission as "helping survivors of domestic violence re-establish their lives," at a Muslim DV awareness event in October

2010.[40] Mildred had a table at the resources fair that accompanied the event. On her table were informational materials that explained signs of domestic violence and focused on the particular challenges of "only" mental abuse without physical scars to prove that abuse ever happened and on strategies for women to overcome past abuse. This goal of her organization is the reason for the organization's name and, as I would learn later, has been her approach to dealing with her own life experiences of abuse.

Mildred was also selling her book, published in 2009, called *Scared Silent: When the One You Love ... Becomes the One You Fear*. I bought the book and Mildred wrote a dedication, thanking me for my support. I would see Mildred Muhammad several more times at DV-related events, including the annual conference of the Maryland Interfaith Community against Domestic Violence (IFCADV) in October 2011, and in 2014, when she was invited by an African American sorority at the University of North Carolina at Chapel Hill, where I teach, to speak about domestic and dating violence. In other words, Mildred Muhammad was (and is) a familiar presence in Muslim as well as non-Muslim DV circles.

When I started reading her book I was in for a surprise. In her memoir, she describes how her husband (whom she married in 1988), after many years of marriage, had abducted their three children after she had sought separation from him in 1999. For eighteen long months, Mildred had no contact with her children and did not know where they were. It turned out later that her husband had taken them to Antigua, and it was not until after his return to the United States that he was found and that Mildred was reunited with her children. In September 2001, she and the children moved to Maryland after she was awarded sole custody in a court hearing in Washington State.

About a year later, on October 2, 2002, a man was shot in a store parking lot in Wheaton, Maryland. He would become the first victim (of at least thirteen others) of the person who came to be known as the DC sniper, or the Beltway Snipers. The latter title was not bestowed until after the perpetrators were captured and turned out to be a man and a boy.

The mastermind behind the killings that frightened and occupied people in the Washington metro area was John Muhammad, the ex-husband of Mildred Muhammad. The killings seemed random, in parking lots, at gas stations, and at bus stops. There was nothing connecting the victims or the locations. Washington metro residents lived in fear and the media coverage of the killings became increasingly frenzied. When John Muhammad and his accomplice,

Lee Boyd Malvo (who was a minor at the time of the crimes), were arrested on October 24, 2002, attention shifted from fear to motive and eventually to the personalities of the two killers.

Much has since been written about the DC sniper case, including a journalistic account by Angie Cannon that focused on the activities of law enforcement officers in the case,[41] a psychological analysis of the personality, life story, and actions of Lee Boyd Malvo by Carmeta Albarus,[42] and Jack Censer's analysis of the media coverage of the killings.[43] There is also a 2013 feature film, *Blue Caprice*, directed by Alexandre Moors, which narrates the relationship and psychological tensions and issues of both Muhammad and Malvo.[44]

I mentioned my surprise when I first read *Scared Silent*. I was living in northern Virginia at the time of the shootings and experienced the fear that had gripped people living in the area. I also followed news coverage of the events and eventually the capture and trial. I do not recall ever seeing any mention of a connection between the DC sniper and domestic violence or for that matter much discussion of the fact that John Muhammad was a Muslim.

Mildred Muhammad's memoir tells the story of her marriage, her divorce, the abduction of her children, her reunification with them, and the killings in DC as a story of domestic violence and its fatal consequences. She asserts in the book (and in a few media interviews that only appeared at the time of the publication of her book) that John Muhammad selected the DC area for the killings because he was looking for her, wanted to kill her for leaving him and taking custody of their children, and that a killing spree could have masked this intent effectively if he had succeeded in his endeavor. She also describes in her memoir conversations with police and FBI agents that indicate that they believed her at the time, even if these claims never showed up anywhere else in literature about the case. Thus, one puzzling dimension of the story of the DC sniper and of Mildred Muhammad is that the claims to domestic abuse, as an important part of the story, never became part of the media narrative.

The other, perhaps equally puzzling, dimension of the DC sniper story is that both John and Mildred Muhammad were long-standing members of the Nation of Islam (NOI). Mildred thanks the NOI, Elijah Muhammad, and Louis Farrakhan in the acknowledgments of her book[45] and repeatedly writes about how significant NOI teachings were for her, both before and after the trauma of her abusive marriage. Albarus asserts in her book on Malvo that

John Muhammad taught Malvo about Islam and made him listen to audio recordings of speeches by Malcolm X and Louis Farrakhan in the car, and that Malvo even got in trouble at the Christian school he attended for preaching Islam.[46]

If at all, the connection to the NOI and Islam, and thus the potential to read the killings as "Islamic terrorism," only appeared in right-wing critiques of mainstream media coverage.[47] Islamophobia pundits such as Daniel Pipes and Michelle Malkin took up the banner at various points, but the label did not seem to stick very well.[48] In late October 2002, the Nation of Islam felt compelled to issue a statement in which Farrakhan acknowledged Muhammad's ties with the NOI, expressed deep condolences to the families and communities of the victims, and recognized the significance of John Muhammad's deployment in the Gulf War and his change of personality because of his experiences there.[49]

So why were the DC sniper killings not discursively linked (in mainstream media coverage at least) to either domestic violence or to Islam? It seems that only a year after the 9/11 attacks, another mass killing by someone with the last name Muhammad and with clear ties to the NOI, let alone fantasies of controlling the nation through fear, would be ripe for the taking by pundits who wanted to link the attacks to Islam and Muslims and keep alive the ever-looming specter of the Muslim terrorist. I would venture that the dominant narrative of Islam as a religion foreign to America, and of Muslims as a primarily external threat, made it difficult to integrate an African American Muslim veteran and his crimes into the story of foreign Muslim terrorist threats.

Indeed, public representations of Muslims after 9/11 were deeply divided between those delinking Islam as a religion from the terrorist attacks (the attacks were un-Islamic) and those emphasizing the presence of Muslims as foreigners and immigrants to then cast American Muslim communities as a fifth column. This narrative of the fifth column is espoused in much anti-Muslim discourse and comes with calls for more surveillance, the curtailing of religious freedoms for supposedly radicalized Muslims, and an emphasis on the impossible "assimilation" of immigrant Muslims into the fabric of American society. Even human interest stories and more positive media coverage of American Muslims emphasize their simultaneous Muslim and American loyalties (think Muslim children waving American flags) but make invisible those Muslims who have been here the longest, and have always been American and Muslim at the same time, namely African American Muslims who constitute an estimated third of all American Muslims.

This erasure of African American Muslims from the representation of Muslim Americans is only possible because of deliberate historical amnesia. It is important to remember that it was in the earlier twentieth century that Black Muslims were surveilled and infiltrated by the FBI because organizations like the Nation of Islam were perceived as a threat to the state. In "The Black Muslim Scare of the Twentieth Century," Edward Curtis chronicles the state's tactics and practices in framing Black Muslims as a threat and designating the NOI a political rather than religious organization. He also argues that such FBI efforts should be read as (partly successful) attempts to neutralize Black Muslim organizations and that one main tactic of their counterintelligence campaign was the creation of a government-sponsored "anatomy of Islamophobia" that would simply be revived around the attacks of September 11, 2001. "The FBI spread this Islamophobia to the mainstream media and its consumers through organized and long-running disinformation campaigns. In summary, Islamophobia was not an ignorant reaction of the public to the presence of Muslims in America. It was manufactured."[50]

Curtis links this manufactured Islamophobia to state responses to 9/11 and notes the differences as well as the recurrence of familiar patterns in such responses. He sees "the disciplining of Muslim American politics" as "a critical component of US statecraft."[51] However, the link between foreign policy concerns and investments such as the first and second Gulf wars, the invasion of Afghanistan, and then Iraq after 2001, and the continued U.S. military involvement in the Middle East made it necessary to shift attention from Black Muslims as an internal threat to Muslims of immigrant background. There are continuities regarding the link between anti-Muslim hostility and racism and the casting of Muslims as racially other, but there are differences in the ways in which certain Muslim bodies are marked as foreign. It is the foreignness of Muslims that can be demonstrated by focusing simultaneously on their cultural difference and their racial non-whiteness.

Neither the cultural foreignness so central to Islamophobic discourses nor the casting of Islam as a religion alien to America can convincingly be connected to the person of John Muhammad. This is why the Muslim label did not stick to him and Muslim communities were likely glad that it did not. My point here is not to argue that he (and his terrible crime) should have been identified as a Muslim in order to vilify Islam and Muslims further but rather that there are specific and peculiar reasons why he was not associated with Islam. As a member of the NOI, his Muslim authenticity could have been questioned (as it has been by other Muslim Americans and the scholars who study them), while African American Muslims have largely been erased not only from public perception of Muslim communities but also in Muslim communal self-representations.

If Mildred Muhammad had been killed by her husband as part of the sniper attacks in October 2002, would anyone have claimed that the murder of his estranged wife and mother of his children was an honor killing?

No "Honor" in Killing

I return now to the debate about honor violence that was brought into this chapter through claims that the murder of Aasiya Zubair was an honor killing and not a domestic violence homicide. Rather than attempting to engage the vast body of literature on honor killings I focus on a particular article from 2014, by Remla Parthasarathy,[52] as a lens for discussing two broad questions: How is the term "honor killing" (or "honor murder," "honor crime," "honor violence") debated and by whom? What are its connections to and intersections with the discursive construct of culture?

Parthasarathy's article, titled "Identifying and Depicting Culture in Intimate Partner Violence Cases," is an important frame of reference here because her arguments are based on a comparison of the ways in which two murders, both by husbands of their wives, both in early 2009, were represented and identified very differently. The first, of Ashkenya Johnson, was labeled a domestic violence homicide, while the second, of Aasiya Zubair, was (by some) labeled an honor killing. Parthasarathy argues, through a careful examination of academic literature on the role of culture in domestic violence cases (thus the title of the article), that Zubair's murder was misidentified as an honor killing because the notion of culture as an explanation for violent and homicidal behavior of men is most of the time limited to communities and families that are cast as foreign and non-white in DV research and practice.

However, Parthasarathy does not deny that the category of "honor killing" exists but rather that it was wrongly applied to the Zubair murder.[53] In her short discussion of honor violence she relies on the definition of the AHA Foundation, discussed below, and argues that it is "a subset of violence against women and has overlapping characteristics with intimate partner violence."[54]

In mapping a landscape of debates about honor killings and "death by culture"[55] as produced, I assume complicated relationships between political projects, academic analyses, and the needs of practitioners and advocates in DV work. There are more than two opposing political sides and more than a dichotomy between academic and public discourses to consider here, and it is precisely the complexity of this landscape that generates the challenges for critique and activism discussed further below.

The AHA Foundation (short for Ayaan Hirsi Ali Foundation) is an organization created and directed by Ayaan Hirsi Ali, a frequent contributor to debates about Islam, Muslims, and reform. Ali, born in Somalia, has written several books, including *Heretic* (2016) and *The Caged Virgin* (2008),[56] in which she represents herself as a former Muslim, critical of gender practices and their foundations in "Islam." She has garnered support from right-wing pundits and is frequently called upon as an "expert" for Fox News and other media outlets on the right of the political spectrum. The AHA Foundation, on its website, is described as follows: "The AHA Foundation is the leading organization working to end honor violence that shames, hurts or kills thousands of women and girls in the US each year, and puts millions more at risk." AHA's analysis of the situation continues: "Global events point to horrifying accounts of culturally-motivated abuse and murder of women and girls around the world. In the US, the number of women and girls experiencing honor violence, coercion and oppression is rising at an alarming rate."[57] Note here the reference to culture in "culturally-motivated." There are references to "Islamism" juxtaposed with enlightenment values that represent Ali's indictment of religion, notable because in its focus on Muslim communities in the United States and Muslim societies worldwide, it becomes clear which religion is the problem.

The activities of the AHA Foundation parallel the more academic efforts of Phyllis Chesler, whose article on how honor killings are distinct from domestic violence homicides (when the perpetrator and victim are Muslim) we have already encountered. In another piece, by Chesler and Nathan Bloom, also published in the *Middle East Quarterly*, the authors compare honor killings among Muslims and Hindus, positioning India and Pakistan as comparable, and extending their analysis to South Asian immigrants to the United States.[58] They conclude that there are significant differences between Hindus and Muslims, chief among them that Hindus kill to maintain caste boundaries while Muslims do so to maintain (unacceptable) gender boundaries, which explains why significantly more men are killed in Hindu honor killings and why the Pakistani government has not done much to address the issue in legal and political terms. The article concludes with the claim that Hindus abandon "the horrific practice when they migrate to the West," while Pakistani Muslims insist on maintaining Muslim-only communities and are only

becoming more radicalized when removed from their traditional surroundings.[59] This assessment not only posits religious difference as synonymous with
cultural difference, but it also lapses into a common construction of Muslimness as pseudo-genetic, that is, certain traits and practices cannot be changed
or abandoned by Muslims because they are embedded in them as Muslims.

Professor of law Kenneth Lasson published an article in 2009 with the
graphic title "Bloodstains on a 'Code of Honor': The Murderous Marginalization of Women in the Islamic World," which delivers the exact picture described
in the title. The piece starts with the murder of Aasiya Zubair and proceeds to
explain the sources of Islamic law and its various applications in countries
such as Iran and Pakistan, to then argue that honor killings (and forced marriage) are based on tribal customs. All his examples and statistics of honor
killings come from Muslim-majority countries or Muslim communities. Here,
again, we find the easy association of Islam, Muslim societies and communities, and a notion of culture that is assumed to be intrinsically linked to religion.
Lasson advocates raising awareness internationally, putting western pressure
on Muslim countries like Turkey (even through the United Nations and the
European Union), and swiftly punishing perpetrators in "the West." He lists
Chesler, anti-Muslim pundit Debbie Schlussel, the already familiar National
Organization of Women (NOW), and Women Living Under Muslim Laws
(WLUML) as important analysts and activists addressing the situation.[60]

A different category of academic writings can be found in surveys of literature on honor killings and honor violence.[61] It is notable that in the two surveys I analyze here, one of literature on honor killings in the Middle East and
North Africa (MENA), and the other globally, the authors assume honor violence as an analytical category reflecting a reality. And they seem to focus on
the literature about Muslim communities and societies and/or a particular region that maps seamlessly onto Muslim societies. Kulczycki and Windle conclude: "Partnerships and coalitions must be built, along with a proactive community discourse. Although the struggle to end honor killings may ultimately
be inseparable from that for democratic rule and especially greater gender equality, work toward curtailing this practice must continue, however incrementally."[62]
I note a peculiar colonial logic in both the necessity to bring democratic rule
to clearly backward societies in the MENA region and the assumption that
gender equality is a clearly defined and universal principle to be applied to all.

The survey produced for the Department of Justice (DOJ) is perhaps most
worrisome, despite its very helpful compilation of a large body of academic
literature. Here, too, the assumption is that honor violence is an analytical

given, not a category to be interrogated for its usefulness and implications. The document contains no discussion of the collected materials and thus leaves it to the reader (here the DOJ) to draw conclusions. It is not too big a leap to expect that the DOJ commissioned such a report for just that purpose and that it will have consequences in public policy and law.

That the landscape is not one of Muslims denying that there is honor violence and Islamophobes insisting that there is becomes evident in an article on TAM, a blog site that publishes materials on American Muslims (TAM stands for "The American Muslim"). Peter Gray, in his " 'Honor' Killings and Political Correctness," discussed the issue through events at the time and responses to them. In part, his political landscape resembles mine here, but he insists on the category of honor killings as meaningful despite its potential to be applied selectively and in both racist and othering ways to particular groups and communities. Gray, with reference to Leti Volpp (see below), accepts that culture talk is used to selectively assign culture as a problem to some communities while assuming that other (mainstream white) parts of societies do not have problematic cultural aspects related to violence: "They are right to condemn this imbalance, but the solution—to equally ignore the cultural aspects of violence against women—is unacceptable."[63]

It is in the link between culture and honor killings that the most problematic assumptions are made. It is worthwhile exploring how this link is drawn and whether it ever was or continues to be useful for our analysis. Uma Narayan, the scholar who appears to have coined the phrase "death by culture" in 1997, argued that "describing and distinguishing between institutions and practices that are 'culturally unfamiliar' might result, often unintentionally, in an understanding of forms of violence against women 'specific' to Third-World contexts as instances of 'death by culture.' "[64] Narayan compares dowry murders in India with domestic violence murders in the United States to reach this conclusion and gestures to the imbalance in the power structures that produce scholarship on these two contexts for violence against women.[65]

Zareena Grewal, in a policy brief after the Aasiya Zubair murder, analyzed media coverage and responses to then argue that

> culture matters in the fight against domestic violence, but not only when the battered woman is of color. Nor does the cultural context always matter in the same way across different cases of abuse ... we should consider the complexity of social life before dividing cultures, family structures, or religions into those that are risk factors for women and those that are not.[66]

Grewal also discusses the feminist dilemma of rejecting violence against women while simultaneously resisting cultural or religious essentializing. She quotes Sherene Razack, who wrote in 2003:

> We cannot have a conversation within our communities about stick figures. To do this is to avoid naming what we know happens ... men commit violent acts in culturally specific ways, there is something about violence that we will not be able to fully describe if we refuse to talk culture outside our communities. Stories involving gruesome culturally specific details will simply be suppressed ... the very secret that gives abusers power.[67]

In their "Culture of Honor, Culture of Change: A Feminist Analysis of Honor Killings in Rural Turkey," Aysan Sev'er and Gökçeçiçek Yurdakul describe the goal of their article as attempting to dissociate "honor killing from a particular religious belief system and locate it on a continuum of patriarchal patterns of violence against women."[68] They argue that "honor killing is an oxymoron, because honor and killing should be mutually exclusive rather than interrelated concepts. A more appropriate term to refer to these murders is patriarchal killings."[69] In their feminist response, they reinscribe the idea of "Middle Eastern cultures," though in distinction from Islam as a religious system, and locate patriarchal killings in poor and rural areas where gender norms and roles are changing the slowest and with the most cultural and patriarchal backlash. State responses are read as part of patriarchal power structure. The authors advocate the delinking of Islam and such murders, working with more modernized and enlightened segments of Turkish society, and with awareness of the responses to "western" interference as neocolonial assault.

In a contribution to feminist literature on domestic violence, Nancy Baker, Peter Gregware, and Margery Cassidy, in 1999, explored "honor rationales in the murder of women."[70] Their discussion of the concept and construction of honor ends with a surprising and very useful conclusion, where they suggest that

> the killing of women by close family members throughout the world can in part be explained with reference to underlying honor/shame systems as a subcategory of patriarchal ideology, and that a similar perspective can be applied to many such killings in English-speaking countries such as the United States. The battering of female intimates at times has been toler-

ated, and even sanctioned, by the dominant culture as a necessary means of controlling female behavior. Femicide is the most extreme expression of this position.[71]

While this conclusion does not refute the concept of honor, it extends it to all patriarchal societies and thus removes the association of the honor with non-western, Middle Eastern, Muslim, or otherwise othered societies and communities. And in defining honor/shame as part of patriarchal ideology, the authors provide useful openings for analyzing and critiquing the devastating consequences of patriarchal systems.

Nadera Shalhoub-Kevorkian and Suhad Daher-Nashif focus their discussion on femicide among Palestinian communities in Israel and argue for "the need to move beyond simplistic 'cultural' explanations of femicide, and pay closer attention to the ways in which structure, politics and economy of death function in colonized spaces and contexts,"[72] which can meaningfully be extended beyond that specific geographical and historical context. In the grand scale on which the majority of Muslim communities experienced colonization by European powers and the ways in which colonial assumptions and the hegemonic production of discourses on Muslims are still embedded in the histories of European colonization, and in their careful attention to the "politics of naming," the authors provide a useful framework to argue against the continued use of the term "honor violence." They write that the term "femicide" is countering the honor killing terminology because there is nothing honorable in such murders. Providing a separate category, especially one that links honor crimes and crimes of passion, allows for a different and less stringent response by different states.[73]

My last example from the vast literature on "honor violence" links the conversation about the utility (or lack thereof) of the honor terminology to legal categories. In the introduction to *"Honour": Crimes, Paradigms, and Violence against Women*, the editors, Lynn Welchman and Sara Hossain, explain how they wrestled with the honor-related terminology. They admit that the terminology is "by no means straightforward," and both its imprecision and its use for exoticizing certain communities are "among the reasons for caution in use of the phrase" (crimes of honor).[74] They also argue that in some contexts the use of the term is productive for challenging notions of honor and that it is difficult to work around a concept, however problematic, that has been so thoroughly established in international law and the work of international agencies including the United Nations.

Through this survey of the discursive landscape of honor as an analytical as well as deeply political category, I have concluded that it produces more harm than use in explaining and understanding particular types of homicide. I find support in the work of Aisha Gill, who has similarly argued that "the term 'honour-based violence' should be abandoned, in favour of situating violence committed in the name of honour within the wider context of" violence against women.[75] The term is permanently tainted by its continued and very intentional use in the ideological and political production of the Islamophobia industry. It is also so deeply associated with Islam and societies identified as Muslim, Middle Eastern, and North African that any attempt at disentanglement is more likely to be cast and read as an attempt at apologetics that ultimately relegitimates the usage of the ascription than to do anything to add nuance or critique. This assessment even holds true in cases where the construct of honor is utilized, as an explanation or excuse, by perpetrators, thus affording it emic status as well as a certain authenticity. Rather, it is the task of feminist scholars in particular to analytically diagnose such constructs as part of patriarchal structures and tools to maintain certain societal structures, power dynamics, and gender roles and to offer alternative terminology in order to change the conversation.

Whither Culture?

I have already gestured toward the easy slippage between religion and culture on the one hand, and culture and race on the other. In the treatment of patriarchal violence and homicide in Muslim communities (and societies), these slippages are especially evident. There is also an additional slippage, or even conceptual intersection, between religion (Islam) and race that has been studied in other contexts but holds significance in work on DV in particular.

Before attending more fully to this triangle, it is useful to return to the concept of culture in general DV literature. Remember, Parthasarathy had argued that Aasiya Zubair's murder was not an honor killing and that nuanced and critical applications of cultural analysis can and should be brought to her case and more generally to DV homicides in communities of color. She has advocated for an approach to culture that recognizes that all societies and communities are affected by "culture," thus moving away from the dangerously racist and anti-ethnic approaches to culture that have dominated DV literature as well as praxis. Leti Volpp was influential in introducing this conversation to DV literature, and her voice adds to the deep analysis of how culture has been used as synonymous with difference in DV work. She writes: "Psychology is used to explain why people positioned as western subjects act irrationally. In contrast, culture is used to explain why those considered non-western subjects act irrationally."[76] This assessment from over a decade ago can meaningfully be applied not only to violence against women but also to acts of domestic terrorism and mass shootings in the contemporary United States.

Parthasarathy considers the development of culturally competent power and control wheels and the attendant need for recognition of cultural contexts for DV praxis.[77] There is, and she acknowledges this, the danger of reifying cultures, even if in the plural, as quantifiable and systematic units that can do more to force individual victims and perpetrators into a set of explanatory assumptions about their "culture" than attend to specific and always overlapping cultural frames. Not only does everyone "have culture" in the singular, the lives of human beings are influenced by a multitude of cultures that affect them. This argument for multiple and overlapping cultures affecting each individual as well as communities of people is arguably not so different from its earlier iterations in the form of identity discourse. The one distinction is that identity constructions provided somewhat more room for agency than is the case for cultures that are primarily approached as affecting people and not as much as continuously being produced and constructed by the very same people.

Going forward in my analysis of Muslim efforts against domestic violence, which were influenced in their most recent history by the murder of Aasiya Zubair and the subsequent increase in awareness of DV but also sharply rising anti-Muslim rhetoric and media coverage, it is clear that culture, religion, and race are not static or immutable categories. They are continuously constructed, and the boundaries between them are negotiated both through the textual production of Muslim DV advocacy and community work and in its practical applications. This statement seems innocent enough, but it carries the deep ethical implications and responsibilities that I have struggled with in this project. For one, to claim that what Islam "is" can be described as an ongoing and thus open-ended discursive formation is academically sound but both religiously and politically complicated. We will see in later chapters that an investment in the stable formation of a reliable and true Islam is an important pillar of the discursive work against domestic violence, and any kind of exegetical relativism[78] has the potential to undermine this work. It also carries the additional burden of opening up the question to who is considered Muslim (in this project and beyond) to the point of deconstruction.

Similarly, pushing back against racist and anti-Muslim rhetoric and hate crimes is more difficult when the construction of racial categories and their possible deconstruction rubs against a very activist and strategic essentialism such as in the Black Lives Matter movement because such attention to the constructed nature of our categories can and is easily being conflated with dismissal of their political power.

Even if the otherness of Muslims in the United States is primarily coded as cultural rather than religious, thus avoiding an honest conversation about which religions count in this society, the implications are tremendous: Muslims as members of cultural communities further the emphasis on the foreignness and immigrant status of Muslim communities; the emphasis on immigrant backgrounds erases the significant presence of African American Muslims as part of Muslim communities with shared histories and complex power and authenticity dynamics; and lastly, in such a cultural ascription, Muslims, Arabs, South Asians, and others join the ranks of other marginalized as well as racialized communities of immigrants who can never be white.

Domestic violence awareness work as well as services to victims exist in the crucible of these constructions and depend on both nuance and applicability to be effective. How can religion, culture, and race be meaningfully incorporated into this work without paralyzing its practical dimensions and thus jeopardizing access to and impact on victims and their communities?

3

Need to Know

EDUCATING MUSLIM COMMUNITIES
ABOUT DOMESTIC VIOLENCE

Today, at a DV awareness event at a mosque, I saw realization grow in an older woman in the audience. After the panel talks and discussions, she approached one of the advocates, with tears in her eyes, and asked for help in finding resources. She had realized over the course of the afternoon that her marriage was abusive and wanted to tell someone before she lost her courage.

THE FIRST STEP in the fight against domestic violence, in Muslim communities and beyond, is to make its occurrence a topic of conversation and move it to the center of communal discourse and attention. For many American Muslims, domestic violence awareness competes with other issues, among them increasing anti-Muslim public sentiment and hate crimes, foreign policy issues, and government surveillance as part of the "War on Terror," not to mention concerns about practicing their religion, living life, and just generally being human.

Efforts to educate Muslim communities about domestic violence and resources to address it are at the heart of the work of many Muslim DV advocates and the organizations they work for. Such awareness work forms one point of a triangle in Muslim DV efforts, combined with offering services and resources as the second point, and educating mainstream providers and the larger public about Muslim needs and perspectives as the third.

In this chapter, I present moments of profound insight and analysis from domestic violence awareness events held in Muslim community settings. I focus on some of the over forty events I attended between 2010 and 2016 in order to offer a deeper analysis of the underlying dynamics and thematic coherence, as well as divergences between events, and the organizations and individuals who organized them. All three themes of this book, namely, religion and culture, interpretation and authority, and gender constructions and critique, appear prominently in these events and thus form the analytical axis of this chapter. My central concern with the foundational ethic of non-abuse as espoused by Muslim activists and advocates appears in a variety of forms as well.

In my commitment not to take for granted previous knowledge, I describe and analyze in order to develop the following lines of argument:

- Raising awareness of domestic violence is necessary both because knowledge is the precondition for action/change and because Muslims are reluctant to acknowledge the issue. This reluctance is more than communal discomfort or a fear of needing to respond to DV. It is clearly linked to issues of public representation and Muslim concerns about even more negative portrayals of Muslims in American media. The latter concern has a direct impact on both awareness events and on the construction of a religious framework for addressing DV.
- Muslim awareness efforts focus on Muslim families as building blocks for Muslim communities and on the needs of children rather than on adult (and mostly female) victims as individuals. In this, they depart significantly from the violence-against-women focused approach prevalent in the American mainstream anti-DV movement. There is significant tension in how this divergence is negotiated vis-à-vis feminist frameworks, Muslim or otherwise, as well as notions of religion and culture as they are constructed and applied.
- Every event, publication, survey, and so forth actively participates in negotiations of what it means to be a Muslim, "what Islam is," and how "Islam" and culture are negotiated as both resources and roadblocks in efforts against DV.

The chapter traces these arguments and provides support for them through a narrative structure that focuses on four particular events and specific moments within them. I also sketch the landscape of Muslim DV awareness work at the time of my fieldwork, realizing that this landscape has shifted since. This sketch then is both a snapshot of and a contribution to a history of Muslim efforts against domestic violence. The last part of the chapter introduces and analyzes several examples of how male Muslim scholars and leaders have developed religious arguments against domestic violence in public speeches and online lectures.

Sketching the Landscape of Muslim Advocacy

When I first started my research, it was Karima who asked me why I was doing it. She seemed concerned but also genuinely curious. My stumbling answer had to do with feminist Qur'an interpretation and gender justice, and it seemed rather grand for the small car we were in. Karima prompted me to think carefully about "why" as an exercise in ethical responsibility and the purpose of knowledge production. Since that day in 2010, I have come to recognize that recording history and bearing witness are two important dimensions of that ethical responsibility. I have already expressed my awe and deep respect for all those who dedicate any part of their life and energy to ending domestic violence. The institutional, political, religious, social, and ethical landscape they work in is as changing as a real landscape.

Imagine a meadow, a forest, a river, and a mountain, over many years, and the ways in which weather, seasons, climate change, and human interference all affect them to be ever changing. How do I even begin to try to capture both the landscape at a particular point in time and the forces that account for its constant change over time? What is the point of such an endeavor? The most convincing answer I have is that this project, like any historiographic and geographic mapping project, allows us to learn, to draw lessons, and to reflect. It is this last aspect that has been most directly formulated by several advocates I interviewed over the years. They reported being grateful for the opportunity to reflect on the trajectories, foundations, and shifts in their work over time—an opportunity that activists often do not have because of the constant and always urgent demands of their work.

What do I mean by the "Muslim" in Muslim advocacy work? I have focused my research on individuals, networks, and organizations that self-identify as Muslim in their public presence and attribute at least some of their motivation for DV advocacy work to being Muslim. For the organizational landscape, this means that I included only those organizations that self-identify in this way. As we will see (in chapters 4, 6, and 7 especially), the Muslim DV landscape also includes Muslim individuals who do not work for Muslim organizations but are involved in such work in the mainstream and interreligious landscape surrounding Muslim efforts. There is also a significant overlap with organizations that focus on different ethnic communities, such as Arab Americans or South Asians, who cater at least in part to Muslim populations among them.

It is important to define what I mean by community. First, I always use communities in the plural when speaking and writing about Muslims in the United States. There is no such thing as a homogeneous, unified Muslim community in this country, and indeed the boundaries of, even a plural, community structure are debated.[1] More significantly, the specific community settings in which DV awareness events take place have to be recognized as constantly changing if not inherently unstable. Yes, there are mosques and community centers housed in physical structures, but Muslim communities are not membership organizations but rather congregations that change constituents as well as leadership, and not least financial structures, depending on people's participation, geographical mobility, and increasingly also interpretational differences.

This point becomes significant when thinking about how "the community" is constructed as a powerful social organization for and by Muslims that regulates gendered behavior and is perceived as carrying expectations and passing judgment. The appeal to community consciousness and the ethic of non-abuse in Muslim DV awareness work is dependent on the notion of a stable and identifiable community. The reality of most Muslims is much more complicated and far less stable with regard to participation, access, and even regulation of individual behaviors. Scholars have estimated that only a minority of U.S. Muslims are associated with a mosque or community center or attend one regularly. At the very least, then, it is important to recognize communal structures beyond mosques as well as beyond physical structures in which Muslims come together to worship and learn.

"Muslim advocates' awareness work in Muslim communities" then is a much more complex affair and encompasses asking critical questions about audience and framework. However, one of the ethical dilemmas I have revisited frequently is whether pushing activists to ask such questions of their work is productive and feasible, or whether this type of self-reflective—and potentially deconstructive—measuring ultimately paralyzes and undermines more than it supports DV work.

There were, at the time of my research, many explicitly Muslim organizations.[2] The (unmapped) landscape they are part of is both always changing and constant in its unchanging commitment to the ethic of non-abuse that constitutes its foundation. The shifts and changes have many causes and may or may not be perceived as a problem. Is it even useful for individuals and organizations that work for change in society to decry change as problematic? Is the problem that neither seems to have control over such changes? There seems to be a strong tendency to think of organizational structures, especially in civic and nongovernmental organizations and networks, as ideally stable when they are, by their very nature, fluctuating and dependent on the initiative of individuals and at the whims of the economic forces they engage with or oppose. In other words, the two driving factors for both continuity and change in Muslim DV work are individual advocates and sources of financial support needed to sustain organizations and services. It may be that the activists yearn for societal change that is accomplished through stable institutional structures in which they work. It is, perhaps, part of human nature to long for a balance between order and freedom, stability and change.

It is then not surprising that at any given time, Muslim DV organizations engage in one, two, or all three of the efforts described in the DV triangle and that such engagement can change. It is also typical that organizations appear and disappear: because the individuals involved experience personal and professional burnout, move their priorities to other issues, or cease activist work altogether. How these meandering paths are created by both agency and circumstance also depends on whether individuals are engaged professionally in Muslim DV efforts and are paid for their work or whether they volunteer and donate their time and work energy outside of paid employment. Organizations also dissolve because they cannot secure further funding or have to reframe their efforts, for example, from providing shelter and services (the most expensive type of DV work) to awareness efforts and collection of donations for DV survivors.

Most organizations I researched had no intentional record or archive of their own history beyond the year of their founding and the individual memories of people involved. While the primary goal of my interviews with advocates was not to recover institutional histories through oral recollection, my questions about such histories allowed for important reflections on their pasts, presents, and futures. Because the eradication of domestic violence is central to all of their work, as is the case for other activist causes, the urgency of the cause makes it almost impossible to reflect, regroup, and strategize. All the oral history fragments I collected point to this sense of urgency, of responding to situations, of dealing with the threats of closure, and of working in the moment. The individual telling of institutional histories also reveals, like all oral history, a tendency and a need to make sense of history in order to invest the present with meaning.

The broader story that emerges goes something like this: discernable and remembered efforts in Muslim communities to talk about domestic violence can be traced back to at least the early 1990s. They were certainly preceded by informal and thus noninstitutionalized efforts on the part of Muslim individuals, often within mosque communities but also beyond, to provide shelter for and support to victims. These early services produced awareness of the need for more organized communal responses, both to provide services and to educate communities. It is here that the ethic of non-abuse, constituted at the nexus of Muslim ethical commitments to justice and early attempts at scriptural reference, appears prominently, and it does so, significantly, first through praxis. One poignant example is the emergence of the Peaceful Families Project (PFP) in northern Virginia.

The Peaceful Families Project

According to its website, PFP was founded in 2000 as a part of the FaithTrust Institute, "a national, multifaith, multicultural training and education organization, working together to end sexual and domestic violence."[3] Since then, PFP has functioned as a domestic violence awareness organization with national reach that has offered workshops and information sessions, has produced and distributed printed and audiovisual resources, and has provided cultural sensitivity training to law enforcement and social service providers.[4]

This official story of how the organization was founded and how it has been operating, however, obscures the much deeper and longer history of the efforts of its founder, Dr. Sharifa Alkhateeb (1946–2004), and the work that her colleagues at PFP carried out after she passed away.

Alkhateeb, who was an active and engaged member of the diverse Muslim community in the northern Virginia area, had been interested in issues of women's rights and social justice for a long time and in 1993 conducted an informal survey among Muslims about incidents of domestic violence. Its results were published in 1999 in the *Journal of Religion and Abuse*, constituting one of the earliest publications on DV in Muslim communities in a mainstream journal.[5]

Upon her passing in 2004, many American Muslim organizations published obituaries, and many prominent members of Muslim communities reverently remembered her activism and achievements. In a deeply moving article, Hibba Abugideiri collected notes on how Muslims, especially other Muslim women activists and scholars, remembered Alkhateeb. Her piece, published in *Hawwa* in 2005, is also a tribute to the difficult path Alkhateeb had taken in challenging gender norms and communal practices that offended her sense of justice. Abugideiri frankly recounts that Alkhateeb met criticism and dismissal of her ideas by Muslim leaders and scholars and that her moments of frustration and disillusionment only spurred her on to work harder. She writes:

> This article serves as a tribute to her achievements, less as a way of canonizing the woman than as a way of inspiring other women to carry the mantle that Sharifa herself inherited. And while in many ways Sharifa was among the forerunners of Islamic *dawah* and gender activism in the United States as early as the 1970s, alongside the founders of the Muslim Student Association, Islamic reform, like other movements, rises out of the activism of pre-existing movements. Islamic reform of women's issues, especially in the United States, is a movement that will outlive Alkhateeb's leadership; however, her faith, foresight, resilience, determination and even stubbornness, coupled with her seasoned experience, serve duly as a celebration of American-Muslim women's deepening spiritual and social consciousness and a collective milestone on our arduous path toward gender justice.[6]

It was Alkhateeb's involvement in interfaith work that created the connection to the FaithTrust Institute, which in turn led to the creation of the Peaceful Families Project. And while the story of the organization and the pictures and reports from events tell a story of valiant efforts and achievements, Alkhateeb also experienced, as an individual activist and as the founder of PFP, a host of the challenges that continue to impact and seriously impede the struggle against DV in Muslim communities. In 1992, Alkhateeb cofounded the North American Council for Muslim Women (NACMW) as an expression of frustration with male-dominated American Muslim organizations. It was NACMW that made DV an issue and encouraged Alkhateeb to found a dedicated organization addressing the issue. Over the years, PFP received funding from the U.S. Department of Justice and some from various Muslim organizations while also charging fees for communal workshops and provider trainings in order to cover the cost of such events.

During the time of my fieldwork, PFP was directed by Salma Abugideiri and Maha Alkhateeb, one of Sharifa Alkhateeb's daughters. Membership on the board that officially ran activities at PFP and an advisory board had shifted and changed over the years and reflected both negotiations about community connections and support and deeper questions and issues of direction, method, and approach. After Sharifa Alkhateeb's death, these negotiations were at times framed as a question of her legacy on the one hand and the changing demands of the efforts against DV on the other.

In June 2015, PFP became a program of the much larger United Muslim Relief (UMR) organization, which resulted in financial support and fundraising through UMR structures and a rearrangement of activities and people involved in programming.[7] Salma Abugideiri said about the move:

> By becoming a program under United Muslim Relief, we believe that we will be able to reach more people and access more resources that will allow us to be more effective in realizing our goal of ending domestic violence. We are excited about the new opportunities that this new relationship presents, and we look forward to joining UMR's existing programs that are working towards improving lives globally.[8]

In 2018, PFP was no longer listed as affiliated with UMR on the UMR website and PFP had created a new website that identified the organization as an independent nonprofit in northern Virginia. The Mission, Vision, and Values statements on the website reflected yet again the focus in the organization on DV in Muslim communities and families; the promotion of "attitudes and beliefs that emphasize justice, freedom from oppression, and family harmony"; and the centrality of religion and culture as either resources or roadblocks in the fight to end domestic violence.

The shifts in affiliation illustrate the complexity of nonprofits and their work in the field of DV prevention, awareness, and education, as well as the challenges that they face in securing funding and access to communities.

Project Sakinah

Compared to the Peaceful Families Project, Project Sakinah (PS) was a relative newcomer to the Muslim DV movement.[9] Originally conceived in response to the murder of Aasiya Zubair in 2009, PS was launched officially in 2011. The project was an initiative of Dar al Islam, a religious education nonprofit organization founded in 1979 in New Mexico. While PS also focused on raising awareness of domestic violence in Muslim communities, in its approach it differed from PFP in that the Project Sakinah team held awareness events that were not only distributing information (as discussed below) but also encouraging and facilitating the creation of local anti-DV initiatives with a team structure, community buy-in, and local stakeholders including religious leaders and existing local organizations.[10] These teams started out with great energy and support from the local communities but proved to be more difficult to sustain in the longer term. Here again, we see the institutional and structural challenges involved in maintaining a high level of awareness activity while struggling with the waxing and waning of funding as well as with people's ability and willingness to stay involved.

Project Sakinah had an active Facebook presence and was still sharing articles, blog posts, and other resources on domestic violence regularly as I wrote this chapter. The website, which in 2015 still contained regularly updated links including local team contact information, by 2017 had settled as a somewhat static resource with little sign of active updating. The page listing collaborators, that is, other Muslim organizations PS was cooperating with, featured an impressive list, including PFP, Karamah, Sound Vision, the Islamic Society of North America, Muslim Men Against Domestic Violence, and the Texas Muslim Women's Foundation. What is notable here is the range of organizations, from those that also raise DV awareness, like PFP and Karamah, to local service providers like the Texas Muslim Women's Foundation, Muslim Family Services of Ohio, and the Hamdard Center in Chicago, to larger community organizations like ISNA, which speaks to the PS team's ability to successfully network in a world of constant competition over resources and to foreground the shared goal of ending domestic violence.

The PS website provided a host of important resources and notably offered books and the *Garments for One Another* DVD from the Peaceful Families Project for sale. I sensed no competition between PFP and PS but rather a strong sense of shared leadership and an even stronger commitment to share resources and tools. One significant contribution made by Project Sakinah was the collection and publication of survivor stories on their website. The team decided to retell the stories rather than retain them as first-person narratives, but even in this form, they were compelling. An example is this short excerpt from Huma's story:

> Scared and alone Huma was caged in that apartment for a few weeks. Every weekend her husband would come to torture her in new creative ways. He would abuse her as much as he wanted and then would leave her alone for another week with a little food and limited means of communications.

One would think that Huma would either die of hunger and fear or at the least would become a mental patient. Neither is true. Hers is a story that belies the stereotypes of women in the Muslim community and speaks to the universal challenges of domestic violence in all communities.[11]

There was some debate among Muslim advocates about the efficacy of personal stories and even more so about the use of graphic images of domestic abuse victims to jolt their communities into awareness. The consensus that seemed to emerge appreciated the role of personal narratives, even if told anonymously or through an advocate, but showed ambivalence toward the shock value of graphic pictures. In 2017, the PS website housed nine such personal narratives under a tab called "Hear Our Stories." One of the original team members of Project Sakinah, Zerqa Abid, had left the organization to focus her efforts on youth initiatives in Ohio,[12] and no new teams were being added to the website. In fact, both the team links and the list of staff members had disappeared.

Another organization, the Islamic Social Services Association (ISSA), which had a significant presence during my active fieldwork, was no longer represented online, and seemed to have ceased active operations, by 2017. It was ISSA in the United States, run by a group of African American Muslim women, that provided the inspiration for PS and facilitated many of the networking events and much of the resource creation and sharing in the 2000s. In 2005 and 2006, ISSA produced several of the brochures and pamphlets I saw circulating in Muslim anti-DV circles during my fieldwork.

Like PFP, PS, and ISSA, every organization I have researched has a story behind its official history, and all of these founding stories center around the efforts, informal at first, of women in Muslim communities who recognized DV as an important and urgent issue. They are stories of speaking against a culture of silence, lobbying against the constraints of dismissive communities, and pushing against the boundaries of male-dominated community organizations and structures. They are also stories of working within those structures and struggling to stay close enough to recognized and acceptable agendas and goals so as to not alienate the communities in which they operated and whom they wanted to reach. The resulting tension between goals and strategies, radical critique and compromise is nowhere more apparent than in events and gatherings in Muslim communities aimed at raising awareness of domestic violence and providing community members with resources and access to services.

To Raise Awareness: Muslim Community Events

Over six years of empirical research, I attended a significant number of awareness events in Muslim communities. Each has its own story, but there are also elements that many of them share. Before embarking on a much more detailed journey into significant moments at several such events, I want to provide a sense of the overall structure and some of my observations about compromise and strategy. In my consideration of these events, I have often thought back to the way Anas Coburn, one of the cofounders of Project Sakinah, described the need for DV awareness: "And the way I would like to frame it in the context of domestic violence is this: some people's lights are dimmed, some people are oppressed, their gifts never manage to be manifested to others, and our whole community loses when this happens. When a woman (or a man) is oppressed within her marriage, the entire community loses."[13]

Events to raise awareness take place in mosques and community centers but also in less institutional settings such as the homes of Muslim community members or, on occasion, in the virtual community spaces created by the Internet. The advocates distinguished between two types of events. In the first kind, the focus would be on the issue of domestic violence in Muslim communities and would raise awareness and offer resources to community members. The second kind would ostensibly discuss healthy Muslim marriages, Islamic norms for families, and issues in Muslim families. According to one Muslim advocate, the distinction between these two types was linked to awareness (or the lack thereof) in a particular community and thus a strategic tool for meeting the community where it was at the time. In some communities, there was awareness of the issue, meaning that community members had acknowledged that DV occurred in their community and were interested in learning more about resources and strategies for fighting it. These communities, or at least one community leader or member in them, were usually responsible for reaching out to an organization to request a lecture, discussion, or resource fair. Such requests usually came with an assessment of where the community was in terms of the DV conversation and what was needed. Advocates then tailored the particular event to those needs and prepared presentations, including PowerPoint slides, handouts, speeches, or discussion forums.

In communities where the majority of members were not willing to have a conversation about DV because they were convinced that it did not happen in their community or because they were afraid to make discussions about DV public and thus affect the image of the community negatively, those who initiated and organized events opted intentionally and strategically for titles and descriptions of events that foregrounded religiously defined family and marriage models and offered advice for Muslim couples, families, and communities. Domestic violence typically appeared in these events as part of a discussion of phenomena that violate the normative Islamic family model developed in the presentation. This was one version of the argument that DV is antithetical to "Islam" and that Muslims should not, under any circumstances, accept any form of abuse.

Some of these events took place in gender-segregated spaces in the same mosque or community center while others were mixed gender and yet others opted for separate and gender-specific programming for men and women. Similarly, speakers often included persons invested with various levels of authority to speak on a given topic. Sometimes there was a panel of speakers, including a legal professional or counselor, a service provider (who could be from a Muslim organization that provided services), and frequently a religious leader or scholar (almost always male) to provide the normative religious framework, complete with references to the Qur'an and selected Hadith traditions, against DV. Each represented one of several objectives of these events:

- awareness of what DV is and how it can be recognized;
- convincing the community that it is a real and urgent issue in this particular community;
- providing access to further information as well as resources to access services (Muslim or otherwise); and
- framing DV as an issue that can and should be addressed from within "Islam."

In many of my interviews with them, Muslim advocates complained that the greatest challenge to ending domestic violence in Muslim communities was the continued and deeply frustrating refusal by Muslim individuals and communities to acknowledge that DV even exists. It was not uncommon in their experience to find Muslims insisting that DV only happens outside Muslim communities or that it is not a big issue and thus should not get any attention.

The refusal to acknowledge that the issue is indeed a Muslim issue, as much as it is one of the biggest social issues in American society, is a tremendous roadblock for advocates as they are frequently accused of bringing trouble into Muslim communities or, worse, being intent on destroying Muslim families. Both reluctance to discuss DV and refusal to acknowledge its existence also explain the often low attendance at DV-focused events and the struggle of organizations that rely on community funding and support. At most of the events I observed the majority of the participants were women with men often hesitantly appearing and leaving before events ended. Walking in and out of community forums and panel discussions appeared to be typical for most events in mosques, but in the case of DV events, the fluctuation was pronounced and made it hard for the organizers to dispense all aspects of the information and maintain a level of conversation with the audience. Events and discussions of marriage and family, on the other hand, often drew large crowds and were in demand in a Muslim community landscape in which marriage and family were frequently discussed.[14]

While the above constitutes a kind of summary and thus generalization from my fieldwork, I more frequently experienced very specific moments of insight as I participated in awareness events. In what follows I attend to this depth of insight and analysis by focusing on small portions of two events that epitomize some of the salient themes of how Muslim advocates raise DV awareness in their communities.

What Is Domestic Violence?

In the appendix to this book, I have outlined in very broad strokes how DV is typically explained and approached in the "secular mainstream." This includes a brief explanation of power and control dynamics, the challenges of leaving abusive relationships (but leave she must), and cycles of abuse. The purpose of sharing mainstream approaches to DV was explicitly not to then measure Muslim approaches to DV against them. Rather, I am interested in whether and, if so, how Muslim advocates draw and rely on these mainstream frameworks, where and why they depart from them, and how they manage to negotiate secular frameworks with or against "Islamic" ones.

I accompanied Safiyah to the home of a woman who holds monthly gatherings for Muslim women in her community. The women had come together one late afternoon to discuss domestic violence. They made the effort to invite Safiyah to speak to them, which meant both that they recognized the existence (and significance) of DV as a communal issue and that it would be helpful to call on a specialist for their conversation. This meant that Safiyah entered the situation as an authoritative figure, but, as we will see, this authority also had to be earned. It was implicit in the invitation that Safiyah was invited to the woman's home because she is also a woman. The woman of the house explained that she had heard a program on the radio about DV during DV awareness month in October and thought that this "is not something that is talked about in Islam."

The house was spacious and several women had brought food to share. The men and boys of the family had been sent away to create a women-only space. The majority of the twenty-five or so women were South Asian, and their ages ranged from early twenties to mid-sixties. The atmosphere was relaxed, and I was only briefly questioned about my Muslimness, which turned out to be important for allowing me into the gathering. After the meal—reception style in the kitchen and dining area—we moved downstairs to a large basement where Safiyah had already set up a projector and screen for watching parts of a video. We all sat on the floor around the room, with a few small children roaming in between.

Safiyah opened the meeting with a question about what those present might know about DV. The answers varied, but all were asking for a definition, a clear sense, especially when a suspected victim does not show physical bruises. One woman repeated that many Muslims think DV only happens to Americans and that "it" does not exist in Islam. Safiyah responded that "it should not exist in Islam but it certainly does." Then she offered this description:

> DV is basically a pattern of behaviors that occurs between one person in an intimate relationship to another person with the intention of power and control. So, that is the definition. But what does that actually mean; what does that look like? In our context, we are talking about husband and wife, but it can also include other people in the family. It is most often the man who is abusive because the men are the ones who have the power to abuse. Women in our context generally don't have much authority or much power. So always the person who has the leadership position is the person who might be at risk for abusing that position. So if the husband, for example, is trying to control his wife through physical violence, which is beating her, pushing her, throwing things at her, or threatening to hit her. It could be any number of forms of emotional violence, which are very common: it could be verbal abuse or verbal violence, which women are actually quite expert at—that we have to admit. Women are more capable at using words, this is really the difference in the brain between men and women; women will use many more words in their lifetime than men ever will. Our brains are designed differently, so that is the weapon that women have. If they use it for constructive purposes, great, but women can also use words to hurt

and to oppress. So that is verbal violence; and men do that as well. There is financial abuse or violence and many other kinds of abuse, but basically the bottom line is: when one person uses the power that they have to try and control the other person's behavior. The emotional kinds of abuse, as you said, these are the invisible kinds, it can create a lot of damage but we don't see anything on the outside. That could be threats, in Muslim couples the threat oftentimes is of divorce: so if you don't do this, I am going to divorce you; if you don't do that, I am going to divorce you. If you don't do what I want, I am going to tell your parents; I am going to send you back home; I am going to put you out; I won't finish your immigration application; I will report you to the INS; I will report you to Child Protective Services ... these are all threats to control another person's behavior. Verbal violence is also name-calling; putting the other person down; sometimes it is making jokes at the other person's expense. Oftentimes a person who is living in an abusive relationship is afraid most of the time, which is the hallmark symptom for being in an abusive relationship. If you have ever been married or are married you know that there is going to be problems sometimes in a marriage, right? That is not what I am talking about when I say domestic violence.

At first glance, this description of what constitutes domestic violence closely mirrors mainstream frameworks based on a power and control dynamic and the presence of persistent fear in the abused person. It also mentions that there needs to be a pattern: in other words, a repeated occurrence of events that induce fear and assert control, respectively. The excursus regarding men's and women's brains and the ability to inflict verbal violence demonstrates Safiyah's engagement with cognitive science claims of the popular variety, and her approval of them, but it also represents a particular gender representation that contradicts much of what else she said in this short speech. In fact, the power of the definition of domestic violence as violence against women is completely undermined by this statement.

The communal dynamic she describes in which men have authority and power and women do not replicates an oft-repeated complementary gender model as Islamic and thus divinely intended. I sensed no critique of this model in her remarks but rather a claim to protective patriarchy, a model in which the power and authority of men, by virtue of their gender, settles them with responsibility for protecting the women around them and explicitly for not abusing them. Safiyah has on other occasions expressed that she does not have a problem with this essentially hierarchical gender model as long as it does not lead to abuse. She also said that she does not care who is in charge in a family or relationship as long as there is no abuse.

The types of domestic abuse this short segment lists are also typical for these types of presentations. It is noteworthy that physical abuse is unequivocally rejected by Safiyah—there are no circumstances in which physical violence can be justified. She identifies the threat of divorce as a specific form of abuse in Muslim relationships, referring here indirectly to the unilateral right of divorce in Muslim marriages. This reference is both basic and puzzling: basic because it reflects, again without critique, the rights of Muslim husbands as regulated by Islamic law[15] and puzzling because the application of Islamic law to American Muslim matrimonial practices is in no way uncomplicated or uncontroversial. Rather, American Muslims exist, with regard to marriage and divorce, in a complicated and partially self-imposed conundrum of negotiating U.S. state law *and* Islamic law, which is not recognized in American courts.

Similarly, references to immigration status and child services assume that American Muslims are immigrants and, also, potentially unfamiliar with the U.S. legal system. While this is true for some Muslims, the universalizing move in her talk clearly addressed this specific event to Muslim immigrants. This last point is not to minimize the abusive potential for immigrant victims of DV; it is rather the universalizing of this specific form of abuse that is at issue[16] and the assumption that the women and girls present all fell into that category, which was not actually the case.

Safiyah continued the program by showing parts of a film, *Garments for One Another: Ending Domestic Violence in Muslim Families*. The ninety-minute film is part of a series of films and educational materials produced by the FaithTrust Institute for different religious communities in America. This particular film was one of the outcomes of the cooperation between PFP and the FaithTrust Institute. It is divided into three parts: "Understanding Domestic Violence"; "Islamic Perspective on Domestic Violence"; and "What We Can Do to End Domestic Violence." Each part contains testimony of victims, explanations and opinions by experts, including health-care professionals and religious leaders, and appeals to viewers to help end DV through the various avenues suggested. Safiyah had elected to show parts of the very moving first segment in which survivors describe their experiences of abuse. Safiyah had cautioned those present that the women (they are all women survivors) in the film had bravely agreed to participate in the project but that their status as survivors may not be known in their communities. She asked participants to keep their identity confidential even if they recognized someone. The making of and content of the DVD program will be explored further in chapter 4; here the most important aspect of the film is the impact on the audience. Several women were clearly shaken, and I was getting the sense that at least one of them might have been a survivor herself. There was a long silence when Safiyah asked for thoughts after watching the excerpts.

On Islam, DV, and Culture: Take I

With a deep sigh, and clearly as affected by the images and words as the others in the room, even though she had seen them many times, Safiyah challenged the women to explain why we should care about what we saw in the film. Then she said:

> Women, not only Muslim women, may not recognize when they are in an abusive situation. But for Muslim women, particularly immigrant Muslim women, if they have been raised in a society where men are allowed to treat women a certain way, where women are raised to just obey the husband and do whatever he says and not to challenge and not to talk back, and not really to think too much, not really voice her opinion, so then many women might feel that this is just the way it is. And I have met women who told me that that's the way my mom was treated, or my aunt was treated, or I saw my grandma getting treated this way, so what's the big deal?

One woman suggested that the biggest concern was that we perpetuate the same patterns and that our children learn the same behaviors. Safiyah agreed and specified that children may grow up and either tolerate or accept their own abuse or become abusers themselves. She also pointed to the women in the film who developed severe psychological and physical health issues. "We also know that children who grow up in homes where there is violence are much more likely to turn to substance abuse, get involved in drugs, to join gangs, to be bullies or to be bullied. A lot of the people in the juvenile justice system are coming from homes that are violent. A lot of the young men are in jail for defending or trying to protect their mother from the assault of the father."

This concern with the impact of DV on children was often echoed at other events. It is noteworthy that concern for the younger generation comes up more readily as a reason to be concerned about abuse than the well-being of the actual female adult victim of such abuse. I have sensed in many of these events an assumption that concerns for families and children as the cornerstones of Muslim communities were considered more significant, not because the individual woman victim did not matter but because advocates looked for convincing arguments and read their audiences as more concerned for families and children than a particular woman. There is at least an implicit pushing back against feminist frameworks that are typically centered on the individual woman as victim and survivor and on her needs. It is also the case that both mainstream and Muslim service providers have recognized that women often will only consider leaving abusive relationships when they realize that their children are in danger.[17]

Safiyah then defined domestic violence within an Islamic normative framework as *zulm*—the Arabic word for oppression and a concept that appears frequently in Muslim discourses on justice.

> As Muslims we have no business treating each other in an abusive way—that is *zulm*, oppression, and next to *kufr*[18] and *shirk*,[19] it is a very big sin for us as Muslims to engage in behavior that oppresses other people. And many Muslim women may not realize that they are being oppressed.... What is the difference between a woman who is afraid to speak up because she is afraid that her husband might hit her and a person who is afraid that when they speak up the government is going to arrest him or her?

She then argued that the husband has a responsibility to take care of the wife, and the children, and that he also has the responsibility to lead the family, in the way that the Prophet led his family. When she asked what we knew about the prophetic husband and family model, the women suggested that he was kind and gentle; that he asked for his wives' (plural) advice; that he respected their jealousy, accepted women's emotional side, and even helped with household chores. She then asked: "Have you heard any stories about a woman or anyone who was afraid of Muhammad?" When no one could come up with a story, she concluded that there are no such stories, which is meaningful and important because the Prophet Muhammad was our Islamic model of the ideal husband.

Having started with the prophetic example, she then moved to the Qur'an as proof text for divine intent with regard to the Islamic marriage model. The verse in question, Q 30:21,[20] would be known to the women in the room from their wedding: "It's from Surat Rum, verse 21 where *Allah ta'ala* identifies the elements that are key to an Islamic marriage and that is why it is read at every wedding. Those elements are *mawadda*, which means love, compassion—it's a very deep level of loving and caring for someone; *rahma*, which is mercy" [she read the verse from a sheet in Arabic and then highlighted the third element]; "*sakina*, which is tranquility for both the husband and the wife. *Sakina* does not mean that the husband is supposed to be pleased in the marriage and it is the wife's job to make it happen. Rather, it is mutual caretaking."

According to Safiyah, men and women are meant to be protectors for one another, which makes domestic violence bad and wrong because it goes completely against being and acting as a Muslim. Here again we see the unequivocal rejection of abuse in a religious framework that does not leave room for negotiation. It is an actualized ethic of non-abuse that Safiyah supported with both verses from the Qur'an and reference to the Sunna. She then stated that Allah dislikes the abuser and all abuse and that it is the right of everyone including women to not be abused.

Safiyah emphasized the importance of teaching this Islamic marriage model to our children, so that when a young woman gets married and she gets mistreated she knows immediately that it is not her fault. She can then resist victim blaming and being cast as a bad Muslim woman. On the deepest level, it is this model of Islamic marriage that defines "Islam" as a resource against domestic violence. Muslim advocates repeated regularly that Islam is not the cause or source of DV but that it instead contains the resources necessary and useful to end it in Muslim communities.

A discussion then ensued between two women, with one arguing that it was a matter of how frequently abuse, especially physical abuse, occurred, and if it was only once a year, then it was not as much of an issue. The other woman disagreed and pointed to the danger and potential for spiraling increase in abuse. Safiyah agreed with both but argued, "We know that abuse never stops on its own, without some kind of intervention."

Another woman referred to cultural frames and the inescapability of abusive situations when there are no alternative options. She explained that it is very different for Muslims who were raised in the United States versus those raised in Pakistan. In Pakistan, people do not educate their daughters, and thus they are financially dependent. When a woman gets divorced by her husband, she has to go back to her parents. In some cases, then, enduring the abuse is the lesser evil. "Most men in our culture and our religion, they think they are always right, and it is always the wife who has to change her ways." She advocated for realistic assessments of abuse versus alternatives, basically saying that standing up to it is not always an option.

Safiyah agreed in principle but pointed to the danger for women in abusive relationships, specifically the danger of being killed. She estimated that at least once a month a woman gets killed in Muslim communities in the United States. She then acknowledged that many women make the choice to stay for the sake of their children or because they have no choice at all. She also defined a particular "culturally specific" form of abuse in Muslim families in which a woman is not abused by her husband directly but by her in-laws, most often the mother-in-law. What little has been written about in-law abuse among Muslims is as invested in culture talk as Safiyah was at this event. Studying and analyzing this form of domestic abuse is challenging both because it complicates the violence-against-women paradigm (when the violence is perpetrated by another woman in a position of power) and because filing it under culturally specific forms of domestic violence runs the risk of reifying cultural explanations for DV that cannot adequately be captured by the mainstream and the DV system in the United States because it is deemed foreign and thus alien.

The conversation then meandered through educating and raising boys differently and making resources available, including non-Muslim services. Safiyah was asked about the possibility of reforming abusers and said that it was only possible through intervention and that it only worked in rare cases. That she deemed it possible at all (she has seen Allah change a few people's hearts) is a radical departure from mainstream approaches and assumptions about perpetrators of abuse. Safiyah did not, however, advocate staying in an abusive relationship hoping for change. She also gestured toward extended families as either potentially part of the problem of abuse, by encouraging or ignoring it, or as part of the solution, by intervening and preventing or stopping abuse. She then employed yet another reference to culture: "Part of our culture is this shame thing: in front of your family you don't want to be shamed and it could be enough of a motivator." Later she also referred to Islamic rights being taken away from women by culture. In most of these references, except the one about shame as a motivator, culture appears as a negative factor, and it is always juxtaposed with Islam, which is never represented as negative. In this framework, the advocates, including Safiyah, lay claims to an "Islam" that is authentic, true, and unchanging, while culture is negotiated and can potentially be changed. Culture also appears as a powerful and deterministic construct that is part of the realities of abused women with no recourse to change.

The event ended with the women and Safiyah sharing broader ideas for solutions that, interestingly, were all suggestions for how to change "culture."

They included changing the ways Muslims think about marriage, supporting spouses getting to know each other better before marriage, and studying the Qur'an to find more support for women's rights, women's humanity, and a better marriage model. One woman suggested that brothers, fathers, and sons needed to be educated about the real Islamic marriage model and about not following cultural models instead. Stories from the Sunna could be a non-threatening way to introduce these ideas.

While each event was unique, each audience different, and each presentation tailored and thus a product of reading the moment and the audience, Muslim advocates actively participated in situational constructions of religion (Islam) and culture. It is both noteworthy and worrisome that few of the events I observed directly engaged with race as a factor or category. This is certainly related to the fact that fewer events took place in African American community spaces, but quite a few events had enough African American Muslims in the audience to make the silence about race noticeable. American racial categories, most importantly Muslim Blackness, are continuously made invisible in many of these conversations. The closest I have observed to acknowledging race, questions of religious authenticity, and racist attitudes and practices in Muslim communities was in the form of discussing African American "culture," often in depictions and constructions that resemble the mainstream ascription of perpetual marginalized otherness to African Americans. Occasionally culture appeared as a descriptor for Arab American and South Asian American Muslim communities in reflections shared by African American Muslim advocates.

In the following section, I present a second example of an event in which both religion and culture appear prominently. Questions of authority are configured differently at this mixed-gender event in a mosque and with two women and one male speaker on a panel on domestic violence. What interests me most here is to further our exploration on how "Islam" is constructed as a stable and authoritative category: through references to scripture, which is expected, as well as in other ways. This authoritative "Islamic" framework is vital for the purpose of refuting the acceptability of any form of domestic abuse in Muslim families. Its construction hinges on assumptions about the existence of a cohesive and historically anchored Islamic tradition (based on the Qur'an and Sunna) that provides advocates with exegetical authority by investing that authority in the texts themselves while limiting the possibility of exegetical relativism or negotiations of a wider range of possible meanings.

On Islam, DV, and Culture: Take II

At an event in a local Muslim community, a prominent imam and two Muslim women advocates, one a lawyer, the other a service provider, spent more than two hours with a group of interested community members, both men and women, in the main prayer room of the mosque, discussing domestic violence in Muslim families.

Malika, the service provider, offered stories of survivors and implored community members to take victims seriously. She also argued that Muslims should not turn to mainstream providers or law enforcement because doing so would confirm the stereotype of the violent Muslim man and negative images of Islam.[21] Najma, a family lawyer and advocate with a Muslim organization, focused on educating imams and community leaders and explained how the American legal system addresses family violence situations. She also pointed out issues with the application of Islamic law in this context.

Imam Akbar then described any form of domestic abuse as un-Islamic, against Islamic law, and domestic terrorism. He quoted verses from the Qur'an on marital harmony and Hadith on how to deal with marital disagreement. He cautioned men to not try to change their wives to be more like them because men and women are different in their natures. He referenced the popular "men are from Mars and women are from Venus" paradigm to explain an Islamic complementary gender model with support from popular science and common sense.[22]

He then proceeded to discuss Q 4:34, the verse so central to Muslim DV work. Imam Akbar focused on the last of three steps, which revolves around the Arabic word *daraba*. He claimed that of the thirty-seven listed meanings in a classical dictionary only one referred to hitting or beating while the other thirty-six all had to do with separating or moving away. This then was his exegetical move away from a Qur'anically sanctioned possibility for hitting a wife in a marital conflict. I gloss the details here to come to the debate that ensued at the end of the event.

The discussion ended with Najma taking the microphone to declare again that clearly there is no excuse for abusing one's spouse: "I don't care if you are angry about culture, I don't care if your parents are there or not there; it doesn't matter. None of that has a place in married life and abuse is not a part of a happy Islamic model of marriage." Here she was interrupted by Imam Akbar, clearly assuming authority, who proclaimed that "it is absolutely *haram*,[23] absolutely unethical, absolutely illegal, and Allah punishes the man who raises his hand against his wife, done deal and period."

It was during the discussion after these statements that Imam Akbar was challenged by an older man in the audience. He started by saying that hopefully he would not be offending the imam, recognizing him as an authoritative figure. He took issue with the terminology Akbar employed in describing domestic abuse as domestic terrorism and accused the imam of playing into the hands of the U.S. government and the American public who already see all Muslims as terrorists. Moreover, he expressed in no uncertain terms that he disagreed with the interpretation of Q 4:34 the imam had offered earlier. Amid steadily rising murmurs from the audience, especially the large group of women in the back of the room, he declared that all classical scholars had understood *daraba* to mean hitting. "The way you chose to interpret the ayah is suitable for your reasons and purpose and that is not acceptable." A woman interrupted and shouted: "Clearly, you can only say that because you have never been beaten." The man continued: "You have to say that *daraba* as going away is only your opinion, don't say that as a categorical statement, that is absolutely wrong." Imam Akbar responded: "I continue to call beating a wife domestic terrorism, whether it happens in a Jewish family, a Christian family, in the United States, in Pakistan, it is terrorism, meaning it is terrorizing these poor ladies and women." Acknowledging the use of the term by the U.S. government he asked: "Give me the right as an educator, as a Muslim, as a human being, to say that it terrorizes women. If you don't know that, *akhi*,[24] you have to go and visit the shelter ... we have to assume responsibility for our own crimes as Muslims. And if we don't stand in support of these women we will be asked on the Day of Judgment about it." On the topic of *daraba* he said:

> I quoted one of the best Muslim scholars in the world who is a member of the International Fiqh Council in Saudi Arabia. He in turn quotes Muhammad al-Ghazzali, Yusuf al Qaradawi, he quotes people in India, in Pakistan, and so many others. So this is not my interpretation, it is not a modern interpretation of *daraba*.... However, there are Muslims who think *daraba* means to slightly beat, I mentioned that. However, I dare to disagree with that interpretation and it is about time we stand up to Muslims who use the Qur'an to abuse women and say no, and not in the name of the Qur'an will we allow anyone to beat up these women. That sister walked out—we should all be walking out [applause]. Women are beaten up every day using that verse in the Qur'an and we allow it to happen.

The event ended there and people stayed to discuss in smaller groups and approach the speakers individually.

My first layer of analysis pertains to the gendered nature of authority. While the service provider and the lawyer, both women, were questioned on particular services and legal situations, and despite the fact that both of them made use of the authoritative category of Islam in their remarks, neither was questioned on their authority to offer such interpretations, but they were also not recognized as authorities on Islam. In other words, their references to what is Islamic about harmonious and peaceful marriages and un-Islamic about domestic abuse, which neither supported with textual references, were not received as authoritative or taken as support for their positions. It was the imam himself who by interrupting Najma assumed more authority, but it was also the male imam qua religious authority figure that was challenged on the basis of his interpretations. While I obviously would take sides in the debate on the ethical and moral wrong of physically and otherwise abusing wives, I would argue that in response to being challenged, Imam Akbar became agitated but not more convincing in his arguments. He referred to the pedigree and standing of the contemporary as well as historical figures whose interpretations he amplified. He paired that reference to others' authority with an appeal to the self-evident evil of physical abuse. He repeatedly referred to female victims as "poor ladies and women" and implored the audience, including his questioner, to see and feel their suffering. And in the end, he threatened God's judgment, of those who abuse women and of those who stand by and let it happen.

His self-positioning vis-à-vis an exegetical tradition perceived as normative and authoritative belies the relative weakness of his position in relation to majority opinion, especially in the premodern context as Ayesha Chaudhry's work has demonstrated.[25] Going even further, I assert that Imam Akbar was actively constructing his very own Islam and was challenged by the man in the audience who espoused a different set of ideas about the content of the box labeled "tradition." The debate between them contained textual and historical references but, interestingly, also geographical ones. The repeated mention of scholars from India and Pakistan (by Imam Akbar) recognized that his questioner was from South Asia and gestured toward his acknowledgment of localized authority structure. The religion versus culture discourse hinges in part on this recognition of localized contexts *as* cultures as well.

To the challenger, the question of textual interpretation and the authority to do so was paramount but also abstract. Perhaps the move toward this abstraction absolved him from facing the fact that he, intentionally or not, supported using Q 4:34 as authorization for the physical disciplining of disobedient wives, a fact that became clear in the response from the women in the audience, including the one who left the room. He was, after all, present at an event to raise awareness of domestic violence. It is possible to assume that he was there to defend physical disciplining of wives but also that he was concerned about the reputation of Muslims in America and wanted to observe the event for that reason. In either case, he actively participated in the construction of an "Islam" that then was pitched against Imam Akbar's, all in reference to shared textual sources but divergent interpretations.

There is also the matter of the woman who left the room. Did she leave because the questioning of the imam traumatized or triggered her? Perhaps. After events like this one, the speakers are routinely approached by women, and occasionally men, seeking help or sharing their experiences.[26] Attending such an event can raise suspicion in the community of being a victim of domestic violence as well. I think that the unnamed woman who left also actively constructed Islam through her act of leaving. I am reminded again of Sa'diyya Shaikh's powerful paradigm of a *tafsir of praxis*, in which she argues that Muslims' actions embody their interpretation of the text. It is especially significant for my project because Shaikh developed this paradigm through research with Muslim victims of domestic violence in South Africa.[27]

Leading the Conversation

In the event just described, we saw both the naturalized assumption of leadership and authority by Imam Akbar and the link between religious leadership and textual interpretation. Even though, as we will see in chapter 5, few (male) religious leaders are trained to address domestic violence and/or actively participate in such efforts, a number of prominent Muslim leaders have taken up leadership positions in public conversations on domestic violence in Muslim communities. They have done so by invitation from women activists in Muslim communities and in response to public attention, such as after the murder of Aasiya Zubair in 2009. There are further questions here of why they assume this authority so much more easily than the women activists, which we will return to in later chapters.

Some of the statements from male scholars and leaders against domestic violence, in the form of public lectures and/or *khutbahs* (Friday sermons),[28] were recorded and then made available online. They appeared on the anniversary of Aasiya Zubair's murder and during the official U.S. Domestic Violence Awareness Month in October. They reached far broader audiences and thus had a significantly wider impact than local community events, especially when the leader in question had a large social media following and was perceived as a religious authority figure. Listening to and watching such sermons and speeches is also possible within the anonymity of the Internet and does not pose some of the risks associated with being seen at communal events against domestic violence.[29]

In my analysis of two selected videos, I am interested in the ways in which Hamza Yusuf and Mohamed Magid, respectively, develop their arguments, what references they make to authoritative textual sources, and how they describe the problem of domestic violence. I selected these two examples from a much larger collection because they approach the issue from significantly different angles and with different strategies but for the same interrelated goals: convincing their audiences that domestic violence is a significant problem in American Muslim communities (i.e., raising awareness); providing the same audiences with tools to recognize that engaging in DV is "against Islam"; and establishing their own authority to define these tools. My analysis is deeply indebted to the work of Ayesha Chaudhry, who in part 3 of her *Domestic Violence and the Islamic Tradition* explores modern interpretations of Q 4:34 and offers important insights into the link between such interpretations and conceptions of the Islamic tradition as patriarchal or egalitarian, as well as universally authoritative or in need of reform.[30]

The two speeches share several common characteristics as well: they are clearly addressed to a Muslim audience (both men and women); they thus assume basic knowledge of the "authoritative" textual sources (the Qur'an and the Sunna); and they are sermons, even if not intended as a Friday *khutbah* and follow predictable rhetorical patterns, including addressing the audience directly, the inclusion of prayers, elliptical quotations from the Qur'an, a particular pathos, and even drama.

Hamza Yusuf: "Removing the Silence on Domestic Violence"

Hamza Yusuf is an American Muslim scholar and preacher who cofounded Zaytuna Institute (with Zaid Shakir) in 1996 and helped transform it into Zaytuna College in 2008. Yusuf begins his sermon with an opening prayer in Arabic and includes quotes from the Qur'an and Hadith in Arabic throughout the talk.[31] He also always includes translations of these quotes into English and relies on detailed discussions of the meaning(s) of Arabic words—thereby acknowledging the acts of interpretation he engages in.

His discussion of domestic violence begins with the already familiar verse Q 30:21, with a focused discussion of the term *mawadda* (love) in marriage, which he links to the purpose of marriage: to establish tranquility. *Mawadda* is the love that is connected to one of the names of God, *al-Wadud*, and thus is the best kind of love. Tranquility can only come from the home, the place where the family dwells, and it is, supposedly, the place where there is no violence.

From there he develops an elaborate argument about humans, animals, and violence among animals and humans. He posits that the purpose of marriage is to make humans more human and less like animals: "Marriage is part of the civilizing process; it's a way they become more human; it civilizes human beings when they enter into a marital contract."

The largest part of the sermon is taken up by Yusuf's discussion of Q 4:34, which he walks his audience through from the beginning to the end, focusing on the key terms we have already encountered in our explorations. He relies on the interpretations of Tunisian scholar Ibn 'Ashur, whom he identifies as the most important scholar of the twentieth century. According to Yusuf, "men are the maintainers of women" and this is the Islamic norm even if there are cases where women take care of men (temporarily and in exceptional circumstances). The overall purpose of human existence is to please God, and marriage plays a very important role in achieving this goal: "That is why there are many Hadiths that Allah loves marriage; Allah loves people coming together; Allah loves that families are built; Allah loves to see a man exhausted at the end of the day who is earning a livelihood to support his family. The Prophet said that the real *jihad* is supporting your family."

In the next step, he asks: What happens when things go wrong in a family? If the purpose of marriage is to live in harmony, then a marriage that does not have such harmony, even with repeated effort from both spouses, might need to be dissolved. But effort within marriage cannot be selfish or greedy and needs to consider the interests of all involved. And divorce is possible and far superior to oppressing another human being. He also warns that a husband should never become like a god: "The husband becomes like a god. What is that? That's not in Islam? What is that? That's not Islam. It has nothing to do with Islam. It's *jahiliyya*, it's patriarchical *jahiliyya*."[32]

Yusuf then responds to "people" who claim that the Qur'an encourages domestic violence and counters them by claiming that only people with twenty years of study of the Qur'an can interpret the text at all, thereby both underlining his own authority and undermining that of others, including grassroots activists who have developed their own interpretations of the Qur'an. Even worse, the people making those claims could also be non-Muslims smearing Islam—echoing the need to defend Islam in anti-DV work.

He then links *nushuz* (disobedience) directly to *daraba*. *Nushuz* is, according to Yusuf, a specific kind of disobedience:

> So, people pick out verses, even translations, there's translations in the Qur'an verse 34, it says that if you fear some kind of disobedience of your wives, it says if you fear—that's not what it means. That's not what it means in Arabic. All of the *mufassirun* [Qur'an commentators] are in agreement that it means if a woman has entered into a state of gross disobedience, and this doesn't mean disobedience to her husband, this means disobedience to God, then the husband is told first to do *fa-'idhuhunna* to ... to admonish them, to tell them please don't do this. And then it said *wa uhjuruhunna*; and then it says leave them in the beds, don't have intimacy with them. Now the third verb in that verse says *wa idribuhunna*. It uses the word *darb* in the Arabic.

Here, he finds it necessary to point out that not even Arabic speakers understand Qur'anic Arabic easily, and that the verb *daraba* appears with different meanings in the Qur'an, followed by the rhetorical question of what this word means. His answer is not really a clear one in that he, relying on Ibn 'Ashur, claims that the verse was revealed to "eliminate domestic violence" and that violence against one's spouse is not justifiable in Islam—because it would mean to contradict the Prophet Muhammad. The Prophet never struck a woman, child, or servant and was sent to us as a mercy, so if Muhammad is the best human being, how could we be allowed to hit spouses?

DV advocates would take issue with Yusuf's description of what constitutes domestic violence: "First of all, I guarantee you that no one has ever hit their wife working out some progressive thing, 'well first I'll try this, and then I'll try this, and then I'll try this.' That's not how domestic violence occurs. Domestic violence occurs when somebody loses his temper and punches somebody. That's domestic violence. So the first thing the Qur'an is telling you is stop and think about this. That will stop domestic violence." This physical attack in anger is not in accordance with the logic of disciplining a wife, which requires both a recognition of her disobedience and the sense of responsibility for her punishment—neither of which is possible as a moment of losing control or striking in anger. And there is of course the missing pattern of power and control.

Yusuf even brings up other preachers who seem to advocate limits to beating and that some women need to be struck to achieve the disciplining goals rather than prohibiting it altogether. Yusuf seems to waver here between wanting to prohibit striking completely and not being able to do so based on the meaning of the word in the Qur'an. In the end, he settles on prohibiting physical harm to a woman and argues that the leaving of any trace on her is not Islamic. In his very last step, he links the suffering of women from domestic violence to possible ways of ending it, and his solution surprised me: he argues that abusers need to be held accountable and punished and that doing so may need to include calling the police.

> And there's people that do these things and these poor women have to suffer the humiliation. Ibn 'Ashur in his *tafsir* says, and I believe this, he says it is absolutely acceptable for the authorities in charge to proscribe a punishment, to proscribe a punishment, for any act of domestic violence. And he says when men are no longer vigilant about controlling themselves … when they use this verse as a means to express their anger, their rage, and their vengeance on a woman, then he says it's the time for the authorities to come in. And that's why any woman who is suffering domestic abuse has every right to go to the proper authorities. If the Muslims won't help her, then she can go to the police or anybody else, because nobody, nobody walking on two feet, not even an animal walking on four feet or crawling on the earth, should ever be humiliated, should ever be tortured, should ever be struck violently.

Yusuf's sermon is notable for both its contents and distribution and has been included in Chaudhry's analysis because he focused his remarks on Q 4:34. In Chaudhry's analysis, Yusuf is among neotraditionalist scholars who need to speak to the values of the communities they address while also preserving the authority of the historical interpretive tradition.[33]

Mohamed Magid: "Let's Talk about Domestic Violence"

The video-recorded lecture by Mohamed Magid is not a sermon but a shorter lecture he offered in the mosque he leads, All Dulles Area Muslim Society (ADAMS), in Sterling, Virginia.[34] Magid, originally from Sudan, is a well-known figure in Muslim communities and served as president of the Islamic Society of North America (ISNA) until 2014, and he is the most prominent Muslim leader to have actively and publicly participated in Muslim anti-DV efforts. I encountered him frequently at events and in conversations with activists. He often mentions his traditional Islamic legal training and the fact that his father was a respected legal scholar in Sudan—both in a clear effort to establish religious authority. Arabic is his native language, which makes the continuous quoting of Qur'anic passages and Hadith easier for him, and perhaps slightly less of a performance of authenticity and authority than for other scholars.

His talk is long-winded and meandering but most notably does not engage with Q 4:34. Instead, he develops his entire argument against domestic violence on the basis of Q 30:21, which also absolves him from having to decide whether *daraba* means to hit, thereby avoiding the ethical dilemma of other neotraditionalist scholars described by Chaudhry.

Magid combines his interpretations of Q 30:21 with other verses in the Qur'an that address marriage, thereby creating a thematic approach to marriage in the Qur'an that was previously the domain of feminist scholars. This thematic framing is necessary for establishing the authority of the text and its clear message regarding domestic violence, namely that it is absolutely unacceptable.

The love, mercy, and tranquility advocated in the verse are elaborated upon in an argument in several steps including that marriage is a contract that should not be taken lightly. The marriage contract establishes rights that wife and husband have, which means duties and obligations toward each other as well. He, too, asks a rhetorical question then and answers it by powerfully bringing home the magnitude of abuse and by rejecting attempts to downplay the issue, including as violence against women:

> The Qur'an says the purpose of marriage is to have *sakina*—tranquility on the spouse. Then what does domestic violence come from in the Muslim community? Can you tell me? What does it come from? Why do you hear about people beating their spouses? Why are you hearing about verbal abuse? Why are you hearing about emotional abuse? Of course, some brothers reminded me, there are some sisters who hit their husbands. That does not exempt them from that. It is not only when we are talking about abuse we are talking about all forms of abuse—but the statistics show 90 percent of abuse is abuse against whom? Against women. Statistics show that. And I can guarantee you it is the statistic in America; it is the statistic in Pakistan; it is the statistic in Sudan; the statistic in Bangladesh; statistic in Afghanistan ... wherever you come from it is, so don't take it personal.

From Mauritania—I saw my brother from Mauritania there. It is the statistic all over the place. No one is exempt. It is happening in every place.

He discusses in great detail the life of the Prophet and the many challenges the Prophet faced in living peacefully with his wives—tranquility requires effort and even the Prophet had to work to have such tranquility in his home. "And what are the ingredients of tranquility? Two things. *Mawadda wa rahma* [love and mercy]. Husband and wife have to be kind to each other." Love is both love of God and love of one's spouse—love of God is reflected in human relationships, and mercy, the willingness to be patient, to overlook mistakes, and help the other person be a better person, is at the center of how one makes a marriage work.

Like Yusuf, he makes clear that a marriage in which such tranquility cannot be achieved should not be continued. Divorce is a legal possibility and is superior to continued suffering of both spouses or, worse, the abuse by one of the other. Openly talking about domestic violence, he argues, is the only way to be a model for others (in America and in the world), and that includes openly acknowledging the problem rather than being afraid for the reputation of the Muslim community:

And therefore, you should not ever say Islam has caused this problem. Islam never causes problems; Islam brings solutions. We say that to media, to everyone. Do not think that Islam is a cause of this problem, because this problem does not know any religion, does not know any race, does not know any social status. It does not know all of that. It occurs at all levels of the community. But the Muslim community, because Allah has ordered us and commanded us to do what is right, we should look to ourselves all the time and say, "We are supposed to be the best community to emerge to mankind." We have to do our best to change our attitudes toward marriage and to think that relationships are based on those principles.

Imam Magid is appealing to Muslim communities here both politically and ethically. And, as in many of his talks, he brings in stories from his experience working as an imam. When he mentions Muslims who say that one has to ask why a man broke a woman's arm or took a woman's life, he responds that asking would mean that there is justification, and to him, there is no such justification.

After many more stories about the Prophet Muhammad, his wives, his companions, his companions' wives, and the examples they offer from their lives for how to resolve issues, maintain marriages, or dissolve them if necessary, he arrives at his final supplication:

> Grant us a gift. Spouses are a gift from Allah; children are a gift from Allah. May they give comfort to our eyes and make us the leader of the righteous. This is my *du'a*, my supplication. This moment I ask Allah to bestow the mercy upon the sisters that have lost a life, very violent, in a very violent way, and that contradicts all those principles that I shared with you, have shaped the core of every one of us, the conscience of every one of us. Why such a thing would take place in the Muslim community? As I said, Islam has no blame in this. Not because they have opened the Qur'an and said, "I am going to do this because the Qur'an says so." But we, the best nation, the best community, we should talk about this issue.

Imam Magid's speech, then, is an example of the normative Islamic marriage model being created and deployed as a counterargument to domestic violence. And his talk also delivers what its title promises: an opening for addressing domestic violence by first accepting that it exists in Muslim communities, second, that it should not exist, and third, that it is not Islamic because it contradicts the tranquil marriage model represented by Q 30:21.

Several other videos, including by Yasir Qadi, Yassir Fazaga, and Zaid Shakir, demonstrate that there is a discernable pattern in the ways in which male Muslim leaders and scholars speak about domestic violence in Muslim families. Each of them would be categorized by Chaudhry as a neotraditionalist; they need to demonstrate their own authority in order to work toward their goal of ending domestic violence, and they are equally invested in maintaining a construct of a stable Islamic tradition with protective patriarchy at its center. And lastly, each of them, by publicly addressing domestic violence, demonstrated their commitment to the ethic of non-abuse. It is worth asking how these male leader figures, all part of a neotraditionalist network, have come to dominate the authoritative discourse on domestic violence in U.S. Muslim communities. Are they given space by (women) advocates because they have authority in Muslim communities and/or do their actual interpretations appear to hold the most appeal for Muslim communities?

From Awareness to Resources and Services

Once a framework for what domestic violence is and how it can and should be recognized in Muslim families is established, and most often, after an "Islamic framework" has been presented as normative, often by someone perceived as an authority figure, awareness events culminate in a conversation about both resources and services available to Muslims in a given community. At times, there is considerable and thoughtful cooperation between Muslim organizations, especially when their work areas complement each other. At other times, the message about services is mainly that there are mainstream services available in particular areas and that Muslims are encouraged to seek assistance when they need it. The discussion at the women's gathering mentioned earlier illustrated some of the challenges that victims of DV face both within their communities and families and in accessing services. We will return to Muslim service providers and the complicated landscape of mainstream as well as other religious services in later chapters.

This current chapter has begun the process of asking how textual sources, especially the Qur'an and Sunna, appear in awareness raising and arguments against DV. It has presented two verses that are prominent in this endeavor, Q 30:21 and Q 4:34. Both verses appeared frequently in awareness events, as did imams and religious scholars to authorize particular interpretations of these verses in line with the Muslim ethic of non-abuse. These presentations demonstrated the centrality of the Qur'an as a source of authority and the negotiations surrounding acceptable and applicable meanings of scripture in Muslim anti-DV work. I feel strongly about emphasizing that in my analysis I avoid reified meanings of these and other verses to then measure grassroots activists against an existing textual tradition claimed as normative or against the interpretations of more "authoritative" male scholars. In other words, I presented here, at least partly in their own words, how advocates and community members represent the Qur'an, their interpretations of its meanings, and its application to Muslim practice as normative without passing judgments of authenticity.

In the next chapter, we move deeper into the lives and motivations of those who initiated and performed most of the DV work under consideration here: advocates and activists, professional and volunteer, almost all of them women. How do they explain their dedication to ending DV? What obstacles and challenges have they faced in carrying out this work? How do they respond when prompted about their perspectives on Muslim and secular feminisms in DV work and broader arguments about gender justice and equality?

The second part of chapter 4 explores how Muslim advocates develop the exegetical and ethical resources that support their efforts, and more specifically how the materials, pamphlets, DVDs, books, and PowerPoint presentations relate to interpretational frameworks, power and authority dynamics, and ideas of Islamic source texts and a stable interpretive tradition.

4

Need to Teach

COUNTERING OPPRESSION, ENDING INJUSTICE, AND PREVENTING HARM

How can domestic violence be invisible? Why can we not see the fear that dominates women's lives, the injuries to body and soul that maim and scar, and the changes in their interactions and relationships? Today I interviewed a woman advocate who disclosed her own abuse, in a matter-of-fact voice, and then moved on to her concern for the women she is trying to protect. Her trust makes this project take on urgency, and I struggle for more convincing words, deeper analysis, farther reach.

THE VICTIMS AND SURVIVORS are on every page, in every interview, in every slide of the awareness-raising PowerPoint presentations and videos. They are present, their stories depressing, infuriating, and often gory in the violence inflicted on their bodies, minds, and hearts. How can one move from the horror of their experiences to the people who have heard their stories and seen their pain? How can memories like this not be all we talk about?

I uncovered memories of my father shouting at and beating my mother while I was trying to go to sleep. For some reason, this only happened at night. During the day, my father was a "normal" husband and father. I would be "frozen" in bed—or under it. I could not get up to help my mother, and I could not get away. I tried to block my ears but that didn't help either. The best that I could do was to "forget."[1]

We do not need statistical evidence to know that the survivors are among us and so are those who are experiencing domestic abuse as I write these words. They are victims and they might not survive. And sometimes the advocates and activists, the service providers, those who volunteer their time and energy, and those who work in a professional capacity against domestic violence in Muslim communities are also survivors themselves. Some have disclosed their survivor identity to me in private; others have done so in public to explain both the need for awareness work and their own involvement in it. Yet others remain invisible victims, out of fear that they might not be taken as seriously as advocates.

In this chapter, I focus on interviews I conducted with Muslims whose work against domestic violence focuses on awareness and prevention. I have conducted more than thirty such interviews and many of them are hours-long conversations. I interviewed some advocates more than once and I have, over the six years of the project, also had many more informal conversations. I write this to explain how I have struggled to do justice to these deeply meaningful conversations, to honor the courage, honesty, and commitment of those who were willing to speak to me as they were doing their important work. Some interviewees have told me that our conversations have been opportunities for them to reflect on their purpose, their work, and their experiences and, in a small way, that might be a way for me to give back.

The interviews are historical and informational as well as deeply personal and they reflect the diversity of voices and perspectives that make up the American Muslim anti–domestic violence movement. There often is no clear boundary between advocates and those who provide direct services—this holds true for organizations as well as individuals. In that sense, this chapter and chapter 6 are organically linked and provide different facets of the same picture—the sketch of a shifting landscape I alluded to in chapters 1 and 3. The following pages offer insights but they also chronicle the scattered nature of DV efforts, the difficulties of developing and sharing resources, and the messiness of the work.

Part of my struggle has to do with retelling their stories without either breaking confidentiality or reducing their work to a function of their personal experiences. Does it help us analyze the work against domestic violence to explain how a particular person came to it and experiences it? I am not sure. In what follows I have selected pieces from different interviews to tell some of the stories and to demonstrate the diversity and breadth of ideas and experiences. There is some indication that shared patterns exist in these narratives; however, I am worried about elevating them to the level of sociological analysis that then lays claim to causality which in turn gives rise to psychoanalytic explanations. Rather, these similarities in their stories may point to the ethic of non-abuse as a reflection of an innate sense of justice and injustice and the ability of human beings to empathize with the suffering of others. To me, these interviews were primarily a demonstration of the many tensions and fissures in the advocates' lives, telling stories of struggle, of frustration, and of meaning-making.

The chapter also interweaves interviews with the materials and arguments that Muslim advocates develop and employ in their efforts against domestic violence. I focus specifically on the film I already mentioned in chapter 3, *Garments for One Another: Ending Domestic Violence in Muslim Families*, produced by the FaithTrust Institute and the Peaceful Families Project in 2007.[2] I promised then that I would offer further insight into its content, message, and structure here.

The ninety-minute film is divided into three parts: 1. Understanding Domestic Violence; 2. Islamic Perspective on Domestic Violence; 3. What We Can Do to End Domestic Violence.[3] I also draw on a short book, *What Islam Says about Domestic Violence*, by Salma Abugideiri and Zainab Alwani, that I encountered at several of the events I attended.[4] In addition, I had access to a collection of PowerPoint presentations from the Peaceful Families Project (most were created by Salma Abugideiri) and the Islamic Social Services Association (created by Bonita McGee), a resource folder produced by the Department of Justice in partnership with Karamah[5] from 2008, and materials from other webinars and events.

I am interested in the interplay between religious arguments against domestic violence, commitments to the ethic of non-abuse, and ideas about causes of and remedies for DV. I insist that the ethic of non-abuse as an embodied practice is much more than the development of a set of arguments that are then applied to anti-DV work. In fact, it is a practice, often not even formulated in words, but certainly not through Qur'an quotes and Hadith references, that reflects a, perhaps innate, sense of justice and dignity for all human beings. This is as close to a theological argument as I will make here: Muslim DV advocates voice their rejection of domestic abuse in terms and words that are born of a God-given sense of right and wrong, of justice and injustice, which is actualized and embodied before they turn to scripture or look for authoritative human voices to interpret God's word for them.

A note on gender is in order as well: as is true for the Muslim DV movement as a whole and the mainstream one as well, the vast majority of the advocates I interviewed were women. There are men in the movement, in larger numbers among advocates than among providers, and they are always noted as important. We see here a particular investment in male authority that validates critiques and demands that women have been making for decades and that only become fully audible when men repeat and amplify them. I am speaking of men involved in awareness work through organizations and not in their primary capacity as religious authority figures. Those religious leaders are almost all men, and their work functions differently in the movement than that of those few men and many women who have founded organizations, put together events, and sown the seeds by formulating the ethic of non-abuse as a religious argument against domestic violence that then received support from religious leaders.

There is a shared story arch among many of the advocates that supports the primacy of an experienced and embodied ethic on non-abuse that is then translated into active work in the community and in a later step a search for religious discourse in order to further effective activism. Advocates often first recognized domestic abuse as wrong (seeing abuse), then became critical of the ways in which Muslim communities address or do not address this issue (communities of silence), and responded by taking action (organizing against injustice) and developing or finding religious arguments. It is in this last part of the story that religious authority, and with that status and authority in communities, became an existential issue for the effectiveness of anti-DV work. At the end of the chapter (and the story arch) I reflect on the connection between feminist ideas about patriarchy and DV on the one hand and acceptance/rejection of such ideas in Muslim communities on the other. It is interesting that *Garments for One Another* follows the exact reverse format—starting with religious arguments against domestic violence and then suggesting what to do about the problem. This order conforms to the way in which we tend to think about thought and action, theory and practice. I see them in a continuous interplay, a cycle in which practice feeds discourse which then in turn affects practice, and the cycle starts with practice.

Seeing Abuse

The film starts with the Arabic recitation (and visual presentation of an English translation) of this part of Qur'an 4:21: *"you have given yourself to one another and she has received a solemn covenant from you."* Then, woman after woman is shown speaking about her abuse:

> "I cannot even remember what the argument was about. But he struck me in the face and broke my nose and cheekbone."

"Listen, Ahlam, one thing you have to understand here is if you want to leave here, it's only going to be through death. Either we live together or we die together and that's final."

"He wouldn't let me work, he would say I can have this friend and not that one."

"You've never had nothing, you will never be nothing."

Then, on a black screen, these words appear: "Alhamdulillah, it never happens to our sisters, it never happens to our mothers, it never happens to us."

This first part of the film, which is most often shown during DV awareness events, directly responds to observations by DV advocates that the first major issue and obstacle for ending domestic violence is to recognize that it exists, not only in the news or in the broader American society but also within Muslim families and communities. The film features eight American Muslim women survivors of domestic abuse, several of them also active in DV awareness work and services, and one young man who bears witness to the abuse of his mother when he was a child, thus representing the impact DV has on children.

This effort to make domestic violence visible, to pull out of the shadows what happens there, is necessary because the invisibility of domestic violence is more than an accidental oversight. Abusers are often masters at hiding their terrible acts, and the reluctance to recognizing domestic violence is often active resistance to doing so. This resistance is part fear of having to respond with actions and part hope that the unbelievable can be ignored. In the lives of the advocates I interviewed, seeing and recognizing domestic abuse took many different forms. Sometimes it was a single event and at other times a slow and difficult process to accept the existence and the many forms and faces of abuse.

Aminah was twenty-two and about to finish college when I interviewed her in late 2011. I met her at a DV awareness event she organized through the Muslim Students Association (MSA) at her college. Because we did not start with a question about how she got involved with DV work, the story of her seeing and recognizing domestic abuse among Muslims did not unfold chronologically. When she started college, she explained to me, she became involved in this issue through her work in a physician's office where she witnessed the effects of domestic violence in patients. She saw patients with injuries inflicted by family members and made the connection to the Muslim community because "they were religious people, you know, guys with beards, women in long dresses and hijab." She described how she would randomly be told by people about domestic violence: the Muslim nurse who drew her blood at a blood drive; the woman who gave her a facial for the first time. At this point in the interview, she declared her efforts against DV to be her calling. She saw meaning in these seemingly random occurrences and perceived their timing as a literal call from God. It was not until later in the interview that she disclosed her extended family's history of domestic violence that she had known about since high school, long before random strangers told her about their abuse. She had an aunt in Pakistan who was abused by her husband for decades, and although the family knew about it, there was no recourse to the legal system, there were no services, and the aunt would have nowhere to go if she left him. She stayed in her marriage, and her sister in the United States felt perpetually guilty about not being able to help. Another aunt, this one a doctor in the United States, was in an abusive marriage and had the means to leave, both financially and in terms of law and available services.

Fadilah was in her early sixties, married with grown children, and had been recommended to me by another DV advocate in her city. Originally from Pakistan, she had been in the United States for thirty years and had lived most of that time in the same community. She described her involvement with DV issues as a function of her standing in the local Muslim and Pakistani communities: "For some reason, since people have known me for a long time, they had confidence in me, they approached me with a problem of domestic violence; I have always been ready to help them out." She recounted eight cases in the past decade in which she interfered in families who had a DV problem. She credited her father with raising her similarly to his son, encouraging her education, and living as an example of a husband who treated his wife well. She saw a cycle beginning with her grandfather of raising sons who respected women and treated them well. There was an argument underlying her story about Pakistani culture as not respectful of women in general and her family's history as a rare exception. In my conversation with her, culture was represented by customs and practices that hurt women and was juxtaposed with what Islam says about women's rights and respect for women.

More than one interviewee linked their awareness of the existence of DV in Muslim communities to the murder of Aasiya Zubair (see chapter 2). This is and is not surprising; many of the interviews took place in 2011 and 2012, so several years after that incident and its aftermath. These interviews indicate, yet again, that Zubair's murder was indeed a wake-up call for Muslims and put DV and its murderous consequences at the forefront of Muslim conversation, at least for a time. It led to the founding and/or expanding of awareness of service provider organizations.

When I interviewed her in 2012, Maliha was forty-six, divorced, and had a young son. She was involved with a mosque in her area and was getting an associate's degree. In 2009, she heard about the murder of a Muslim woman in upstate New York (Aasiya Zubair), and in the same month she received a call from a community member about counseling for sexual abuse. It was then that she started doing research about domestic violence and came across her state's coalition against domestic violence.[6] After reading the materials and resources provided on the coalition's website, she said:

> I realized that I was a statistic. I had asked my husband, who was from India, for a divorce in 2007, and the divorce became final in 2008. But I told myself that I was not a statistic. When I was reading the stuff online I realized that my marriage had been abusive. He used to call me names and threaten that he would destroy me—it devastated me emotionally that I had been abused like that.

She felt the need to write a poem about her experiences and shared it with a group of Muslim women on a discussion forum. In response, she was contacted by a woman in her community who asked her whether she would be interested in organizing a committee for the mosque on DV. She had not been actively involved in the mosque while she was married, in part because her husband discouraged her from participating. I did not point out in the interview that isolating victims is one important abusive strategy but Maliha brought it up herself later in the conversation. Her involvement in the mosque through the DV work was a mixed blessing, but it enabled her to take control of her religious identity (she had converted to Islam when she got married) while at the same time putting her into a complicated position in the community. As we will see, advocates against DV are most often not welcomed with open arms when they insist on bringing abuse issues out into the open.

Abdullah, whom I interviewed in 2011, dated his realization of the problem of DV among Muslims back to when he was in college:

> In 2002, when I participated in this Muslim youth program and there was a group of us who wanted to meet to talk about social justice issues and there were a couple of sisters there who talked about the problem of do-

mestic abuse in the Muslim community. Now I was raised in the Muslim community here and I went to university close by and I worked with the MSA there. When I heard that, I was shocked, "domestic abuse in the Muslim community, this is a joke, right?" It was there that I realized that I had been sheltered for a long time and I began to see. They set me straight and said, "of course, this is a huge problem." And they began to share stories with me, "I know this sister and this happened to her, and I know that sister and this happened to her," and I was shocked. It really affected me. And I was hurt and felt like all this time I never knew about this. These were people I was shaking hands with and this was a real problem.

He became actively involved in work against domestic violence in 2009, also after the Aasiya Zubair murder. His involvement lasted several years and focused on what Muslim men can and should do against DV.

One of the most heartbreaking stories was told by Safiyah at an event and then in more detail in an interview with me in 2011. She was doing an internship as a counselor and had not thought that she would be doing work related to DV. She was matched by her organization to a Muslim woman and sent there for her first client assessment.

She had called wanting help for her depression and she was homebound because of her infant child. I was sent to her home, knowing that she had been abused and that she was depressed. When I got there, she showed me her baby. Her son must have been about two and he was in a glass crib, the kind they have in hospitals, with all sorts of tubes and wires coming out of him. She told me that she had been severely abused during her pregnancy and that there was a history of abuse before that as well. And then when she had the baby and he was neurologically impaired, her husband said it was not his child. And this boy was beautiful, Juliane, with these big brown eyes, gorgeous face, mashallah. So the husband said it wasn't his child and left her. Her family wanted her to institutionalize him and she refused because of the shame of having a child who would never be able to walk or to feed himself or talk. I remember visualizing my own son running and jumping and knowing that this boy was not ever going to. And I just sat down and started to cry. I asked her how she coped and she brought down her Qur'an and she started reading to me verses that brought her comfort.

This story helped Safiyah realize the importance of focusing on domestic violence in her work. The woman and her son left a lasting impression, and she stayed in contact with her beyond that first assessment. Eventually the woman had to put her son in an institution because he became too big for her to care for him alone. Safiyah supported her along the way and was, several years later, invited to her wedding.

When I asked Safiyah whether she tells this story for a particular purpose at awareness events, she said that she never plans on telling particular stories. She says a *du'a* (supplication) before she starts a presentation or event and when she meets the group that will be her audience, the stories come to her when they need to. This particular story has been important for her in convincing Muslim audiences that DV is real and happens in their communities. She did not explicitly mention communal silence in the interview but described her work as important to convincing Muslims that this is a problem they need to address.

Communities and Families of Silence

It is no coincidence that so many books about domestic violence in religious communities mention silence in their title. Rabbi Abraham Twerski's now classic *The Shame Borne in Silence: Spouse Abuse in the Jewish Community* from 1996, and *Silence Is Deadly: Judaism Confronts Wifebeating* by Naomi Graetz represent the concern in Jewish communities, as Anne Weatherholt's *Breaking the Silence: The Church Responds to Domestic Violence* does for Christian communities. And Mildred Muhammad, whose story we encountered in chapter 2, called her book *Scared Silent*.

Maliha recalled that the response to her efforts in her community included attempts to ostracize her and tell others to not associate with her. She was grateful for every person who showed up for any of the DV committee meetings and even more so when more than one person showed up for the first awareness event at her mosque. She had been told that earlier efforts had failed because people simply would not come to meetings and events, thereby effectively refusing to acknowledge DV as a community problem. The divorce from her husband added to her ostracization because community members both blamed her for the failure of her marriage and suspected that she was out to now destroy other marriages.

Fadilah said:

I am very sad that the Muslim community here, predominantly from Pakistan and India, they don't have anything to offer. It is shameful to admit that they don't want to offer anything. They have resources; they have money, but this is not part of their charity. It was a few friends and family that were ready to financially help.... I do not believe in any culture, it's something that you have but it is not important; Islamically, a woman has rights, culturally, our women have no rights. So, the majority of this community—they were saying that I was trying to break somebody's home—some thought that I was too rebellious, too westernized. Of course, those are the people that don't know about their own religion.

Soraya, an Arab American Muslim advocate in her thirties, told me the story of a woman she encountered around the time she started to be actively involved in a DV organization:

The very first person they called me about was a young Moroccan woman who did not speak a word of English. She had a six-month-old baby and a seven-year-old boy. They were living in a homeless shelter, with her husband, and the idiot beat her in the shelter, on camera. When that happened, he was kicked out and they were moved to a women's shelter.... This woman was amazing, she was in her early twenties, she didn't speak any English, she had no skills, no support network, no education, but she was so strong, incredibly sweet, she was a good mother, she wanted the best for her kids, and she was willing to do whatever it takes to make that happen. I never saw her cry; I never saw much in terms of weakness in her. I think I would be a basket case in that situation. I think of myself as a strong person, and I don't think I could have done what she did. Exactly where do you start? She couldn't get a job, we tried in so many places. She was inspiring to me in so many ways and we would talk often, she would confide in me. We still have a relationship and I check in on her.... She went back to him and it killed me that she went back. She didn't go back because of herself, she went back because she wanted a father for her kids, because the only family she had were going to disown her if she didn't go back. She would have been cut off from everything in the world that sustained her. From what she has said, she would threaten him that she would leave if he started to cross a boundary. Now they live in a small apartment and she is thrilled that her life is moving toward normalcy again. I met her husband and I didn't like him. My readings were not good readings—this was a really traditional, patriarchal man. She was telling me that things were okay but in a defensive way. Something was not right. She knows all the resources and she is choosing to be where she is right now. I just hope that

that doesn't involve any serious abuse.... She is still inspiring to me even though she went back. She was willing to persevere against all odds. She is the invisible victim; she is what could be in both ways.

In almost every interview, the hesitation and often resistance of communities as well as families to acknowledge that domestic violence happens in our communities were brought up. It is a source of frustration for the advocates. This refusal to acknowledge the problem in several cases took the form of undermining and ostracizing the advocates as individuals and community members. For women advocates, there were layers to this strategy: community members would speak badly about them behind their backs; they would warn others, especially other women, away from them; they would approach their spouses or fathers to ask to control their women; and they would refuse to speak to them.

In response to the rejection and insistence on silence many advocates have faced, they developed a number of strategies. One was to confront communities, leaders, and individuals with the stories, faces, and voices of the victims. This is evident in *Garments*, which allows the viewer to hear and see the stories of abuse. The women are visibly shaken by emotion, some in tears, and some eerily calm when they recount physical, emotional, financial, and spiritual abuse in their lives. In the two later parts of the film, the survivors become representations of the possibility for survival and "journeys to healing." There is no downplaying here of the effect DV has had on the women. In the interviews, advocates were hesitant to share stories of abuse, their own or those of others they had encountered. Most often, references to abuse stayed general and I had to ask about specific stories. This may be related to the fact that the existence of DV in Muslim communities was the starting point of my research and I needed no convincing. In awareness events, there emerged a wide range of options: from focusing on the retelling of one particular story, to telling several stories, to inviting a survivor; in at least one case there were posters with graphic images of physical abuse. The advocates were loath to sensationalizing abuse stories or recounting them for any kind of consumption as is often the case in media coverage of abuse.

A book published by the Peaceful Families Project in 2007, *Change from Within: Diverse Perspectives on Domestic Violence in Muslim Communities*, contains academic essays about facets of DV in Muslim communities (including outside the United States), strategies and solutions including "the Islamic paradigm," and, significant for us here, four survivor stories, including the one by

Jennifer Mohamed cited in the beginning of this chapter. Written in the first person, they represent the reality of domestic abuse and are meant to be used as resources for raising awareness among Muslims.[7]

Another strategy to break the silencing acts of communities is to address domestic violence through a topic that American Muslim communities are interested in and want to discuss: marriage and family. It is no coincidence that some organizations have names such as the Peaceful Families Project, Healthy Families Initiative, Muslim Family Services, and Domestic Harmony Foundation. There is a clear focus on the family, both as a strategic move and as a reflection of an investment in Muslim families rather than women or individuals. This theme of families and communities as the focus of DV work, both advocacy and services, weaves through the Muslim DV movement and is explored further below and in chapter 6.

The "Hear Our Stories" feature of the Project Sakinah website was another attempt at breaking communal silence.[8] Several of the stories were originally published on the blog of Zerqa Abid, one of PS's founders. I conclude my discussion of the problem of silence and rejection, which enables abuse, with a quote from one of the stories, by an anonymous woman survivor:

> Now how are the Muslim communities bad? Let me explain ... I am not supported by them at all. They think that, because I filed for divorce and did not give a chance (as if 10 years is not enough chances), I am destroying my children's lives. That I'm selfish for putting my life over that of my children. A woman will be sent straight to heaven if she patiently takes the abuse because that's her reward! All this bullshit and more, I have heard from Imams, from so-called friends, and strangers.[9]

Without attempting to validate the interviews through other research or statistical evidence, it is clear that a community's refusal to recognize domestic abuse as such and to express concern and rejection is not a neutral position. In a manual for physicians from the earlier days of anti-DV work (1992), the American Medical Association argued: "Silence, disregard, or disinterest convey tacit approval or acceptance of domestic violence. In contrast, recognition, acknowledgment, and concern confirm the seriousness of the problem and the need to solve it."[10] This statement, intended as a reminder to physicians in the 1990s, still rings true for American society in general and the Muslim communities at the center of this book. And it reminds me of a quote from South African social justice activist and Bishop Desmond Tutu, often posted as a meme on social media as a reminder of our shared responsibility: "If you are neutral in situations of injustice, you have chosen the side of the oppressor."[11]

The advocates I interviewed had particular perceptions of the boundaries of their communities, which usually were drawn around mosques and community centers. It is in these contexts, with assumed communities of Muslims connected by a shared space, a shared history, and often a shared set of religious ideas and interpretations, that domestic violence is addressed. It is even harder to break the silence, identify victims, and offer resources to them when such communal frameworks do not exist. Some recent studies have claimed that the majority of American Muslims are in fact not associating with a mosque on a regular basis and while there might be alternative communities, virtual and embodied in their place, it is indeed more difficult to aim awareness work at them.[12] On the other hand, there is far more openness to acknowledging domestic violence as a Muslim issue on social media and in communities that are sustained through social media. In a very practical way, Muslim DV awareness is achieved simultaneously through events in physical spaces and by disseminating information online and on social media. All of the organizations I have studied have a website containing information and resources. Social media–based communities also allow victims and survivors (as well as advocates and providers) a degree of anonymity that can be paramount to their safety. It is noteworthy that the websites of organizations that provide services to DV victims almost never contain information about the people who work there in order to protect them. This is in addition to often choosing to not list the address of the office where the organization is located and meets with clients.[13] Perpetrators of domestic abuse are a threat not only to their intimate partners and their children but also to those who help victims and survivors.

Working against Injustice and Oppression

For some advocates, awareness came through a single event like the murder of Aasiya Zubair; for others it was a gradual process of recognizing events, conversations, and silences as part of domestic abuse patterns in the lives of people in their families and communities; and yet others were victims and recognized their abuse as domestic violence while it happened, or in Maliha's case, much later. The shock, surprise, and frustration for many of them was the bridge that connected their ethical sense of right and wrong and their recognition of DV in Muslim communities to actualize the ethic of non-abuse that then leads them to their activism.

I interviewed Muslim advocates who worked in a professional capacity within the DV field or in the organization through which I met them and others who volunteered their time and energy for organizations, networks, or, in some cases, specific events.

Aminah took her realization that DV awareness was important (and her calling) and organized an MSA event at her college:

> I asked others in the MSA if they knew anybody who is going through DV and surprisingly everybody did know someone or had heard about someone. So why are we not doing anything? Because we assume that the older generation is doing something, we assume it is not our place. That we are imposing ourselves in their lives when there is a Hadith that says when you see an evil you are supposed to stop it with your hand, if not then with your mouth, if not then in your heart. We have extremists using that exact Hadith and skewing it and applying it to the worst situation, yet when it comes to doing good, we are backing down? Everyone related to that thought and agreed with it, so we decided to organize the event for DV awareness.

She made sure to involve college social services and organizations and remarked that the response was overwhelmingly positive. The event in 2011 was attended by approximately sixty women and no more than ten men. It featured a Muslim DV advocate from a local organization, someone from a Muslim shelter in the area, and several representatives of college social and mental health resource facilities. Aminah thought that it was important to provide the women with resources and, recognizing that men might have had different reasons for not showing up, she later initiated a "Muslim men-only" event, with a male religious authority figure. She did not attend that second event but remarked that it focused on Muslim men as leaders in communities but also in their families and the responsibilities that come with being leaders. Neither Aminah nor the male speaker would have called this move a sign of protective or benevolent patriarchy, but I did. Even if Aminah had recognized a men-only event focused on leadership as a benevolent patriarchy move to involve young Muslim men in DV awareness work, would that have been a problem? The event reached the people who, in her view, needed to be reached and thus accomplished its goal. Aminah did not share my concern with benevolent forms of patriarchy supporting marital hierarchy and thus potentially enabling a power and control dynamic that amounts to domestic abuse. Here again, we see how important it is for advocacy work to be grounded in the reality of a particular community. How can advocates negotiate their ultimate goals and their value commitments with the communal realities and power dynamics they encounter?

Abdullah had known about DV for years and always found that he was too distracted by his studies and then his job, he told me. It was in response to the Zubair murder in 2009 that he took the accumulated energy and frustration he felt and created an organization for Muslim men who wanted to speak out against domestic abuse. It existed mostly online, via a website, and solicited signatures from Muslim men in the United States and statements from male religious leaders in order to raise awareness. Abdullah's involvement with the organization lasted for several years and his recollections were marked by the limitations he felt, a lack of interest on the part of too many Muslim men, lack of funds to set up a more impressive website, and eventually lack of momentum to keep going.

When I interviewed Maryam and Jamilah together in 2012, both were married, had children under the age of fifteen, and were working/studying full time. Jamilah had been involved in sexual assault awareness work in college. She became Muslim around that time as well as married a fellow student from Algeria. She lived with him in Algeria for several years and it was there that she heard from her sister-in-law and friends about cases of domestic abuse. They would be mentioned in private conversations and the defining characteristic of each story would be shame. At this point in the interview, Jamilah paused and then said: "My mom was a victim of domestic violence by my father, so I grew up with it quite a bit. He was never physically abusive toward me but to my brothers. I think that is where most of my passion comes from." This narrative move from recognizing domestic abuse in the outer circles of a person's social network to sharing their most personal live experiences with me, which is also a move from recognizing DV to recognizing its impact on the self, appears in many of the interviews. It functioned as a protective mechanism and spoke to the complicated dynamics of interview situations and the fact that sensitive topics required trust building. In some interviews, the full realization of the extent of abuse also created emotional situations and left me wishing that I had better support and coping tools.

Maryam told me about her experience in her first marriage of being kept away from her child for two years because her son was abducted by his father and taken to another country. She got divorced, managed to reunite with her son, and then married an Arab American Muslim with whom she had another child. Maryam got involved in DV awareness work in her community after one of her best friends was abused by her husband and confided in her. She did not make an explicit connection in the interview between the abduction of her child as an act of domestic abuse and the story of her friend who was abused psychologically and physically in her marriage.

The organization they founded with another woman in the same community was their response to an increasing number of calls from women who were looking for assistance. The organization was small but had managed to receive some funding from their state DV coalition and other mainstream funding sources. The six women who were mainly involved in 2012, when the interview took place, were all volunteers and took turns taking phone calls from abuse victims and tried to raise awareness through events. This made it even more impressive that they also managed to organize and hold a workshop on DV for local area imams and religious leaders. They explained that they recognized the necessity of this training when they approached imams for support for their work and were met with much dismissal and, yet again, silence. They also invited a speaker from another Muslim DV awareness organization to offer them a training session on DV in Muslim communities and on how to more effectively provide services.

These layers of work and efforts are important to recognize as well as analyze carefully. This local organization trained local imams in a full-day workshop that ended with a pledge to work in their communities against domestic violence and provide access to information and resources to victims. They also held a series of public DV awareness events in area mosques, to which they invited Imam Mohamed Magid, a nationally recognized leader in Muslim DV awareness work whom we already encountered in chapter 3, and several speakers from national organizations such as the Peaceful Families Project (PFP) and the Islamic Social Services Association (ISSA). With the experts already in town, they also put them to work training women in the community as DV awareness advocates. The bulk of the funding for these events was procured from the state coalition and several state grants. The women wrote the grant proposals and succeeded. As I will discuss further in chapters 6 and 7, the question of funding is central to the ways in which Muslim DV advocates negotiate their relationship with the state, mainstream funding agencies, and Muslim communities and donors who all have different objectives, funding structures, and expectations. In the case of this organization, it was somewhat

surprising that state funding was given to an explicitly Muslim organization—
the separation of religion and the state remains an important principle. The
argument for funding them revolved around the necessity to raise awareness
of mainstream resources and services in a community that was perceived as
reluctant to access those services.

In the decidedly longest conversation I had with any of my interviewees
on this topic, Khadijah discussed the dynamics of volunteer work and professionalization. Khadijah, who is African American and grew up in a Muslim
family, was in her late thirties, had been a social worker for many years, and
had worked in a mainstream DV shelter for several of those years. When I
interviewed her, she was working for a social services office in a non-service-
related capacity. She had founded a local Muslim organization related to DV
in her twenties, got involved in DV awareness work with a national Muslim
organization, and then helped put together another Muslim organization that
collected resources and connected DV advocates and providers throughout
the United States. She noted the difficulties involved in nonprofit work as a
dynamic typical not only for Muslims and listed some of the major challenges: the need for proper management, especially financial management to
ensure viability of the organization; a focus in the work on systemic changes
rather than personalities, which she saw as problematic but typical for Muslim organizations; the overcommittedness of a small number of advocates,
many of whom volunteered their time and were not paid; and the problem of
proper training for advocates, not only in the basics of DV awareness but also
in recognizing boundaries, practicing self-care, and focusing on victims and
survivors.

Khadijah perceived the rotation of DV advocates (in and out of active
work) as necessary and healthy to ensure that organizations did not get stuck
in feeling good about their efforts but focusing on the goals. She commented
several times on the problem of being too territorial about resources and ideas,
and saw the self-importance of some advocates and leaders as detrimental to
the cause. She recalled episodes from her own experiences where she had to
admit that an organization or model was no longer working, or where the
atmosphere in an organization had become too toxic to be productive and
beneficial. She also remarked that it sometimes felt easier to work in a mainstream organization or office and that the particular dynamics in Muslim organizations, including questions of gender and authority, made it especially difficult: "While these are issues in all organizations, I think, being Muslim and
working with Muslims creates this higher expectation that we should all have

the same goals and get along, and it doesn't always work that way. The higher expectations just lead to higher levels of frustration."

Unlike other advocates I interviewed, who emphasized the idealistic motivation and ethical responsibility of the work they were doing, Khadijah described her volunteer work on the board of the Muslim awareness organizations in more practical terms: "I always say that this organization has a product to share and it is not so much the resources on DV, but it is platform building. It is helping to connect people and giving Muslims a sense of where the mainstream DV movement is going. We need to be a part of it. We need to build alliances and connect with people and then we can connect people with resources and services. That's our product." Part of this product was a plan to produce an annually updated list of Muslim providers and services. She described it as understanding the landscape of Muslim DV work, which would be essential for strategic planning but never happened. As far as I know, neither the directory nor the mapping project ever came to fruition and the organization had ceased its activities before I finished writing this book.

Khadijah's organization saw its primary mission as data sharing, training advocates, and capacity training. They organized several conferences, spoke as representatives of the organization at public health and service provider workshops, and had begun to discuss the necessity for what she called "surveillance," perhaps an unfortunate term in the climate of the "War on Terror" that has seen American Muslims put under state surveillance and active interference in community affairs. What she meant was something that I had never thought about before even though I have worked in nonprofit organizations in the past. She pointed out that every well-run organization needs oversight to hold its participants accountable for their goals, achievements, and, importantly, financial management. This accountability was not always in place in the organizations I studied and led to accusations of fraud, but it also broke communal and donor trust and led to high turnover rates in employees and volunteers. It may also help explain the waxing and waning of organizations in just the six years I actively observed them.

She also discussed the issue of professionalization of DV work, especially services:

> We had this big debate about professionalizing at this one conference. You know what, you want people to have quality services, and I don't care how that happens. We don't want it so that a person gets re-victimized because you are more concerned about some other thing. It is not about you feeling

okay, that shifts the focus away from the survivor/victim. You can provide culturally sensitive services but "competent" is a big word. It's been used in other movements to push out volunteers, to push out those who have experienced what they are fighting against, like what has happened in drug prevention. It started with volunteers, former addicts, and then they required those letters behind their name rather than that specific experience. What matters to me is excellence and accountability and not professionalism. I started out as a volunteer and trained to become better so I could provide better services.

There were fewer advocates in my project who both identified as Muslim and worked for mainstream DV awareness organizations rather than specific Muslim ones. This does not mean that Muslims tend to work in Muslim contexts but rather came about because of my focus on religious frameworks against domestic abuse, which led me to particular groups, networks, and individuals. At more than a few awareness events, I saw mainstream organizations sending Muslim representatives in recognition of the need for trust building in Muslim communities.

What happens when advocates cannot do the work any longer? There is extensive research on "compassion fatigue" and "burnout" in doctors, nurses, and providers of various social services including DV services.[14] Advocates burn out in similar and different ways: they lose momentum and energy from investing too much in the cause at one time; their life circumstances change; they move; they lose the support of their families, especially spouses; and they experience secondary trauma through being confronted with story after story of abuse, including horrific physical and emotional violence and the deadly consequences of it. The danger of being re-traumatized is especially great for survivors of abuse who have become advocates. Only one of the advocates in my study told me about leaving her organization and distanced herself from DV awareness work during the course of the study. She told me that she continued to struggle with a deep feeling of guilt for abandoning Muslim DV victims, which was exacerbated by the fact that she had joined the movement after learning that her mother was abused by her father. She justified her leaving by the danger she felt continuing would have posed to her own physical and psychological well-being.[15]

After this important excursus on burnout and reasons for leaving the DV movement, we now return to what Muslim DV advocates identified as the causes of domestic violence and how they analyzed the relationship between

Islam and culture. In the next section, I focus on one representation of "the Islamic marriage model" and analyze references to the Qur'an, in particular the problem of Q 4:34, to reflect on the dynamic interplay of patriarchy, feminist ideas about hierarchy, and religious authority.

DV, Islam, and Culture

What is assumed by the authors when a book is titled *What Islam Says about Domestic Violence* or when a segment in an education video is called "The Islamic Perspective on Domestic Violence"? It lays claim to Islam as a stable, recognizable, and essentialized tradition, which in turn encapsulates the construction of authority through the Qur'an as scripture, the Sunna of the Prophet Muhammad, and, to a lesser extent, the interpretive textual corpus, especially Islamic legal interpretations. This claiming of "Islam" is in the broadest terms a product of modernity and developed in response to Muslim experiences of colonialism with its destruction of Muslim institutions, systems of knowledge production, and the perceived loss of political control and religious life as taken for granted.

American Muslims are part of that historical development, but they have simultaneously shaped and been shaped by mores, specifically American religious history. It is no coincidence that talk of Abrahamic religions and religious pluralism in the United States often uses Islam as a litmus test of inclusivity and the possibility of shared histories, dogmas, and, perhaps, the dangers of secularism as the antithesis of religion. On the other hand, Muslims have struggled to be accepted as part of the religious landscape of the United States. One side product of the struggle for acceptance and the pluralism project as well as Muslim efforts to rethink and reform religious interpretations and practices for changing times and circumstances is the emergence of a reified concept most often called "Islam." In academic as well as popular literature, this takes the form of "according to Islam," "in Islam," and even "Islam says." Behind those expressions lurks the ongoing struggle for political representation and religious authority, as well as the complicated possibilities of multivalent Muslim voices, perspectives, and interpretations.

There are, however, very specific dynamics at work in different spheres where "Islam" is called upon in this way. The work of Muslim DV advocates is one such sphere, and there is both complexity and urgency in the investment in Islam as authoritative and stable, which in turn leads to the construction of "culture" as its opposite.[16] Throughout this book, it becomes clear that within

Muslim anti-DV work, Islam and culture are not deployed in uniform ways. In chapter 6, I demonstrate that service providers recognize both religion and culture as potential roadblocks and resources, which necessitates a nuanced approach to the construction and deployment of both. In chapter 7, we see that the religion/culture resource/roadblock dynamic is represented in yet another way in the context of awareness work in mainstream circles and law enforcement, as well as in interfaith work. The advocates in Muslim communities and those raising awareness are the same individuals and organizations, and their deployment of the religion/culture dynamic in different contexts points to their ability to recognize both the structures of the DV movement and the need for authoritative construction and referencing in the different contexts they operate in.

Mustafa, a convert in his fifties, worked for one of the awareness organizations. When I asked him about Muslims and DV, he said:

> The issue is a human issue, it is not a Muslim issue. The way I think about it is, a long time ago I gave a talk to college students on Islam and they asked, "what about Islam and women?" and my response was, "men tend to oppress women." The Muslims got their style of doing it, Americans have their style, different parts of America, you know. People wield power. For me it has been interesting to see. Obviously the Muslims have particular wrinkles. I would be interested to know, for example, how the mother-in-law as perpetrator, how that goes down in Hispanic culture. I don't know if it's so much a problem in Arab families, it is certainly in South Asian families. And then there is textual stuff, like the verse in the Qur'an with *daraba*, that everybody gets hot about.

Leaving the reference to Q 4:34 for later discussion, this statement on the cultural particularities of power and control while assuming a common humanity is instructive. The connection with religion becomes clear in the next paragraph:

> If you want to go to the deepest level, one of the things that is being revealed there is that people don't know their *deen*. There is a problem that arises because of literacy. Everybody has their translation of the Book, and the Arabs think that they know what the words mean, but that meaning is very particular in that cultural context. And now it's all seen through this postmodern lens that none of the Muslims will admit they got. So now people don't know what a community really is anymore.... It is useful to

have a frame that speaks to Muslim experience and in general that is to talk about oppression.

When I asked Maliha about the causes for domestic violence, she kept evading my question. This evasiveness came in part from her worry that she did not have the "Islamic" knowledge to explain a proper religious position to me, as she told me in a later conversation, so instead she referred me back to DV 101 training materials, power and control dynamics, and the oft-repeated fact that there is domestic violence in all communities and all layers of societies. For Muslim advocates this quite often is also their chance to refer to statistical evidence: in this instance, to point to the fact that Muslims are no different from other people in American society, as far as we know from limited statistics. This argument can go both ways: Muslims are not better than others in this regard and need to acknowledge DV in their midst, but they are also not worse than other Americans, thus Muslims are neither especially prone to violence nor is their religion responsible for DV. Maliha did say at one point that she was sure that the Prophet Muhammad did not abuse his wives. An imam had told her that, and it was very important for her to hold on to that knowledge.

I have already quoted Fadilah distinguishing between the existence of rights for women in Islam and the lack thereof in Pakistani culture. When I asked her about Islam and DV, she said:

> For me this is about the status of humanity. Oppression and abuse are not okay in any situation. But these people are Muslims and I would always ask them, "Do you even read your Book?" Believe it or not, they thought it is okay sometimes for the husband to beat the wife and control her, and it's the duty of the wife to take care, not only of the husband, but his whole family, and to be obedient to them. So I had to clarify to them that this is not what Islam says.

She thought that culture was dominant over religion and that, often, religious arguments did not do enough work to convince Muslims otherwise. Muslims, she said, were too often ignorant of their religion and did not want to change their ways. Even if something was a two-hundred-year-old custom, it could still be wrong.

Nabilah, an African American advocate who had converted to Islam when she was in her forties (she had just retired when we spoke in 2012), told me that she had volunteered in a YMCA women's shelter in the 1980s, long before she became a Muslim. It was very hard for her and she never engaged in direct-service work after that. However, she told me that she had always been aware of the existence of DV and, to her, the question of what DV might have to do with Islam made no sense. She did not see it as a problem coming from Islam, nor did she necessarily look to "Islam" for arguments against DV. Instead, she focused her efforts against DV in the community she was part of, which happened to be Muslim.

I found this pragmatic approach most prevalent in my interviews, which often made it necessary for me to ask about the link between DV and Islam. When advocates did make the connection unprompted, they typically did so in an attempt to rescue Islam from any association with DV. This took the form of, "DV is not a Muslim problem, but there are Islamic solutions." They categorically refused to acknowledge that there could be something "in Islam" that allowed for any form of oppression, especially domestic abuse, which they saw as injustice and oppression within the family. This insistence on the disconnect between domestic abuse and Islam was also at the center of the normative Islamic family model they constructed. Those advocates who produce awareness materials, including PowerPoints, for events, books, and articles, and films like *Garments for One Another*, were especially invested in the development of such a construct, which they used both as an entry point for conversations on DV in Muslim communities and as the foundation for their arguments against DV. Below I discuss one such Islamic family model in detail.

An Islamic Family Model

In the chapter on family structure, the authors of *What Islam Says about Domestic Violence* assert that "Islam presents a comprehensive model for all aspects of life. Many of the guidelines and principles taught by Islam form a framework designed to prevent individual and social problems at all levels of society."[17] One of the coauthors of the book, Salma Abugideiri, shared with me one of her PowerPoint presentations titled "The Islamic Model of Healthy Families," which she created for a workshop for Muslim DV providers in 2009. Obviously, unlike the book, the slides would have been accompanied by Salma's explanations and discussion with the audience. One of the first slides states that "applying Qur'anic teachings & following model of the Prophet (pbuh) prevents major problems" but also that it is important to think through cultural practices in relation to Islamic teachings: "Many cultural practices are un-Islamic."

Further slides focus on the obligation of Muslims to worship Allah and to recognize both their createdness as God's representative on earth and their bond as a community. One slide references Q 4:1, a verse that tells Muslims that they were created from a single soul; that they have rights over each other; and that God is watching them.[18] Based on Q 49:13 and Q 9:71, the relationship between men and women is explained as one of mutual responsibility and caretaking, but it first emphasizes that men and women were created by God differently and that one can only be superior over the other based on their God-consciousness.[19] Or, as stated in *What Islam Says*, "equality from the Islamic perspective means equal in value but not necessarily identical in nature."[20]

Marriage is then described as a beautiful union and linked to Qur'an 30:21, a verse that, together with Q 4:1, is part of most Islamic marriage ceremonies and has been discussed before. The verse reads, "And among His signs is this, that He created for you spouses from among yourselves, that you may live in tranquility with them, and He has put love and mercy between your (hearts)—verily in that are signs for those who reflect." Tranquility, *sakina* in Arabic, as well as love (*mawadda*) and mercy (*rahma*), are represented as the foundation for the relationship of the ideal Muslim couple.

Three more verses from the Qur'an—on the treatment of spouses (Q 4:19); on relations between couples (Q 2:187); and the encouragement of consultation between Muslims (Q 42:38)—appear on later slides in the presentation and they form the foundations for how Muslim spouses should relate to each other: through "mutual caretaking, loving, and nurturing; by practicing mutual consultation for decisions, with respect, kindness, mercy, and humility."[21]

The next four slides are connected by their referencing of different parts of Qur'an 4:34, the contentious verse in the Qur'an that has animated so much debate about gender roles, marriage, and family.[22] I intentionally do not connect the expansive existing exegetical literature on the verse into my analysis of the advocates' exegetical work here because I have found that they rarely reached for these textual sources in order to arrive at their own interpretations. They occasionally used selected ones to support their own presentations of the meaning of Q 4:34. They were acutely aware of the existence of this literature but also recognize the complications it presents for their work. More than once, advocates said in interviews that they wished they could just not talk about that verse. Mustafa was quoted earlier as saying that it was a hot topic of discussion.

On Salma's slides, the entire verse reads as follows:

> Men are the protectors & maintainers (*qawwaamuun*) of women, because Allah has given the one more (strength) than the other, and because they support them from their means....
>
> ... Therefore the righteous women are devoutly obedient (*qanitaat*), and guard in (the husband's absence) what Allah would have them guard....
>
> ... As to those women on whose part you fear disloyalty and ill-conduct (*nushuz*), admonish them first, then refuse to share their beds, and lastly *wadribuhunna*, but if they return to obedience, seek not against them means of annoyance, for Allah is Most High, Great.

Part 1 appears on a slide titled "Who's the Boss?" and explains that Allah is the Creator of both spouses and that each is individually accountable for their actions. *Qiwamah* is explained as an added responsibility of men to their wives, which does not mean that they can or should be dictatorial. Dictatorship and tyranny in the family are declared to be oppression. In *What Islam Says*, the Islamic paradigm is presented as based on God-consciousness (*taqwa*), doing good (*ihsan*), justice (*'adl*), and equality (*musawa*).[23]

The second part of Q 4:34 appears on a slide titled "Obedience" and explains that each spouse must be obedient to God but that the word *qanitat* does not imply that wives have to be obedient to their husbands. The husband is, however, the leader of the family and in his leadership he should follow the model of the Prophet Muhammad. The last part of Q 4:34, which has garnered the verse the moniker "the beating verse" in popular discourse, is explained on a slide called "A special verse for a specific case." It explains that the verse can only be applied in a situation involving immoral behavior and that the steps listed in the verse, namely communication, separate beds, and then *daraba*, have to be followed in order and that these steps imply increasing levels of intervention. Two key terms, *nushuz*, here translated as disloyalty and ill conduct, and *daraba*, which is not translated in the Qur'anic quote, are at the center of the argument. The slide also points out that the word *daraba* can have multiple meanings, including "to leave, separate, strike, tap." The fourth slide in the series does not contain quotes from Q 4:34 but rather picks up the term *nushuz* as it is employed in another verse in the Qur'an, 4:128. In that verse, *nushuz* is interpreted as cruelty and is applied to the husband, and it encourages a wife to seek an amicable separation in case of marital discord.

The final two slides of the presentation address arbitration in cases of family dispute, citing Q 4:35, the very next verse after 4:34.[24] It argues that the verses need to be read together to get a fuller picture of God's intent for Muslim families, and Salma is emphatic that arbitration *cannot* be used to address situations of spousal abuse. The final slide points to divorce as an option in family situations where no other solution can be found. Divorce is presented as a peaceful dissolution of a marriage that is regulated in the Qur'an, without mentioning Islamic law, to prevent injustice, especially to women. Verses 2:229 and 65:6 are quoted in support of the possibility of divorce and reasonable treatment of the (former) wife.[25]

The most notable dimension of this presentation, as well as of the same model in *What Islam Says* and in the *Garments* film, is the primary reliance on the Qur'an. The advocates, here at PFP, selected particular verses in the Qur'an to create and present this marriage model. Their presentation of "the Islamic family model" represents a thematic approach to the Qur'an by pulling together Qur'anic verses that address gendered creation, marriage, and family. Without reference to "scholarly" authorities or exegesis in textual form, Salma presented these interpretations in translation to Muslim audiences on more than one occasion. Only once, in the discussion of *daraba*, do we see the possibility of a spectrum of interpretations but it does not amount to exegetical relativism. Salma's reliance on the Qur'an as a "clear message" from God makes it possible to argue, based on the authority of the Qur'an as the literal word of God, against any form of abuse in a Muslim marriage. In communal discussions, as we saw in chapter 3, this insistence on a clear anti-abuse meaning can be challenged by community members. I have previously argued that criticizing this insistence on a singular meaning of the Qur'an in a specific activist context should not be represented as a manipulation of scripture or as an erasure of the wide range of possible interpretations. It is, however, an ethical dilemma for me as a researcher and fellow activist:

> I want to return here briefly to the question of interpretation. In studying exegetical frameworks for anti–domestic violence work the charge can be brought forth that activists find the interpretations that best serve their goal of eradicating the practice of domestic abuse. Hermeneutical moves that interpret away the meaning of "*daraba*" in Qur'an 4:34, or selective emphasis away from 4:34 and towards other verses in the Qur'an that put forth an Islamic marriage model based on tranquility, and mutual respect, in which husband and wife are described as "garments for one another"

(Qur'an 2:187). Here, too, the danger of exegetical relativism is real, as the possibility of many valid interpretations undermines the authority of the text as well as the advocates trying to stop domestic abuse through their insistence on certain meanings over others.[26]

My own impulse to critique is not borne from a need to deconstruct the advocates' constructions or even the academic tendency to analyze to destruction but is rather a product of my own feminist approach to gender roles and models for Muslims. As a Muslim feminist scholar and activist, I am concerned about the implications of a family model that legitimates patriarchy as God's intent and endorses hierarchical family models as long as the husband and leader of the family does not abuse his power and inflict injustice and oppression on his wife and children.

That I am not alone in this critique and concern became evident in several of the interviews with advocates who discussed the discrepancy between their own ideas about patriarchy, gender roles, and Muslim families and the necessity of compromising on those positions in order to both reach what they saw as the mainstream of Muslim communities and endorse an authoritative family model in order to be perceived as authoritative through the authority of the Qur'an itself.

Patriarchy, Feminism, and Hierarchy

When I discussed causes of DV with Soraya, she pointed out that the organization she worked for did not identify as a feminist organization but that she as an individual and advocate did. She also said that she did not broadcast this self-identification but that instead she was quiet about it in order to not jeopardize the reputation of her organization as well as how she was perceived by the Muslim communities she worked in. She remarked at some point that it was hard enough to gain acceptance as a Muslim woman who did not wear hijab. The issue of the Muslim authenticity of women advocates, represented by their choices about hijab, came up frequently in conversations, with the general opinion being that wearing a headscarf was almost a precondition for any acceptance in mosque-based communities. Conversely, in mainstream DV spaces, acceptance as a Muslim DV advocate seemed easier to accomplish without hijab, reflecting the widely shared stereotype that women with hijab are obviously and especially oppressed.

Soraya's analysis of the causes of DV was deeply invested in critiques of male privilege as the foundational structure of society—not only Muslim societies but all human societies in the present. Men and boys, she said, are raised to expect a particular and privileged role in society and are encouraged, or at least tolerated, when they react to the loss of that privilege in specific ways. There is a spectrum but the main setup of these structures is ubiquitous. The spectrum goes from a left extreme in societies where gender roles are a choice; to the average, where women have traditional roles but can negotiate some; to the right extreme, where powerless women and abuse are the norm and there is little resistance from women to the situation.

When we discussed her organization's approach later in the interview, she explained that Islam was at the center of what she called a positive model (like the Islamic family model above) and that this worked because Muslims would not relate to a presentation or workshop on domestic violence that they perceived as based on a concept foreign to Islam. "They don't like to talk about domestic violence because they cannot see that it exists in their community because Islam says that it doesn't exist, or that it is not justified in Islam and therefore it is not a reality for them." She made a distinction between domestic abuse and domestic violence, with the latter term generating more resistance and argued that what worked best was "using terms straight out of the Qur'an. People react to something very differently when they feel like it is a particular approach—my religion is saying this is what your home environment and community should look like and here are the tools that we can give you, based on Islam, that we can give you to make sure that is what happens." She argued that audiences at awareness events would react negatively if they identified a term or concept as western (or, even worse, feminist) rather than authentically "Islamic."

She went on to explain that religion is linked to culture: "That is one of the beauties of religion, you can personalize it and make it part of your culture but I feel like they [immigrant Muslims] have taken some of the negativity that has nothing to do with Islam and that comes from immigrant culture, including patriarchy, which exists here but not on such a blatant level. There is something very powerful to saying you have the right to do this because patriarchy is part of Islam. That is something very powerful." When I asked whether she thought patriarchy is part of Islam she said:

> I think Islam came to an extremely rigid, close-minded patriarchal culture that was very abusive and oppressive to women. (I am glad this is anonymous, this is my opinion, not that of the organization ...) I think that some of the wisdom behind Islam is that it came gradually. On a personal level, do I feel that there are Qur'anic verses that are anti-woman? Yes. Can they

be interpreted in other ways? Yes. Is there a certain point to which you get when, no matter how you choose to interpret it, it's kind of leaning on the side of men? To most Muslims, no. There is a sense that Islam must be perfect, that it is infallible, but to me only God is perfect and infallible. Religion is one thing, implementation something else.

It was at a webinar in 2012, which was aimed at mainstream service providers, not Muslim communities, that I first saw direct references to feminist Muslim scholarship in Muslim advocacy materials. The list of resources at the end of one PowerPoint presentation included books by Amina Wadud, Kecia Ali, Asma Barlas, and Nimat Barazangi—all four prominent American Muslim women scholars who have engaged in feminist analysis, reinterpretation, and reconstruction of gender roles in Muslim societies and communities.[27]

I did have an encounter with a male advocate and an imam at a DV awareness event where the advocate asked me what I had done research on before this project and I responded that I had studied prayer leadership in American Muslim communities. In response, he exclaimed: "I hope you didn't study these feminists who want women to lead prayers. That is not Islamic!" Ironically, the woman-led Friday prayer in 2005 in New York City, led by Amina Wadud, was indeed at the center of my earlier project and book.[28] My response was vague and got me off the hook in that particular situation, but it alerted me to the potential risk if my interlocutors realized my ideas on feminism, patriarchy, and Muslims. It would not have been difficult for anyone to find out through a simple Google search, but the incident brought home to me that even for me as a researcher, my position as a feminist engaged in "reform" work has the potential to jeopardize my access to the communities I study.

Reflecting on Authority

This chapter has focused on the stories, experiences, and discursive constructions of Muslim advocates against DV. I have intentionally drawn on those aspects of the interviews that are most closely linked to awareness work in Muslim communities. In other chapters, we will meet these and other advocates who also train and engage imams and religious leaders, and in mainstream education and interfaith DV efforts. Here, I was primarily interested in how they came to be involved in this particular work (as volunteers and professionals), how they recognized DV in Muslim communities as a first step, and what forms their response to this realization had taken. As individuals involved in organizations, they both participated in existing structures and shaped them through their involvement. One question, which runs through this chapter and connects it to the next, is what role authority in its different forms plays in their efforts. How do the advocates, who are not religious leaders and scholars, acquire the space necessary to carry out their work? Who or what authorizes them to engage in their own interpretations of scripture and their adjustment of existing "DV mainstream" resources to the Muslim contexts they work in?

The distribution of, claims to, and recognition of authority structures is complex. Several women advocates told me explicitly that they had developed their own frameworks and ideas but recognized that they would not find traction in Muslim communities without the support of male religious leader figures.

Others lamented the hostile responses they received from communities, not only undermining their authority but questioning their status as Muslims as well. Two of the male advocates I interviewed recognized that their role, even though they were not religious leaders or scholars, was important precisely because they were perceived differently by communities and taken more seriously. Even if they advanced somewhat controversial opinions, they would never be challenged in the same way as women advocates.

This, then, is the perfect closing to this chapter and the opening for the next. In chapter 5, I explore how Muslim advocates against domestic violence have involved imams and religious leaders in their efforts, and how those leaders in some cases double as advocates. Specifically, I examine the dynamics of women advocates training male religious authority figures and of bringing together male leaders who are vying for leadership among one another, as well as the question of how the Qur'an, Islamic tradition, and Islamic knowledge were reconfigured in that context.

5

To Lead and to Know

RELIGIOUS LEADERS AND SCHOLARS IN THE WORK AGAINST DOMESTIC VIOLENCE

Do male religious leaders shiver at night from the weight of the responsibility on their shoulders? So much depends on their willingness to recognize DV as an issue, to see it happening in their communities, and to support the work against it. Most do not do any of these things and we need to appreciate the few who do, benevolent patriarchy or not.

THIS QUOTE FROM my research notes, tinged with frustration, reflects one dimension of my struggle with addressing domestic violence in a deeply patriarchal (American) society and in/through religious arguments and interpretations that wrestle with that same patriarchy in Muslim communities and families. This chapter focuses on religious scholars and leaders who have chosen to participate in the work against domestic violence. I open this chapter with excerpts from public statements by three of these leaders in order to introduce the discourses and framing of the issue of DV they have developed, thereby also providing a reminder of the discourses discussed at the end of chapter 3. The three statements, all acknowledging the issue of domestic violence in Muslim communities, were recorded upon the request of and in support of Project Sakinah (PS) and contained explicit calls by these leaders to help the organization reach the worthy goal of ending domestic violence in Muslim communities. Imam Mohamed Magid, the imam at the ADAMS Center in northern Virginia (and in 2011 president of the Islamic Society of North America, ISNA), Nouman Ali Khan, the founder and teacher of Bayyinah Institute for Arabic and Qur'anic Studies, and Dr. Yasir Qadhi of al Maghrib

Institute were all well-known figures in U.S. Muslim communities, well-traveled public speakers, and seen as both authoritative scholars and representing correct knowledge of "the Islamic tradition."

Imam Mohamed Magid

In the Muslim community we have an issue of domestic violence. It is not a problem of the larger community only, but I, as an imam and as a counselor, I have had many people who came to me with the issue of violence in their homes. Many sisters seek help and refuge in *masajid*, asking imams to help them through a difficult time.

Nouman Ali Khan

Abuse is an unspoken about, not much spoken about issue in our community, but it is a sad reality, so we should try to address it collectively and take responsibility ... Inshallah, we can prevent more and more abuse from happening.[1]

Dr. Yasir Qadhi

Domestic violence is a topic that is unfortunately taboo in our communities, we don't want to talk about, we'd like to ignore it and sometimes when cases do surface we try to cover them up. Domestic violence is not going to go away simply by ignoring the issue.... We need to take a stand as a community on this. There is a zero tolerance policy on this. No man who beats his wife is a man. No man who mistreats a woman whom Allah has blessed him with is a real man. Such a person is not following the laws of Allah or following the Sunna of the Messenger of Allah.

The short videos of Project Sakinah's website were meant to underscore the significance as well as the urgency of the problem of domestic violence, and who better to authorize and support anti-DV work than religious leaders and scholars in American Muslim communities?[2] Project Sakinah took a specific approach to raising awareness in Muslim communities: they offered online resources, but at the core of their activities was outreach to local, usually mosque-based, communities who would be encouraged and supported in their efforts to build a local Project Sakinah team that would in turn be familiar with the local community situation and thus able to tap into local resources and address specific challenges. Because local PS teams were created through awareness and outreach work from mosques, their approach required

the endorsement of at least one local religious leader. In addition, PS advocates recognized the important role imams and community leaders play at
the front line of communal needs for DV services.

During my fieldwork, I interviewed imams and community leaders, and
I observed them at community events and in imam training sessions on domestic violence. Some of my interviewees were well-known leaders nationally (and even internationally), while others did their work primarily in their
local community. Some of them, as we have seen in previous chapters, have a
significant public and online presence as well. While I focused on their work
within local communities, it became clear very quickly that, in the U.S. context, there is no clear boundary between imams, community leaders, and religious scholars. We have already encountered religious leaders and scholars
in the chapter on awareness work in Muslim communities, including some of
their constructions of the Islamic tradition, their interpretations of scripture,
and their implicit claims to protective patriarchy and the ethic of non-abuse.[3]

As in each chapter of this book, I weave my analysis and arguments around
the central themes: authority and interpretation, religion and culture, and
gender roles. I also reflect on the formations of protective patriarchy central
to my analysis and consider possible feminist critiques. Quite naturally, the
relationship between leadership and authority emerges as significant to a discussion of Muslim religious leaders and scholars in work against DV. Are they
leaders because they have authority, or do they have authority because they
have leadership roles? Where do scholarship, pedigree, and interpretation
come into this relationship? And further, what does it mean in the context of
DV to make claims to and thus construct an unchanging Islamic tradition that
in itself carries the authority that the scholars and leaders are invested in?

I argue that in Muslim DV efforts the leadership roles of imams and scholars are taken for granted and that they are assumed to be male. In the history
of Muslim efforts against DV, women, and often women survivors, were the
engines of change, the carriers of the burden of awareness work, and the providers of informal services. It was only later, in the process of forming organizations and then trying to gain traction in communities, that religious leaders
and scholars began to appear. How and why did male leaders and scholars become central to the project of ending DV in Muslim communities and what
role did religious authority and interpretation play in the process? It is clear
that it is indeed important to involve men in DV efforts—after all, not only
are they half of the community but they also constitute the majority of perpetrators of domestic abuse. But is there a link between this argument and the

significance of male Muslim leaders supporting anti-DV work? It appears from my interviews tracing the history of DV efforts in Muslim communities that (mostly women) advocates intentionally amplified their own message against DV, including as we have seen their own interpretations of texts, by inviting and convincing (male) scholars and leaders to become allies and supporters.

In terms of the agency of Muslim leaders, I argue that they, too, are motivated by the ethic of non-abuse. This, of course, only applies to those who participate in DV efforts, which is a minority among leaders in U.S. Muslim communities. Those who do participate in the movement either bring the ethic of non-abuse to their interpretations and arguments or are convinced by advocates to support this ethical framework after being educated about it. There is an evident tension in the ways in which speaking out about DV draws leaders into the vortex of discussing marriage and family and through that, inevitably, gender roles. There is risk involved in speaking about DV because doing so can pose a threat to their communal authority. On the other hand, if a community is in support of anti-DV efforts, not taking leadership on the issue can also undermine leadership roles and authority. Imams and scholars walk a fine line of negotiating their leadership roles and authority in relation to the textual interpretations and arguments for peaceful families they put forward. They do so in a communal landscape that is complicated, only partially institutionalized, and formed by the American context in which Muslim communities function as and beyond congregational structures.

On Community Leadership, Authority, and Power

How does one become the imam of a community, or a leading Muslim scholar who is recognized across the United States as significant in his contribution to Muslim thought and practices? On the level of local leadership, the imam of a mosque, depending on the size of the congregation, the affluence of the community (and thus its ability to sustain a mosque and imam), and his "knowledge of Islam," can be a very influential and important figure on one end of the spectrum and the person who comes to the mosque primarily to lead the community in prayer on the other. Imams can be anywhere on that spectrum, and the United States has seen congregational models where the mosque board had most of the power, financially and ideologically, while in other congregations it was the imam who determined direction, practices, and finances as well. American Muslims were caught in a complicated situation for institution building because (Sunni) Muslims historically did not have a clear hierarchical structure of religious leadership or scholarship. In the absence of ordained leaders, theologically as well as liturgically, it was a complex and difficult task for Muslims to build institutions that resembled both traditional mosque settings in Muslim-majority societies and that attended to the very different needs of Muslim-minority communities as religious organizations in a secular state context.[4]

One way to assess the importance assigned to imams as local leaders may lie in the ways they are compensated for their work. In discussions at the ISNA convention, in online and offline communal conversations, imams have pointed out that there is no financial reward in leading a community and that basic needs like health insurance are often not met through their financial compensation. It arguably says something about the value and perhaps even authority invested in an imam as leader by a community that they are not adequately compensated for their work. At a deeper level, this is a reflection of the relative power and authority an imam may have with regard to advocating for a particular communal issue such as domestic violence. If a community, as we have seen in earlier chapters, refuses to acknowledge that DV exists among them and needs to be confronted, then how precarious can the status of the imam become if he continues to push for addressing the issue? Even if, say, the women in a community or women affected by DV in a community appreciated and supported that imam, they themselves would not have sufficient power to prevent his marginalization if the more powerful men, often affluent and providing financial support for the mosque, were critical of his stance.

Based on anecdotal evidence (relayed by my interlocutors) and without direct statistical backing, it is safe to state that the majority of imams in the United States do not acknowledge DV as an issue in their communities, that DV contradicts Islamic teachings, and/or that they have any responsibility as frontline providers. The advocates and providers I worked with expressed continuous frustration with this situation and recognized the importance of imams in their work. This assessment is supported by a small study, carried out by Maryam Al-Zoubi in Chicago, in which she found that the majority of the imams she interviewed were reluctant to acknowledge DV as an issue and were uninformed about resources available to victims and survivors. They supported maintaining Muslim families at (almost) all cost and tended to send women back to their husbands and counseled them to be patient and obedient when they were approached for help.[5] There is research that supports the claim that victims of DV in religious communities frequently approach their religious leaders to ask for spiritual as well as practical support—it is safe to assume that this holds true in Muslim communities as well.[6]

The imams whose interviews, occasional public appearances, and presence in imam trainings I analyze here are among the few who *do* acknowledge DV, who want to do something about it, and who offer various levels of exegetical support, as well as counseling and other services. The fact that they are a minority among the presumably several thousand imams in the United States has to be appreciated and highlighted while also holding them accountable for the predominantly patriarchal frameworks they put forward in their interpretational efforts and spiritual care practices.

The chapter structure follows my earlier argument that practice plays a role equal to discourse in DV work, and this is true for imams as well. In the next section, I explore my interviews with nine imams. I demonstrate through close attention to two interviews that there is an inherent logic to the ways in which imams address DV in both practical and discursive terms. The themes of this book emerge organically from the interviews and are discussed in the section in order to demonstrate the range of approaches and practices among this group of imams. In the next section the imams are discussed as learners: in their relationships to other imams learning with them and as recipients of knowledge, both practical and theological, from DV advocates. I reflect on moments and conversations in several imam trainings as sites for analyzing themes that have not previously been highlighted in this book and/or that are specific to the work and discourses of religious leaders.

Interviewing Imams

Imam Aziz

On a sunny Friday, and after I had attended the Friday prayer at his mosque, I was ushered into the office of Imam Aziz.[7] He insisted on keeping the door open and had invited one of his male congregants to stay in the room for the interview for propriety reasons. Imam Aziz was African American and in his late sixties. He had converted to Islam as a young man and in the Nation of Islam. He followed Warith Deen Mohammed in the 1970s toward what he described as the transition to "al-Islam" and had been the imam of this congregation since the late 1980s. He was also a Muslim chaplain in the prison system.

His role as the imam was closely linked to the institutional history of this mosque, which had begun as a basement prayer community and had grown to the building they had at the time of the interview. He led prayers and offered Friday *khutbahs,* as well as lectures and educational sessions. He also performed marriage ceremonies in the mosque. He described his activities as a community counselor, as someone offering advice, and he wanted to make sure I correctly understood his role. The masjid's policy was to require two or three premarital counseling sessions before any of the imams (there are several others who work in that capacity) would perform the *nikah* ceremony. These sessions focused on commonalities and differences in attitudes, expectations, religious commitment, background, and family histories. They were designed to introduce the potential partners to each other as full human beings and provide them with the opportunity to walk away if they discovered any serious incompatibility without losing face in the community. He explained that men and women have different roles and responsibilities but that in al-Islam they are equal because they were created from one soul.[8] Marriage was ordained by God for Muslims, and it was an important expression of respect for God to treat each other well in marriage.

When I asked about DV in his community and in his many years as an imam, he replied that he had seen unfaithfulness in marriage and examples of mental cruelty but not instances of physical abuse.

> It has not been presented to me, in most cases, as physical abuse. I have had people come in and say they got into a tussle or fight, and sometimes it was the sister who started the fights and he said I didn't want to hit her back. If you have a brother who threatens her or hit her, yes, but never to the extent that someone has come in all beat up and with bruises, I haven't seen that.

I was taken aback by this statement, because I had interviewed women advocates in the same community who definitely had stories of physical abuse to tell and who had offered informal support and services to abused women. The women's bathroom in this mosque had informational flyers posted that offered women access to services through a local (Muslim) organization working against DV. He continued: "We have ways of letting people know that we are not going to tolerate that among the community, and if it does happen, even if we have to intervene and call the police, we won't take the law into our own hands, because we live in America." He then offered that what did happen in his community was that people would get married and then realize that they did not get along well, so they got divorced. It was relatively common to then marry someone else in the same community and thus create what he called "blended families."

When I asked about religious arguments against DV, he described Adam and Eve as the first Muslim couple who were created from one soul and were called by Allah to be kind to each other, to live in peace and tranquility.[9] The Prophet Muhammad never struck his wives but rather walked away when there were disagreements. He also encouraged his followers to forgive and move on. Imam Aziz then made the connection to culture and explained that a lot of issues in marriage were culturally based and had nothing to do with Islam. Things are done in different ways in different countries but Muslims in his mosque were formed by the political and social environment here: the women knew that they had access to the police. "We preach and we let them know in no uncertain way that it is unacceptable and un-Islamic to do that and I don't care what they read in the Qur'an, to strike women lightly. The term 'daraba' can be translated as 'strike' but it also means to separate. For how it should be applied I look to Muhammad, the Prophet."

We returned to his discussion of divorce and conflict resolution in marriage, and he pointed out that the reality of marriage can be difficult and that it is part of the human burden and a test of how one bears it. For Muslims there were additional challenges when they married someone from a different cultural background with different ideas about religion (note the mapping of understandings of religion onto culture). He told me that he did offer marriage counseling (or advice) but that he had also referred people to outside services. He had concerns that non-Muslim services might not be able to attend to questions of religion adequately. He did not know of a shelter he could send women to (and had never done so) but thought that it would be easy to find out.

When I asked him whether he grants Islamic divorces, he explained that the *nikah* ceremonies they perform are also civil ceremonies, which then means that a civil divorce also counts as an Islamic divorce and he was not needed for that decision. He had, however, heard of cases where a woman was forced to accept/offer a *khul*, a divorce request in which she has to forfeit her dowry, and the divorce needs to be accepted by the husband to be legally valid. He acknowledged that divorce is both harder to get for women and harder on them in terms of communal perception. He ended the interview by emphatically disavowing polygynous marriages and swore that there were none in his community.[10]

Imam Ramzi

I met Imam Ramzi after an awareness event at his mosque. He was excited to be interviewed. Ramzi was in his late fifties and described his background as Palestinian, but he grew up in the Gulf. He had lived in Arab countries, Europe, and the United States and described himself as an immigrant Muslim. He had volunteered at mosques and had been an imam for some time before he realized that he needed more training in order to fulfill the multiple roles an American imam had to play. He had been taking classes on chaplaincy, pastoral care, and counseling in order to be a better imam. He described his experience with DV on three levels: in the larger society where he had been approached for support by family and friends; when he volunteered in the community, which made interventions easier because it was less official; and in his capacity as imam, which included both *khutbahs* on the issue and being approached by victims and their families.

He went on to describe three of the nine cases he had been involved in as an imam in more detail. One involved a couple whom he saw as having marriage problems but he did not think there was physical abuse. In two other cases, he heard about physical as well as sexual abuse in the relationship. He felt overwhelmed and was worried that he could not uphold the "do no harm" rule he saw as central to his role as imam. He described the Islamic marriage model as based on tranquility and with the best of manners. Couples are encouraged to hold on to their marriage and make it work, but not at all cost. His model of marriage counseling consisted of four steps:

1. What is the problem?
2. How did you get to this point?
3. What is the best possible solution?
4. What steps can be taken toward #3?

He described cultural differences through the example of a couple in which the wife was an African American convert, who shared the above marriage model and knew her rights. The husband, a recent immigrant from Pakistan, had no understanding of how to properly treat his wife and was shocked when she questioned his behavior. He then asked me (and himself) how important religion was in this scenario.

He got upset when he described the attitude of another imam who encouraged men to get another wife if they were not happy with their current one—effectively threatening a wife with divorce if she does not obey. He distinguished between "bad marriages" and "abuse" and assured me that he could tell the difference when he saw it. The most difficult kind of abuse to track was emotional abuse because the harm is not as evident as in cases of physical abuse. He pointed to the importance of both premarital counseling and suggesting separation and eventually divorce in cases where there is no hope. This, he said, followed the Islamic guidelines in the Qur'an, but couples often could not accept divorce as a possibility because they saw it as bad and un-Islamic when that stigma was clearly cultural.

Imam Ramzi brought up the centrality of the Qur'an as well as the Prophet Muhammad for the Islamic marriage model and insisted "roughing up your wife is not something that Islam condones." When I asked why he thinks Q 4:34 is there at all, he explained that "Islam leaves the door open for a wide road and anywhere on the path is still the right direction." He knew of examples where "a light beating" was a one-time thing and not systematic abuse and based on the verse such a one-time event could be acceptable if the woman was not too badly hurt. He conceded that the verse could be misinterpreted by men to condone their behavior but insisted that the "right meaning" can be determined through the example of the Prophet. DV in his view was a cultural problem and not an Islamic one and that in both interfaith settings and the American media the two have been conflated for too long.

According to Imam Ramzi, there are two conflicting marriage models: the Islamic one and the western one. In the Islamic model, the man is the breadwinner and if he loses his job that can cause problems with his masculinity, while the woman is the family builder who takes care of the children. This model is not lacking in equality but is complementary in nature. This is the model that most Muslim families follow. (And it replicates protective patriarchy perfectly!) In contrast, the western model is based on a 50/50 share assumption in which both partners work and a woman's caring for children is seen as a sacrifice. This is why issues and conflicts only arise in western-style marriage in which women insist on working outside the home. (He did not seem to see the irony of this in light of the fact that I was one of those women working outside the home, interviewing him.)

The interview ended with him offering me his thoughts on a number of his imam colleagues. He was critical of most of them for not being willing to openly discuss DV in their communities and pointed out that, unlike him now, they all lacked pastoral care and counseling training. He commented on their command of Arabic as an important marker of religious authority and the ability to both study and interpret "the Islamic textual tradition." All eight imams he discusses were identified as immigrants from Muslim-majority countries. I concluded that either he did not know any imams who were born in the United States, including African American ones, or he did not consider them to be religious authority figures.

He also offered me a paper copy of a book review he had written of Ingrid Mattson's *The Story of the Qur'an*. As I reflected further on this somewhat curious move, I decided that he had tried to impress me with his scholarly achievement and that there was meaning in his wanting to impress me, the "secular" albeit Muslim woman scholar, with his academic achievements and in the fact that the book he had reviewed was written by a Muslim woman scholar.

Analyzing the Interviews

These two interviews provide a glimpse of both the dynamics of my conversations with male religious leaders and the wide range of ideas and perspectives espoused and practiced by American imams. In the nine interviews I conducted, several themes were central to the ways in which the imams approached their work: the existence of DV in their community and their work related to the issue; thoughts on the role of imams and the question of authority; several, very similar, versions of the Islamic marriage model and its roots in the Qur'an and Sunna; and lastly, the recurring distinction between religion and culture.

Imams Addressing DV in Their Communities

All nine of the imams I interviewed recognized that DV is an issue in Muslim communities. They were, after all, recommended to me as conversation partners because of this recognition and the resulting efforts of their work. Some, like Imams Khaled and Salman,[11] had been at the forefront of both local and national-level efforts against domestic violence while for imams at the other end of the spectrum, DV was something that happened but not in their particular communities as we saw with Imam Aziz. At this latter end of the spectrum, I wondered whether the imams I interviewed did not acknowledge DV cases in their communities because they did not trust me and would not want to discuss them in an interview in order to not make incidents public. Denying DV could also be an effective means for avoiding necessary conversations about their skills and knowledge and through that the creation of needed services in the community.

All of the imams interviewed offered some form of premarital counseling and emphasized the importance of this service and of taking it seriously to make sure that Muslims found partners they were compatible with in order to avoid conflicts later in the marriage. Some linked compatibility to checking for red flags about domestic abuse potential. They expressed concerns about the state of marriage in Muslim communities—"American Muslims are becoming like other Americans, with high divorce rates and other problems"—and emphasized the centrality of Muslim marriages and families to sustaining and growing healthy Muslim communities in the United States.

All nine imams had given *khutbahs* and lectures in their communities on harmonious Islamic marriage and the example of the Prophet Muhammad for Muslim marriages. Only three had ever given a *khutbah* on DV and only two told me that they regularly offered *khutbahs* on the topic. They described, similarly to the DV advocates in chapter 3, the responses from their communities ranging from blaming them for airing the community's "dirty laundry" and creating discord in Muslim families to explicit support for the *khutbahs* as well as the services the imams provided. This range of communal attitudes was also the main reason why some imams offered *khutbahs* about healthy Muslim marriages but not DV explicitly. Part of their work had also been to support, directly or indirectly, the efforts of advocates and organizations in their local contexts to create awareness of DV and support victims. In some mosques, DV survivors were provided with certain services through a social service committee that used *zakat* (Muslim charity) funds to finance their activities.

Several of the imams commented on their own lack of skills in directly offering counseling and conflict resolution services. Some had taken measures to remedy this shortcoming, while others cited their own lack of skills and knowledge as a reason to refer people to other services. There was a clear lack of knowledge about mainstream services evident in the majority of the interviews with imams, and in some cases this lack was somehow combined with negative opinions about those services. Two imams claimed that in mainstream shelters women were actively turned away from Islam; they were being proselytized to become Christian; and there was the additional danger of "being turned into a lesbian."[12] They also expressed concern that mainstream services are based on feminist ideas (the fear of becoming lesbian could be linked to this) and aimed at, intentionally or not, breaking up Muslim families. These fears were echoed in some of the conversations with Muslim providers (see chapter 6) and they seemed to circulate in Muslim communities more broadly. This is worrisome because it effectively hindered Muslim women's access to mainstream services especially when the first person they approached was their imam.

On the other hand, several imams commented that they were regularly approached by abused women because they had a reputation in their communities as supportive of DV victims and open to intervention in abusive family situations. This extended to DV victims from outside their own communities. Imam Amir pointed out that in those situations, where the family was not part of his own community, it was more difficult to intervene and keep track of the situation. Within their own communities, imams reported being trusted with sensitive information but in return they were expected to intervene productively. None of the interviewees specifically mentioned the fact that as frontline providers, like police officers and service providers, imams are potentially also at risk for threats and physical injury from abusers when they interfere.

All imams claimed that they did or would encourage victims of domestic abuse to not only come forward—"there is no silencing in our communities"— but more importantly call law enforcement in for help. Imam Khaled put it this way: "111 is asking you to call 911" with 111 representing God.[13] At DV awareness events, I had gotten the impression that there was significant mistrust toward the police. This lack of trust was explained as a function of immigrant Muslims' earlier and mostly negative experiences with the state and the police in their countries and the equally complicated relationship of African American Muslims with the American state and police.[14] In the context of both the "War on Terror" since 9/11 and a longer history of state surveillance and infiltration in Black Muslim communities in the twentieth century, this general trust in law enforcement expressed by imams was surprising. It may have been more of a function of their performance as law-abiding religious leaders in the interviews with me than actual trust in the police and with it the American legal system as a successful arbiter in domestic violence situations.

Unlike in mainstream DV work (as well as my own perception), the imams did not all or consistently represent domestic violence as gender-based violence or violence against women. Some imams, like Salman, insisted on describing DV as violence against women, while others brought up repeatedly that at least sometimes women also abuse men, both physically and psychologically. While Imam Ismail[15] acknowledged that there was a clear power imbalance and also statistical difference between men and women as perpetrators of DV, others claimed that women were more often abused physically, while there was equal or even more emotional abuse of men by women. Throughout my ethnographic work, I encountered many situations in which Muslim men, often in leadership positions, would joke about women abusing men as some kind of corrective to the impression that women are always the victims of abuse and men the perpetrators. These comments and statements were not only hard to stomach, but they also mirrored a tendency in academic literature on DV that constitutes a backlash against feminist analyses of DV as a product of patriarchy. The same backlash can be observed in online discussions of DV and in the emergence of men's rights organizations.[16]

I asked in each of the interviews, as I did in interviews with providers and advocates, about motivations for taking up DV as an issue and cases/stories that were particularly important in realizing the significance of the problem. The answers, if there were any at all, varied but, strikingly, none of the imams told a specific story that involved the kinds of heartbreaking details about physical abuse, injuries, fear, and terror I heard from the women I interviewed. It seems possible that the male imams did not want to present emotional investment in these cases or that they did not relate to the women victims and survivors in the same way. It could also have been a performance of their masculinity rather than an inherent difference in the way Muslim women and men tell stories of abuse and how they were affected by them.

The Role of the Imam and Issues of Authority

Assumptions about male authority and their naturalized stepping into leadership roles are at the core of the self-understanding of imams and community leaders as well as scholars. I describe these assumptions as naturalized because they do not even have to be mentioned, discussed, or justified. Such arguments are only necessary in conversations about women in leadership roles or as scholars.[17]

Hibba Abugideiri has argued that it is insufficient to discuss women as leaders only in relation to women's issues. Based on her exploration and then rethinking of the role of Hagar in sacred Islamic history, Abugideiri analyzes notions of "Islamic leadership" in American Muslim contexts as gendered and based on historical and traditional assumptions that such leadership is naturally male and needs to be qualified with the attribute "female" only when women lay claim to leadership roles. In a move that represents Hagar as gendered and defined by her biology as a woman, Abugideiri represents her as God's chosen agent: "Her maternal strength, her courage, constancy, and self-initiative as messenger—all derived from her *taqwa*[18]—provided her with the necessary qualities not only to fulfill her sacred mission but also become an aspect of the mission itself."[19] She criticizes models of Islamic leadership that "represent the invisible construct, certainly assumed to be masculine, to which the qualifier 'female' must be added in order to shift focus from larger issues of Islam to issues exclusive to women."[20] In this model, women are confined to certain types of activism and thus limited in their leadership, but they feel compelled to participate in it because it is their only access point for leadership roles. We may conclude that women, through their participation, legitimate this system continuously, because they have an investment in addressing certain issues, like DV, rather than seeing changes in leadership roles as their primary goal. It can be a particular, politically conscious version of what Deniz Kandiyoti has described as the "patriarchal bargain" women enter into in patriarchal societies and communities.[21] More importantly, though, it is the patriarchal system itself that naturalizes men's access to leadership roles and forces women to struggle for access, and often fail.

In the invisible construct of normative male leadership that imams are part of, they seem to have no obligation to interrogate their own claims to authority. In practice, as reflected in the interviews, the imams participate in a leadership and authority competition with one another, as reflected in Imam Ramzi's thoughts on other imams. In gatherings of imams, such as imam trainings, or when a national leader appears at a DV awareness event in a mosque, the tension between the authority and knowledge of the different imams was usually quite palpable.

As outlined above, with regard to addressing DV in Muslim communities, as well as gender issues broadly, imams and scholars walked a fine line between being leaders of change and being leaders in preserving the status quo. Inspired by Abugideiri's discussion quoted above I have wondered whether we should take for granted the assumption that activism (of women at least) makes someone a leader. What if the role of a community leader is to keep things in place and not change them in any direction? Imams and scholars risk the support of their communities, and thus their very livelihood, if they espouse ideas and goals that their communities are not in agreement with.

In the interviews, I also noticed a significant tension with regard to imams *as* scholars—namely as knowledgeable about "the Islamic tradition" including their ability to quote the Qur'an in Arabic on the spot, in conversation, and in speeches. Such quoting of the Qur'an would not only require memorization of significant portions of the text, but the imam would also need to have them thematically memorized in order to recall such passages on demand and in context. Such knowledge of the Qur'an goes far beyond traditional modes of Qur'an memorization.[22] This ability to quote the Qur'an and to reference particular Hadith or stories from the Sunna, and, in some cases, legal scholars' opinions on certain matters, was present to varying degrees in the imams I interviewed. The ways in which they highlighted their traditional training (if they had any) and their abilities demonstrated that they saw a clear link between religious knowledge and religious authority. Ramzi and two other imams also gestured toward a different kind of knowledge, namely of counseling, psychology, and pastoral care, that related to the different functions of imams in the American context from those in Muslim-majority contexts.

The most dramatic moments of thinking about imams as leaders and authority figures occurred when the imams told me about important men in their communities who were perpetrators of DV. The communal significance of Muzzammil Hassan, the murderer of Aasiya Zubair, shone a spotlight on the continuous support he had received for his Bridges TV project but also for his succession of marriages in the same community despite communal knowledge of his earlier abuse of his wives.[23] Imam Ramzi offered the example of one of his teachers who taught him Qur'an recitation and was close to him. When Ramzi found out that he was very cruel and abusive to his wife, he distanced himself from him even though the teacher kept trying to find ways to reconcile, with his former student, but not with his wife. Imam Ramzi told him he would reconcile with him only if he stopped his behavior and when that did not happen, Ramzi stayed away. The same person was finally exposed in the mosque community and was pushed out. Later, community leaders heard that he had moved to another state and perpetrated violence against his wife there as well. He was also a well-liked figure and Qur'an reciter in a national Muslim organization. Before a meeting of the organization, at which he was scheduled to recite from the Qur'an, a woman from the community approached the convention leadership and exposed him. His appearance at the event was then canceled and Imam Ramzi thought that it was good to see that kind of response. He also mentioned that there was an initiative among some Muslim organizations to consider requiring background checks before hiring someone as an imam.

Several of the imams struggled with situations in their communities in which leading community members with significant authority as well as financial power were exposed as abusers. Some communities managed to bring the abuse into the open while others chose to interfere privately and quietly. There was an ongoing debate among advocates and imams about the virtue of exposing abusers versus intervening within the framework of the community. Stories circulated about serial abusers who moved from place to place and could start anew in each because the new community did not know about their earlier abusive behavior. The alternative strategy, to work with the abuser and either limit the abuse or reform the perpetrator within the community, assumed the possibility for both guided self-reform and DV interventions outside the American legal system.

These avenues of intervention, both different from simply ignoring and/or denying domestic abuse in Muslim families, were intimately linked to the question of what the imams thought the causes of domestic violence were.

Religion and Culture

The imams were quick to point out that DV is an issue in all communities and thus is not directly linked to Islam. They decried media portrayals of Muslim men as violent and Islam as a violent religion and pointed to the few available statistics to argue that DV incidents in Muslim communities were generally on the same statistical level as in other segments of American society. Their use of U.S. statistics as a frame of reference was strategic as well as convincing and placed Muslim communities squarely within the fabric of American society. Ismail told me about a panel at a national Muslim convention in which a speaker made the argument that precisely because Islam is portrayed as a violent religion in U.S. public perception and media, Muslims needed to demonstrate that Islam is against all forms of violence and domestic violence especially. In other words, addressing DV in Muslim communities, rather than reinforcing existing stereotypes of Islam and Muslims, would provide a means of alternative representation.

I encountered few references to Muslim-majority societies except, as we will see, when they discussed the distinction between religion and culture. Several imams accused other imams they knew, who were all "from overseas," of supporting abusive and violent behavior in husbands and telling women victims that they needed to be patient and return to the family home, and that they could not or would not confront the abusers. They made this claim

repeatedly in order to assert that they themselves had the right kind of authority on the issue of DV, which in turn was a measure of their own righteousness. I was offered contact with additional imams whom I should talk to and
warned away from others who did not know anything about DV or were, even
worse, doing damage to Muslim families and communities by ignoring, denying, and even supporting the abuse they knew about.

As in the events and interviews discussed in earlier chapters, the interviews
with the imams reliably and frequently referenced the important distinction
between religion and culture. The imams responded with varying degrees of
clarity to my question about the causes of DV in Muslim communities. The
most comprehensive and organized list came, not surprisingly, from Salman,
a leading figure in anti-DV work among American Muslims and a frequent
speaker on the issue. According to him, there were five causes of domestic
violence:

1. a lack of Islam in an individual or family—a lack of faith and religious
   knowledge;
2. a "holier than thou" attitude that he described as a form of spiritual
   abuse—abusers think that they have the right and obligation to
   discipline their spouse and think that will get them to paradise ("they
   might end up in hell instead");
3. life stresses that are managed badly causing anger, loss of control, and
   then abuse;
4. alcohol and drug use even in Muslim families despite the religious
   prohibition of both; and
5. wrong expectations about marriage including generational differences
   in practices and expectations, which can lead to abuse including abuse
   by in-laws.

This list, however, does not foreground a clash between Islam as against
DV and culture(s) producing justifications and frameworks for abuse. Neither
does the list mention gender roles and thus patriarchy of any kind explicitly.
Instead, Imam Salman complicated, at least in my interview with him, the existence of a clear and stable Islamic tradition and instead emphasized the possibility of both varying interpretations and potentially wrong interpretations
and their consequences. He commented on men who use the Qur'an to abuse
their wives spiritually as well as physically, based on the idea of making them
compliant Muslims, who might think they will go to paradise for taking such
responsibility, but they will instead end up in hell. This raises interesting

questions about human accountability in this world as well as in the next. In other, public contexts, he has presented precisely the kind of framing repeatedly discussed here: Islam as against DV and culture as the problem. This is another version of the dilemma about exegetical relativism and ambivalence versus unequivocal and universalized claims to a religious tradition in the service of ending domestic violence. Imam Salman could see the nuances and probably even recognized the constructed nature of his "Islamic tradition" but chose to present it as clear to his Muslim audiences in order to achieve the goals of his activism.

Imam Khaled presented culture as significant in a different way. He claimed that different communities (he had introduced them earlier as African American and immigrant Muslims) "are no different in the frequency of or attitudes toward domestic violence particularly among men." Differences among women, according to him, are a function of "being culturally adapted to America." If they come from a culture where physical and verbal abuse are the norm, they will be accepting of such treatment, while in America the cultural norm is "don't you ever put your hand on me." Men will say when a woman pushes back against the abuse that she has become Americanized. Here we see culture deployed in order to describe the American context, and while Imam Khaled did not represent American norms as negative, other men might. He pointed out the complex relationship with the American state and the varying degrees of trust or mistrust of the system that inform different choices when it comes to calling the police. He also referenced the connection between male privilege and DV, which, according to him, is exacerbated by socioeconomic status. Men who rise in socioeconomic status also show a growing sense of entitlement (perhaps code for patriarchy?), which can express itself in the abuse of women in their lives. This goes contrary to some theories about DV as especially prevalent in economically deprived segments of society, but he thought this gap might be explained by reporting rates. I was intrigued by his thoughts on male privilege, which lined up well with the power and control model—and perhaps even feminist ideas about gender justice instead of protective patriarchy—even if he did not frame his analysis as an explicit critique of patriarchal control of gender roles, women, and families.

Imam Ahmad, originally from Somalia, repeated several times that DV had nothing to do with Islam. The perception that it is connected to Islam comes from the media,

> but that is not true. You know, sometimes it's cultural things that have nothing to do with Islam. So I always educate the community and I tell

them that it is not Islam that tells you to abuse your wife or your children. That is against Islam. But there are some cultures and traditions that say that women can be abused by men and they think that is part of Islam, but it is not.

Imam Jamal, who was in his forties and African American, explained his entire life trajectory as a quest to find the real religion of Islam and as a series of steps, first as a student and then as a leader, to distinguish Islam from its cultural influences and interpretations. He studied overseas for "many years" in order to receive a proper Islamic education and recognized while there that the interpretations he learned were informed "by their culture" but that he could formulate his own Islam free of such constraints. His goal was to be a model and leader for "indigenous imams" who would represent a truly American Islam without cultural interference.

According to Imam Jamal, domestic violence happens because Muslims bring cultural assumptions about the treatment of women to their marriages, families, and communities.

> These assumptions, by generational repetition and over the years, have be-come Qur'anic in the minds of the people who practice it as a cultural norm. Domestic violence is something you could see in Muslim societies because they have been doing it for so long, they don't see anything wrong with it. They don't have another frame of reference. They feel that it got to be Islamic because everyone is doing it.

After laying out how a direct approach to the Qur'anic text, with the requisite knowledge of Arabic (which he had), can help change this misunderstanding, he also explained that sometimes men commit DV because they do not know that what they are doing is abusive. That, too, is part of culture: "Culture is the big bad wolf in Islam right now." As an educator and leader, he felt called to offer his knowledge to other Muslims so they could both learn to distinguish religion from culture and help end DV in their families and communities.

The interviews were rich and complex, and each of the imams both per-formed for me and revealed facets of their work and their life history in their narrative. There were moments when I was infuriated by casually made misogynist remarks or jokes about DV, and others when I admired the person across from me for their resolve, their courage, and the enormous efforts they had invested in this cause. They wanted to impress me, I have no doubt, and they did. They might not have shown as much emotion in their conversations with me and saw the interviews as a form of publicity, but there was great earnestness and concern in much of their demeanor. It is useful here to remember that male religious leaders are also public representations of Muslim masculinity, which is usually maligned as essentially violent and inherently other in much American public discourse and media representations. Despite their apparent authority and power in Muslim communities, which is already tempered by intra-Muslim debates about DV, they are also at the receiving end of surveillance and state intervention and racial and religious profiling, and they are continuously measured by their willingness to assist the state in reporting and controlling "radical elements" in their communities. This relative vulnerability of their position vis-à-vis Muslim communities on the one hand and the state on the other was put on display in the imam training sessions I observed over the course of my research.

Training the Leaders

Awareness work and training of imams were identified as among the great priorities in my interviews and conversations with Muslim advocates. That made sense considering how often imams are approached as frontline providers for both religious advice and practical support. There was consistent lament about imams who provided counseling and services even though they lacked basic skills and understanding of DV dynamics but even greater frustration with the fact that many imams were not even interested in addressing DV in their communities.

The imam training sessions were organized by various Muslim advocacy organizations during my fieldwork, and I observed several full-day sessions between 2010 and 2014. They required preregistration and were not considered public events. I thus refrain from identifying either the imams in attendance or the speakers and organizations involved in the event. I identify them by pseudonyms as I have done throughout the book.[24]

This description for an imam training in 2016 offers a good window into the purpose and structure of such an event:

> This training is meant for imams who are sensitive to the existence of domestic violence among Muslim communities, like other faith groups, and hope to become vocal catalysts for anti-abuse advocacy. Successful participants will better understand the dynamics of domestic violence and have new tools for responding to the complex and challenging cases that they may face as leaders. In addition, participants will identify ways in which

they may support each other in their efforts to deal with the ramifications of domestic violence in their respective communities.[25]

After describing the basic structure of the trainings, I offer several thick descriptions of moments and conversations that reflect some of the underlying themes and dynamics in these events. The trainings were organized by local advocates who felt that it was important and necessary to offer training for imams in their area and involved workshop leaders from outside Muslim organizations. The attendees at these events were self-selected—they were interested enough to spend a day or more of their weekend at a training and in some cases travel to the venue, and they were willing to discuss DV, including in their own experiences and communities. At each of the trainings, the majority of the leaders present were foreign born. This may be due to the fact that the majority of imams in the United States lead communities of different national origins and/or the fact that imams in some communities need such training more than others.[26]

The training sessions were structured as follows, and involved both Karima and Imam Salim as presenters of various sessions. They had worked together in many capacities and had developed this particular format, which they "took on the road" when asked to do so by local advocates or communities.

Welcome	Local advocate
Qur'an Recitation	Imam attending the training
Program Overview Imam Experiences with DV	Karima (woman advocate)
What Is Abuse?	Karima
Survivor Stories	From *Garments for One Another* DVD
Discussion & Debrief	Imam Salim and Karima
Relevant Theological Concepts Role of the Imam	Imam Salim
Islamic Family Law & DV	Imam Salim
Counseling Interventions & Mental Health Issues	Karima and Imam Salim
Signing of Proclamation & Evaluations	

The sequence of sessions and topics walked the imams through several steps: reflecting on their own experiences with DV in their communities, presumably one of the reasons they would attend a training; acquiring a working definition of forms of domestic abuse; bringing home the urgency and reality of DV through survivor stories; offering an authoritative scriptural framework *against* DV and resources from within Islamic law; and providing first steps toward counseling and intervention skills. These components follow a structure very similar to the *Garments for One Another* film discussed in chapter 4. The Peaceful Families Project developed this important resource, but I saw the film recommended by other organizations and witnessed segments of it being shown in many events including imam trainings. In reflecting on my notes and the recordings of the trainings, I am struck, yet again, both by my own reaction to some of the content, including contributions from the imams, and by the fact that these events confirmed the internal cohesion of the anti-DV arguments in Muslim contexts and the significant range of possible opinions, ideas, and perceptions.

But What about the Women?

Karima opened the session with a short self-introduction and explained how she got involved in DV advocacy and service work. She grew up in a home that functioned as a shelter for community members with abuse issues, and her parents—she realized later—provided counseling, a safe space, and other interventions. She herself recognized the prevalence of the issue in Muslim communities and decided to acquire training as a counselor: "my parents were naturally good at it, but I needed to have that professional training." She established her professional authority in this moment and continued throughout the day to base her contributions and arguments on her experiences and professional knowledge as a counselor. She also communicated that professional training was a vital component of effectively working in communities, thereby encouraging the training participants to engage.

After Imam Salim explained how he got involved, which was not personal in the way Karima framed her introduction, the imams one by one shared some of their perspectives on DV. Each represented his authority as an imam based on work experience and Islamic knowledge training, in this order, and shared some of his views. Of the nine men present, four, during their brief initial remarks, brought up that men are not always the perpetrators of domestic abuse:

#1: "In my society, where I grew up, ladies basically lead the family; she is the boss, she can't be beaten at all. It is even difficult to even verbally, to say anything to the ladies."

#2: To my surprise I found that it was not the women who were beaten
      but the men who are beaten here [some of the others chuckle]. In
      many cases, there is this drama, when the woman calls the police,
      they come right away; the man cannot say anything; he is always
      guilty. Some men, they get beaten by the woman and they have to
      call the police first, before the wife calls the police, otherwise he is
      already guilty. I told the men, how do you manage [more chuckles],
      you see the men weeping and crying, and because of the kids I am
      staying; it is because of the kids. So that is my experience with that
      and we are still dealing with it."

#3: "I have come here to learn, from a practical point of view, what really
      happens and how we can help those who are affected, whether those
      are men or women. Sometimes, this issue is overblown from the
      women's side when men are totally neglected. In many cases, men are
      also abused. Women will threaten their husbands, or they will totally
      abandon the husbands. So they disregard the rights of the husband."

#4: "In my masjid, it is the opposite, it is the women abusing the men.
      It's destructive when that kind of thing happens. Back home, where I
      grew up, cases like that are very rare, it is always the men abusing the
      women, but it is the opposite around here."

What are we to make of these remarks—prominently formulated as the
imams introduced themselves to the group and established themselves as
conversation partners? Empirical evidence demonstrates that women are the
overwhelming majority of victims of domestic violence including DV murders, which has led state efforts to be framed in terms of "violence against
women."[27] What happens when imams overemphasize the prevalence of DV
against men is a not so subtle shifting of the framework that centers on the
critique of unequal power dynamics in a hierarchically structured patriarchal
family.[28] It makes it possible to endorse a patriarchal family model but curi-
ously seems to undermine the notion of protective patriarchy and dominant
Muslim masculinity at the same time. If men are abused by women, then they
are clearly not in control positions, not even the protective and maintaining
kind, in their families. It may also distinguish different Muslim men from
one another in terms of their masculinity, which is tied to their not only protecting and maintaining their wives but also not being dominated, let alone
being abused, by women.

At this training event, the existence of male victims of domestic abuse continued to be brought up, by both the trainers and the attendees. The remarks

in the beginning set the tone and framework, which existed in great tension with the emphasis, provided by both Karima and Salim, on women as victims and the severe danger of women being killed as a result of imams not interfering and not providing or referring victims to services.

Karima both challenged and reinforced this when she offered an overview (on a slide) of forms of violence in order to distinguish domestic abuse from other types of violence. She referenced the introductory comments by the imams in her explanations of the slide's text.

1. *Intimate terrorism*: "This is where the person who is abusive or controlling is using violence as a tool with the objective of dominating the other person. It is done in such a way, over time, and with a variety of control tactics that the person who is the victim really feels terrorized even if there is no physical abuse. This makes it a case of domestic violence—a case of intimate terrorism. The majority of perpetrators here are men and the majority of victims are women."

2. *Violent resistance*: "This is the case where it may even reach to a homicide where the person is reacting to the other person trying to exert control and might try to fight back, physically, and may get injured in the process. Sometimes after many years of living with an abuser, a woman may decide that the only way to save her own life is to kill the abuser. That is a case where she is not trying to control him; she is trying to protect herself. Here it is the woman in the majority of cases who is trying to resist her abuse."[29]

3. *Situational couple violence*: "If you do any counseling, you see a lot of this. The couple are just having a fight and then the fight gets out of control and there can be violence, whether it is name-calling, or hitting, or some kind of threat. But the violence is not for the purpose of controlling the other person, it's more that the person who is angry is out of control. Either the man or the woman can be escalating the fight to the point of violence."

4. *Mutual violent control*: "There are very few cases, and I had one recently that was very troubling, each of them was determined to control the other person and they were both violent and it was very dangerous. In those cases, they are both abusive; they both fit the profile of the intimate terrorist and they are doing it to each other. In these cases I would advocate for a separation or a divorce, but they seem addicted to this type of behavior, so it is very difficult."[30]

Karima complicated the picture the imams had presented and perhaps intentionally did so without directly confronting them. Her typology could also be read as moving away from a framework that focuses on violence against women. There was ambivalence that was related to Karima's authority as well as her objective to get the imams to care about DV. She could not afford to antagonize them, but she herself also embraced the potential of a protective patriarchy framework for DV efforts in Muslim communities. On several later occasions throughout the day, it was Imam Salim who brought the focus back on women as the primary victims. On the other hand, it was also Karima who repeatedly brought specific cases to the conversation and who insisted on describing them in some detail—without mincing words in her descriptions. Both insisted on making explicit the realities of DV in Muslim communities to get the religious leaders present involved in anti-DV efforts. The same purpose was served by watching the segment of the *Garments* film containing survivor testimonies that were intended to make real the statistics and abstract descriptions of DV as a societal problem and to shock the viewer into action.

Protecting Children and Families, and Women's Faith

There were moments in which women as individuals, with rights and agency, were subtly moved away from the focus of the training. This happened on several occasions when the discussion shifted from the abuse of wives by their husbands, physically, emotionally, spiritually, and financially, to children and by extension to Muslim families.

In one training session, the participants watched a part of *Garments* titled "What about the Children?" It demonstrated the negative effects of domestic abuse on children, both directly as victims and, indirectly, through the witnessing of abuse through the testimony of Muslims who experienced such trauma as children.

In commenting on the domestic in domestic violence, Karima had said earlier: "If you attend any trainings in the general public sphere, they are generally talking about either spousal abuse or intimate partner violence, in a dating relationship for example. I broaden it and I also include child abuse. Generally, child abuse is considered as a separate topic but in our context it is important, so I include that as well. And given that we often live in extended families, our domestic context is also much broader than you might find elsewhere."

There were murmurs of *Astaghfirullah* (I seek Allah's forgiveness), which I took to reflect a sense of responsibility for such trauma happening to Muslim children. Karima then commented that this was difficult to watch and the participants nodded in agreement. They expressed anger that this happens and described how important it was for Muslim children to grow up in healthy Muslim families in order to make them good Muslims. This communal responsibility for the perpetuation of Muslim families and thus the community itself seemed of great concern and appeared as an argument, in the film and at many events, as an incentive to care about DV in ways that the plight, suffering, and even murder of women did not elicit. The trainers also reminded their audience that children witnessing domestic abuse could make them more prone to being victims as adults and/or to becoming abusers themselves.[31] Karima added several stories from her own practice to illustrate the long-term mental health effects of family abuse on individuals including children.[32] On several occasions, the protection of children was highlighted as a reason to intervene in an abusive situation that the imam came to know about. Karima pointed out that children are often the reason why women stay in abusive situations but emphasized that by witnessing abuse children also become victims. It is this danger to children that can become an important argument for leaving an abusive situation.

Imam Salim described the two most important relationships for Muslims as the vertical one between the individual and God and the horizontal one between people, especially spouses. A correct understanding of God as the Creator, Provider, and Protector can help a woman get away from an abusive relationship. She could recognize the oppression inflicted upon her by her husband as against God's intent for people in this world and would see that God would not want her to stay in such a relationship. He then shared another story:

> One of the biggest problems with abuse is, especially for a person who is religious and comes to the masjid, it weakens the relationship with God. *Subhanallah*, some sisters leave Islam. *Wallahi*, there was one sister, she was married, she had been Muslim for thirty-five years! She became Christian again and took her two children back to church! She convinced her oldest daughter to convert with her. She had a Muslim name! Because her husband was abusive, abusive, abusive, and claimed that he was super religious. Every imam she went to told her to stay with him. Some of her life she even wore *niqab*, and her coworker asked her why she is staying with

her abuser. She felt Islam failed her, so she left the whole Islam. [Murmurs of *astaghfirullah*!] That is chaos and it is very important for us to know the seriousness of our job!

Here, Imam Salim declared the imams responsible for keeping the faith of abused women and their children, and thus emphasized the importance of women and children as part of Muslim communities. The woman in his story was another woman who left, this time not the room but the religion and the community altogether and she took her children with her. The story was a cautionary tale and its aim was to shock the imams and bring home their responsibility for interfering in abusive situations. In a similar vein, the *Garments* film shows one survivor reflecting on her abuse and her relationship with God:

> I did have this sneaking suspicion that I would find out that Islam wasn't for me, and that God really did believe that my husband was right. And so it was through my reading (of the Qur'an) that I realized that it wasn't that God was for either of us but that God was ultimately merciful and just, and that God did not want me to stay in a relationship that is unjust, and that I had to have the strength to leave what is not good for me.[33]

When Imam Salim told the story about the woman who left Islam, the training had reached a point at which the imams were discussing issues of confidentiality but more importantly, the inevitable moment, so familiar from any conversation about abuse, where several of them pointed out how difficult it is to determine whether abuse is "actually" happening, especially when "there are no visible bruises."

One imam related that some abusers are so smart that they will not leave bruises in places where they would be visible to someone else, and Karima debated whether intelligence had anything to do with it. The imams appeared uncomfortable with interfering in Muslim families based on "one side of the story" and cited the need for "real evidence" of abuse. Imam Salim argued back that 99.9 percent of complaints about domestic abuse are true and that imams, when they are approached, need to always first believe the woman. According to him, a woman has so much to lose when she comes forward that it is very unlikely for her to make up claims of abuse. It is her reputation as a wife, the reputation of her family, and the reputation of her children as future marriage partners that are at stake, not to mention her life as she exposes her abuser. Sometimes women would even go so far as to not report abuse because they are worried about the reputation of their abuser.

Imam Salim also argued that not believing a victim breaks the trust that community members should have in the imam and would lead to other women victims not coming forward. When they do, it is not enough to "talk to the husband" despite the possibility for self-reform. The most important aspect of the imam's work was to show her that there are options and that she has to make choices and decisions ("also, don't make decisions for her!"). Several imams related that they had found out about abusive situations through their wives, who were approached by victims because they felt more comfortable talking to another woman. Some imams involved their wives in counseling and conversations to make the women feel comfortable, maintain propriety, and offer a modicum of confidentiality by not having other community members present.[34]

The imam trainings, like other awareness events in Muslim communities, oscillated between a focus on women as individual agents and victims and a focus on Muslim families including children. The latter focus created significant tension both with mainstream American approaches to DV and with feminist Muslim frameworks of gender justice. It felt wrong to me, every time it came up, to have to argue that Muslim families were important and that Muslim children needed to be protected from DV, both from witnessing and experiencing it, to grow up as good future Muslim adults who would in turn perpetuate the Muslim community. It was, though, the protective patriarchy frame at work and it was, admittedly, productive for getting the imams on board. Despite their presence at the training events, the teaching units, lectures, and conversations all conveyed the necessity of convincing religious leaders of the severity and consequences of domestic abuse in Muslim families.

The focus on Muslim families also leads to different approaches to intervention: in the imam trainings, more so than in interviews with providers, there was a commitment to the possibility of couple counseling. This approach ran counter to mainstream approaches because they focus on women as victims/survivors and on safety. Couple counseling runs the risk of misreading the power and control dynamic in a relationship and thus jeopardizing the safety of the abused spouse. It also assumes that reconciliation is not only possible but the desirable outcome of an intervention in a domestic abuse situation. In mainstream approaches, to the contrary, separation and, ultimately, divorce is the only solution that guarantees the safety of the victim. This demand for separation is one of the reasons for American Muslims' suspicion of mainstream services (and law enforcement) because they appear intent on destroying Muslim families with this approach.

The second important dimension of a reconciliation-based approach to DV is the possibility of a (self) transformation and thus reform of the perpetrator. Here, too, there is significant tension with mainstream approaches in which a perpetrator of abuse is assumed to always be a perpetrator. Some of the Muslim approaches counter this assumption with a theological framing of the self as in constant need of self-reflection and improvement. Once a Muslim individual recognizes the error of his behavior and aligns himself with the will of God, through the Qur'an and the Sunna, and through understanding ethics and law, then each Muslim has the potential to atone for mistakes and even sin and ask for God's forgiveness. In a second step, they are expected to transform their behavior as well. Here, imams are called to "out" abusers in their communities, but not expel them, so that the community and its leaders can hold the individual accountable for his behavioral transformation. The alternative, abusers moving on to other communities (or back to their country of origin) and continuing the patterns of abuse because they are not known to the community, appears in many stories as a recurring problem in communities across the country. On occasion, I have heard an imam acknowledge that such accountability, in early stages, might include physical disciplining, or the threat of it, by men in the community—"to make him realize how it feels to be hurt." This form of communal justice is claimed to have been successful in some cases and bypasses the criminal justice system, which is not always trusted to do the necessary work.[35]

One imam shared that he brought couples together in his office and discussed their marital issues with both of them. Sometimes he even left the room to give them an opportunity to talk out issues between themselves. He would only counsel couples separately if he recognized signs of intimidation by one spouse of the other in his presence. Karima cautioned that this is where tools, such as a lethality assessment, are not only useful but lifesaving, and that it is part of the responsibility of an imam to have training and tools available to them. Imam Salim brought that point home when he emphatically stated:

If you hit your wife, that is not your own private business, it is everyone's business. People say, who are you to intervene in my family, and as I say in my *khutbahs*, the injustice to a person, it is not a private matter.... We have to stand with the women and children.... Safety is number one, not to second-guess a woman, because for sure we all know cases where we couldn't second-guess, because the women lost their lives. We all know cases, in Buffalo, Aasiya Zubair who has been killed, in X, in Y, and in all of our communities. These are real examples of people who lost their lives! And there are some people who have become handicapped, who were injured and there is permanent physical damage. I know an imam, he feels responsible that a sister lost her eye, because the first time her husband hit her, the imam sent her back home and told her to be patient and a better wife. And then he hit her again!

Karima then described several cases in which domestic abuse "broke" a woman by causing mental health issues ranging from depression, anxiety, and anorexia to intentional physical self-harm and active or passive suicide attempts.[36] Here again, we see the moving back and forth between concern for women and concern for families, children, and communities. I cannot accuse the trainers in these events of not caring enough for victims and survivors, and yet sometimes that care, outrage, and concern, or for that matter, gruesome and shocking stories of abuse, are not enough to convince others, including the imams, of the severity of the issue.[37]

"In Islam, We Do Believe in Divorce"

In order to prevent further harm or another DV homicide in the Muslim community, there is, sometimes, no option other than divorce.[38] The imams were hesitant about this option and expressed that they might be perceived by their communities as marriage breakers if they suggested this option. A discussion ensued about how such a claim can lead to further danger for a woman talking to the imam—she could be seen as a marriage breaker by association. There was also concern about the possibility of remarriage for divorced women, regardless of the reason for the divorce. A woman who is divorced because of abuse in her marriage might still be seen as partially responsible for the breakdown of the family and thus would not be considered fit for another marriage. "That is just how the communities are, we have absorbed these cultural norms," said one of the imams.

Imam Salim pushed back and suggested support groups in the community for single women and then proudly declared that his own wife had recently organized a first meeting of single mothers in their home, which was aimed at helping them find ways to remarry. He then seamlessly moved from this declaration to the fact that the Qur'an mentions divorce as an option for Muslim couples in cases where reconciliation is not possible. In the *Garments* film, in a segment titled "Is Divorce an Option?" Imam Mohamed Magid can be seen saying: "Tell them: Listen, she is not a slave in this relationship. This relationship has to be mutual respect, mutual love. If you guys cannot make it, there is another word, it is called divorce. In Islam we do believe in divorce!" Zainab Alwani, one of few women scholars I saw directly involved in the Muslim DV movement, has argued that scholars and leaders should not per se encourage divorce in order to avoid pushback. Instead, they are to simply encouraging peaceful families, which is best for women and men, as well as their children.[39]

When discussing Islamic law in the imam training, Imam Salim went even further and pronounced that if a woman approaches an imam for help in a case of domestic abuse, he has the responsibility to grant her a religious divorce. He outlined the foundations of the Islamic marriage model as based on mercy, compassion, and tranquility, repeating Q 30:21 and references to the Sunna. He also pointed out that a family or marriage in which one of the spouses is oppressed and treated unjustly is "not an Islamic marriage."

He then offered a rundown of Islamic legal rules and injunctions, distinguished by which school applies them, regarding reasons and circumstances for divorce. In addition to the unilateral divorce, *talaq*, in which a husband pronounces the phrase *talaq* (I repudiate/divorce you) three times, there is the option for a woman to ask for an annulment of her marriage. This option is called *khul'* and requires the intervention of a Muslim judge or legal scholar. Imam Salim did not need to explain the details as he assumed the imams were all familiar with these basics. He nevertheless listed the main reasons for an annulment: abuse, neglect, impotency, and mental illness. He then reasoned that cases of severe spousal abuse are not *khul'* worthy but should result in an immediate divorce without the woman having to return her dowry (the main condition for *khul'*). Instead, the imam should pronounce the *talaq* on behalf of the husband/abuser because that is the right thing to do.

Also, in cases of DV in a family, the mandatory waiting period, *'idda*, which requires maintenance of the wife and her staying in the same house, needed to be rethought, he argued. It is clearly not an option for an abused woman to stay with her abuser, so she needs to spend the waiting period somewhere else where she is safe from abuse. He also claimed that an abused woman is entitled to maintenance, at least according to the Maliki school.

He mentioned that withholding a *talaq* from a woman is in itself a form of abuse, which is why it is so important for an imam to pronounce a divorce (and not an annulment) in abuse cases. Not doing so can result in situations where the woman wants a divorce but has not been granted one and the abusive husband continues to approach her for sex (which is his right as part of the marriage contract).[40] If a man lies about abuse, the imam should rely on the woman's testimony, making her swear in the name of God, and he can take into consideration testimony by other adult Muslims (but not children and non-Muslims). The utilization of withholding (or in other circumstances threatening) divorce appears regularly in survivor testimonies and awareness events. It is exacerbated by the complex role of Islamic law in the lives of Muslims in a minority context such as United States. The majority of the imams have "Islamic knowledge" training of some kind, but many of them, even those who work as imams full-time, are not trained Islamic legal scholars. They lack the necessary knowledge and qualifications to apply Islamic law in their communities, most importantly in the case of divorce, which had led to an Islamic legal vacuum.

The situation is especially confusing because officiating at a Muslim wedding ceremony, the *nikah*, does not require similar legal qualifications. Several work-around options have been deployed by imams and communities: to strongly encourage an Islamic marriage contract that stipulates the woman's right to a divorce under certain circumstances and without an Islamic legal scholar or judge, and/or to recognize a civil divorce as simultaneously an Islamic divorce (by following the law of the land on divorce).[41] Imam Salim advocated for imams to help women file a civil divorce, be knowledgeable about divorce law in their state, and do what they can based on the maxim that sometimes divorce is the only solution. On occasion, especially when the marriage was contracted in another country, the divorce also needed to be acquired from that country's legal system. Facilitating divorce proceedings then, perhaps ironically, becomes one of the most central functions of the imam.

Reflecting on Authority and Authenticity

"Alhamdulillah, Allah has blessed me with knowledge, Allah has blessed me with the experience of knowledge. I have learned from my teachers, I have the honor to have learned from one of the greatest teachers of our time, X, and the mufti, Y, he is also my teacher. I also consult with them on many occasions." This is how one of the imams introduced himself to the people gathered at the training. This set of claims to authority based on authoritative sources of knowledge, which form a chain of knowledge transmission central to Islamic knowledge production, is quite typical for the way in which religious leaders and scholars perform authority as well as religious authenticity.[42]

The imam trainings were gatherings of religious scholars and leaders who all, in complex and fascinating ways, tried to impress one another and jockeyed for positions in a hierarchical structure of authority to be established. Such hierarchy only partially exists in Sunni Islam (Shi'a Muslims have hierarchies of religious scholars), and recognition as a significant scholar or authoritative leader has to be granted by a following of lay Muslims and/or communities. In a gathering of imams, though, all the men in attendance had some authority, which they leveled at one another and performed in a variety of ways. The presence of women, including one woman with significant professional authority as a practitioner, was either tacitly ignored in their competition or perhaps fueled it to some degree because the women could be impressed by such performances.

One imam told the story of how his wife of now thirty-five years, in their first week of marriage, called him, punched him in the stomach so hard that he fell to his knees, coughing, and then proceeded to tell him that she could always defend herself. She had been a karate trainer for Muslim girls in the Nation of Islam. All the imams laughed together at the story and, repeatedly, throughout the day referred back to it by telling him that he should have been in the *Garments* video or that he was proof that men are abused as well. Arguably, the story itself does not show the man as authoritative or masculine, but the laughs about it as well as the continuous joking references to it marked the space of the training as male. They also asserted the masculinity of the other imams. I found nothing funny about any of the abuse stories, regardless of whether they involved women, children, or men as victims.

When Karima was presenting on forms of abuse, the imams frequently contributed to the conversation, often by interrupting her, thus both challenging her authority and asserting their own. They confirmed what she said as well, so authority was distributed in a complex way when she spoke. She was the professional expert in the room and the imams, albeit reluctantly at times, deferred to her authority and superior knowledge in some areas. Karima actively encouraged the imams' participation and repeated several times that they were the experts in their communities and that their knowledge as well as their commitment were extremely important. She was, of course, encouraging them to stay involved, feel important, and commit to the work only they can carry out in their communities. She also referred to Imam Salim as the religious expert and authority with regard to questions of Islamic law and the Qur'an even though she had her own thoughts and ideas about religious arguments and texts.

Knowledge of the Qur'an and Sunna went hand in hand with the performance of superior knowledge of Arabic, which was the native language for only a few of the participants. The Arabic required was Qur'anic, and thus classical Arabic, and being a native speaker of modern Arabic or one of its dialects would not have provided the necessary qualifications and thus authenticity. Throughout the training sessions, the performance of Arabic proved central. It appeared naturalized in the ways in which Imam Salim and the other imams quoted verses from the Qur'an as well as entire Hadith, or phrases and words from both. Sometimes they would translate them after citing them in Arabic and at other times inclusion in the circles of authenticity depended on one's command of the language. There were never any references to which chapter and verse from the Qur'an they were quoting, let alone references to books of authentic Hadith that the cited traditions came from.

In one instance, a discussion of the now familiar verse 4:34 in the Qur'an turned into somewhat of a battle of Arabic sentences between four of the imams and Imam Salim. They were literally throwing them at one another, with the intention of "winning" the argument, which was about the permission in the Qur'an to "strike" one's wife, possible other meanings of *daraba*, and, finally, the example of the Prophet in never striking a woman or child and declaring those among his followers the best who are the best to their families. I had never before seen religious leaders and scholars refer to one another as living religious authorities. Usually, they each assumed such authority and authenticity that it could not be enhanced by referencing one another. They also cited their teachers and scholarly authorities in Muslim-majority countries who are assumed to have more authenticity, and of course a long history of exegetical textual traditions, however selectively.

The imam trainings were rich and complicated sites of exploring the frameworks of gender roles, religious interpretation, and authenticity. They challenged the imams present as well as the trainers to perform various types of authority, reference religious source texts, offer or repeat interpretations of them, and bring home the significance of DV as a communal issue to be very concerned about. They challenged me to carefully consider the potential and the problems with protective patriarchy as a strategic tool as well as deep conviction at the heart of DV work in Muslim communities. Yet again, the victims and survivors were present at all times, even when their presence made the religious leaders uncomfortable.

The interviews with imams were very different research situations in which I observed the imams performing certain models of masculinity, authority, and authenticity as well. They appeared intent on impressing me with their knowledge and their community work while also dismissing me, the Muslim woman scholar, as neither an authentic scholar nor a relevant authority. They were also, more than advocates and other providers, concerned about the "image" of the Muslim community when discussing domestic abuse. Some of the imams will make another appearance in the following chapter where interviews and observations form the foundation for a discussion of various forms of Muslim-specific or Muslim-led services for victims of abuse.

6

To Support and Defend

PROVIDING SERVICES TO
MUSLIM VICTIMS AND SURVIVORS

Some days, she said, she was afraid that she could not do this work much longer. She had seen so much pain and suffering, so many bruises, so many tears, and so much despair. She also found it harder and harder to trust the men around her—if the statistics are true and one in four women is abused, then one in four men is an abuser. How could she ever let her nieces get married? She had also given up hope of finding a husband again; men do not want anything to do with women who do DV work.

I MET FATIMA at a Muslim community convention where her organization had an information table with brochures and flyers outlining the services they provided to victims of domestic abuse and stalking. The color purple dominated their information materials and so did a focus on families as the foundation for Muslim communities. Fatima was in her fifties, wore hijab, and in response to my request to tell me something about herself described her own growing up in a South Asian Muslim family, in South Asia and the Gulf, and eventually coming to the United States in order to marry a South Asian American man. She was careful to not describe her marriage as abusive but instead told me about how difficult and horrid her divorce had been and how it left her, alone with small children, to fend for herself. She held up her father both as a role model for how to be a good Muslim man and as her supporter and defender during and after her divorce. She eventually found work and raised her children by herself. Years later, she started recognizing the problem of DV in her Muslim community and over several years explored possibilities and searched for allies in her struggle to create a Muslim DV service organization. Her story was a familiar one in how she described the obstacles, the rejection from community leaders, and the accusations of wrecking families and destroying Islam from within. Parallel to these efforts in her community, she worked with mainstream agencies as a volunteer. It was in this context that she realized the specific needs of Muslim women. At one point in the story, she said: "And I saw Muslim victims who cannot go to the shelters because they can't eat the food, they can't do their *wudu*, they can't pray. It is not an option for them but they are in danger. Most nights I just cried after I got home from these visits."

In this chapter, I focus on Muslim service providers of many kinds and on the organizations in which they work. Muslim service providers, in different ways from advocates and community leaders, not only are at the front lines of the struggle against DV in Muslim communities but also most directly and persistently interact with the mainstream DV landscape/movement. Service providers are at risk themselves in more acute ways as their direct contact with victims and survivors can also become contact with perpetrators who are a threat not only to DV victims but also to anyone who supports those victims.

It is therefore necessary to sketch my perception of the mainstream DV services landscape in order to then situate Muslim organizations and individuals in relation to this mainstream. As I did in the chapter on community awareness, I introduce the reader to several of the existing organizations, the services they provide, and the ways they interact with the mainstream, both on the level of networking services and on the level of funding and outreach. In this chapter, too, I am interested in the stories of the individuals who perform this vital work, at great personal sacrifice and risk to their safety. There is an even greater demand for confidentiality, and in this chapter I have opted for the creation of composite stories that combine the experiences of several interviewees, thereby obscuring features that would expose their identities. Toward the end of the chapter, I introduce several very public Muslim service providers through their presence in mainstream and online media.

I conducted interviews with Muslim individuals who worked in DV services, both in explicitly Muslim organizations and in various mainstream ones. They provided services such as emergency room care, legal support, and counseling in their primary professional capacity as nurses, doctors, lawyers, and therapists. In the latter category, the individuals themselves identified their religion as an important factor or motivation for their specific investment in

helping Muslim victims. It was often impossible to neatly distinguish between
DV advocates and service providers, not only because many DV organizations
did both but also because the experience with providing services to victims,
Muslim and otherwise, often animates the advocates' drive to raise awareness.

I explore the significance of their religious convictions and identities for
the work they perform and for the ways in which they relate to their clients
on the one hand and to "the system" on the other. As will become clear, in
both, there are assumptions involved and constructions employed to account
for the ways in which religion/Islam is presented. Muslim advocates and providers see and represent it as a (potential) resource to victims and survivors,
while in mainstream DV work religion is primarily identified as a roadblock
to addressing DV effectively. Islam, as we have already seen, tends to be identified as an especially profound roadblock with much less potential as a resource. This perception is clearly linked to negative representations of Islam
and Muslims in the American public square. In working with Muslim clients,
service providers take great care to distinguish between what "real Islam says"
about domestic abuse and what they deem to be cultural issues masquerad-
ing as religion. Their ethic of non-abuse is directly linked to a framework of
religious ethics, whether formulated as such or in response to perceived critiques of Islam. And their rejection of any form of domestic abuse is indistin-
guishable from religious convictions and guidance for ethical living in this
world. The linking of the ethic of non-abuse to their religion strengthens the
ethical framework itself by linking it to a divine power and thus beyond individual conviction or a human-centered framework of good and bad, right and
wrong.

I conducted both personal interviews with providers and more organizational ones in which interviewees introduced me to the work of their organization including services they provided, sometimes a bit of institutional
history, and information about funding structures and community interactions. I include in this chapter materials collected at Muslim conventions and
conferences, awareness events, online sources such as websites for different
organizations, and the occasional news item or Facebook post to throw a
wider net. The interweaving of these different sources provides another degree
of confidentiality. It is noteworthy that provider organizations, not only Muslim ones, typically do not list individuals working for them on their website,
let alone individualized contact information for them. This is both a safety
measure and reflects the high level of turnover due to burnout of both pro-

fessionals and volunteers. Domestic violence and women's shelters do not disclose their physical address in order to make it as difficult as possible for abusers to track down victims.

In the interviews and observations, I noticed again the power of the protective patriarchy paradigm and how it brushes up against feminist approaches in mainstream organizations while seemingly working adequately in combination with the power and control paradigm that provides the foundation for DV work. One significant point of tension is a focus, in Muslim DV work, on the family rather than the individual, which in both very practical and broader philosophical ways chafes against the liberal focus on individuals and their freedoms, responsibilities, and choices. The power and control paradigm at the center of mainstream DV work itself relies on a specific notion of subjectivity and individuality as well.

There is a very specific point of great tension that emerged in the work with providers: the boundaries around identifying, individually or as an organization, as Muslim, and offering services to Muslims and non-Muslims, or to Muslims only. If an organization was indeed animated by a commitment to "Islamic" frameworks for identifying and combatting DV, how would such a framework affect the potential for working with non-Muslim clients? Do such normative frameworks not also potentially alienate Muslim clients with differing normative frameworks, for example feminist ones, more conservative ones, or even sectarian differences? Is this ever an issue the other way around, or a kind of Islam exceptionalism? What assumptions need to be made about the Muslimness of a client and the significance of religion to their lives in order to offer them religious resources? On a very practical level, that of funding, Muslim service organizations also had to make a choice between serving all clients and thus being eligible for at least some state and federal funding on the one hand and focusing on services for Muslims only and being dependent on Muslim communities for financial support on the other.

The services these organizations offered range from shelter, transitional housing, and financial assistance to legal support, vocational training, job searching, and counseling for the various forms of trauma caused by the abuse. Some organizations provided these services themselves while others functioned as clearinghouses that connected clients with the services they needed and helped them navigate a very complex and deeply confusing system of possibilities, gaps, and challenges.

Navigating the Maze of DV Services

It is no coincidence that academic articles on DV services have titles like "Roads to Nowhere"[1] and "Map of Gaps,"[2] even if these two particular articles address the very difficulties of finding and navigating the complex structures of DV services, and the very lack thereof, in the context of the United Kingdom. It is impossible to offer here a comprehensive picture of mainstream DV services in the United States, which becomes even more complicated in its connections to and overlap with organizations run by Christian denominations and a few Jewish congregations. I will attend to the dynamics of religious and interfaith work, and the participation of Muslims in it, in chapter 7, where I also analyze the challenges of religious DV work in a secular state and public system. Here, rather than attempting the impossible, I have opted to describe service structures in one particular county where I conducted some of my fieldwork. The focus on Montgomery County provides some idea of how "the system" tended to work, but it also might make it look better than general reality because the county was nationally recognized as a model for how to help victims and survivors of DV access and navigate services.

Let us imagine a situation in which a friend has just disclosed that she has experienced prolonged physical, emotional, and financial abuse by her husband. She has small children, is financially dependent on her husband, and is afraid of what is going to happen to her if she tries to even bring up the abuse to him or if he finds out that she has told someone else. We want to believe this friend and help her, so we attempt to find out about available resources and services. Most services are local, as they need to be accessible to the victim in need. Resources, such as information on what DV is, warning signs, and so forth, are available online but service providers operate on the local level, not least because DV policies, funding, and laws are often determined on the state or even county level.

When I Googled "Montgomery County MD domestic violence resources" in 2017, I found the following links first: the county's circuit court with information on what the court does and how to access the Family Justice Center (to be explained shortly); the sheriff's office resource page with a list of services, phone numbers, and explanations of who does what; and then three more links to the Abused Persons Program, the Family Justice Center (both county run), and the Maryland Network against Domestic Violence (statewide and similar to state coalitions of DV organizations in all states).[3]

There is, first of all, a clear link here to the justice system and thus to the law. The courts and law enforcement agencies play an important role in responding to disturbance calls, arresting perpetrators, issuing restraining orders, and processing criminal cases. Much work in the United States within the framework of violence against women has focused on criminalizing domestic abuse[4] and increasing conviction rates as well as punishments for documented abuse. Documentation, such as petitions, medical records, and police records, continue to play an important role in any attempts to move DV cases toward legal attention, recognition, and prosecution.

The other, and perhaps historically older, focus of DV service work was the concern with the emotional, psychological, and physical impact of abuse on women and children. Feminist scholars and activists recognized the interconnected nature of their efforts in the legal field and criminal justice on the one hand and the provision of services to victims and survivors on the other. Both on their own were limited in their ability to change societal norms, which perhaps may account for the depressingly high levels of domestic violence in U.S. society over the past fifty years.[5] Martha Fineman, a feminist legal scholar and coeditor of *The Public Nature of Private Violence: The Discovery of Domestic Abuse*, wrote in 1994:

> When societal norms are in a state of flux (as they certainly are in regards to matters of sexual intimacy and gender relations) the law tends to become identified as a significant site of contest. Competing societal factions seek to codify their worldview, thereby giving legitimacy to the stories they tell about what are appropriate ideals and values. Policy formation and law reform in this regard are inevitably political.[6]

A 2011 report prepared by a group of lawyers, scholars, and activists for the UN special rapporteur on violence against women, Rashida Manjoo, evaluated the legal situation in the United States. Three of the initial statements in the report are especially significant here:

- Government sources indicate that one-third of women in the United States experience at least one physical assault at the hands of an intimate partner during the course of adulthood. Due to feelings of shame and fear of retribution that prevent women from reporting assault, this statistic may significantly underestimate the incidence of domestic violence in the United States. The historical characterization of domestic violence as a "private" or family matter may also contribute to the under-reporting of domestic violence.

- Not all women in the United States experience domestic violence with the same frequency. The data suggests that although the domestic violence epidemic cuts across the lines of gender, race, and immigration status—affecting women and men, African Americans, Latinas, American Indian and Alaska Natives, whites, and immigrants and U.S. citizens—it has a particularly pernicious effect on groups which lie at the intersection of these categories: poor ethnic minorities, immigrants, and American Indians and Alaska Native women.

- While poor minority and immigrant battered women in the United States are among those most in need of governmental support and services, including domestic violence services, these groups are chronically underserved. This greater need for an effective government response is due, in large part, to the social, familial, and financial isolation experienced by many minority and immigrant women. Nationwide, black women report their victimization to the police at a higher rate (67%) than white women (50%), black men (48%), and white men (45%). African American women account for 16% of the women reported to have been physically abused by a husband or partner in the last five years, but were the victims in more than 53% of the violent deaths that occurred in 1997. A recent study found that 51% of intimate partner homicide victims in New York City were foreign-born. Another study determined that 48% of Latinas reported their partners' violence against them had increased since they immigrated to the United States.[7]

Many of the points made above are about the prevalence of DV in all communities, but different rates of reporting and very different experiences of interacting with law enforcement and the court system depending on ethnic and racial background and economic status are at the center of a growing literature on various aspects of domestic violence. My goal here is not to summarize this literature but to offer reminders of how important the multiple and overlapping identities of victims are for how they understand and access DV services.

Here we return to Montgomery County and more specifically to the Family Justice Center. The center was a county effort, ideally making the navigation of the system easier. The Family Justice Center was created to offer access to services in one location, thereby addressing the concerns of service providers with the myriad difficulties victims and their families faced in finding out about and then navigating available services. The website described the mission of the center as follows: "Co-located in one space, we are a collaboration of public and private county agencies seeking to provide services to families impacted by domestic violence, in a family-friendly environment. The Mission of the FJC is to promote safety, well-being, and healing for victims of family violence."[8] Translation services in a number of languages were available, and the goal was to allow victims and survivors in need of various services to connect with representatives in one building, which also offered child care and spiritual support.

Women could walk into the center during opening hours and ask to be introduced to representatives of organizations that provided emergency and temporary housing; they could meet with a lawyer to talk about legal options for divorce and child custody; they could file for a restraining order; they could explore options for financial assistance including food assistance; and they could begin, with the help of case workers and counselors, to think about their options for professional training or employment with the goal of achieving economic independence in the future. They could also take another first step and report the abuse to the police and/or acknowledge it to a social worker.

If we could convince our friend from above to come with us to the Family Justice Center, at least, she might have transportation there—we could drive her. The obstacles to addressing DV come in many forms and they might not look too daunting to us, but in combination they compound the challenges and dangers in seeking support as a victim. There is the lack of money for public transportation to get to a service organization, much less access to a car, or a place to leave their children while navigating the system; and there are other issues such as no house key (an abusive isolation technique); no Internet access (and the threat of being discovered looking for help); and being tracked electronically by their abuser through their phone, a car's GPS, and so forth—each of these can be a hurdle as well as a serious threat. As I so often heard in Muslim awareness events: women are at the greatest risk of being killed by their abuser when they decide to leave the abusive relationship—taking the victim's life is the ultimate act of control—and women leave on average eight times and return to their abuser before they get out for good, if they ever do.[9]

But what happens if our friend is African American and/or is Muslim and wears hijab? Or if she is of immigrant background and does not have U.S.

citizenship and her abuser is withholding vital documents about her immigration status from her? Or if she does not have a high school degree and
finds it difficult to read forms and interact with authorities, is afraid of the
police herself, and/or convinced that the legal system is more interested in
deporting her than stopping the abuse? Or what if reporting the abuse leads
to the arrest of her husband, the abuser, who is also the sole breadwinner?
What if the judge and social worker think that she is being abused because
she and her husband are Muslims and their religion allows such abuse? What
if she is blamed for the abuse? Any and all of these scenarios have happened
to victims and only scratch the surface of the challenges the system poses to
someone as deeply traumatized as a victim of recent and continuous domestic abuse in its many forms.

Once a victim reports or acknowledges her abuse and approaches various
agencies for services, she has at once asserted her agency and is at great risk of
being re-victimized by the agencies. Service providers should, in theory, not
limit her agency and choices but in practice often do, both through the im-
posing weight of their institutional structure—recognized as authoritative
and experienced as overwhelming—and because service providers continuously struggle with their impulse to protect victims versus allowing those
same victims to make decisions for themselves, including returning to the
abusive situation.[10]

Montgomery County and its Family Justice Center are not representative
of the ways in which the DV service landscape presents itself to victims in
need. In most locations, there is no centralized space to connect to services,
and there is significant overlap between state, county, federal, and nonprofit
and religious organizations in the services they provide, the populations they
may serve or exclude from their services, and their accessibility, service crite-
ria, funding, and effectiveness of programs and services. As a scholar with
advanced education who has tried for years to acquire a grasp of how the system might work, I have had to admit that it was deeply overwhelming and
often daunting. In addition, with all its overlaps and duplicated efforts in some
areas, the DV service system, at the intersection with other social, legal, and
financial services (after all DV is not the only social ill in U.S. society), also
has gigantic gaps through which victims and survivors routinely fall.

On the systemic level, the anti-DV movement with its various branches
involving lobbying, public policy work, research, advocacy in communities,
and, not least, direct services was complex and the subject of much research
and assessments itself. The literature on domestic violence, gender-based vi-

olence, violence against women, and so forth is so expansive that it is impossible to account for. However, there are important and critical lines of inquiry that I see as necessary for the later analysis of Muslim service providers in this chapter.

The Battered Women's Movement:
A History and Reflection

Rather than starting with a short history of the battered women's movement at its inception in the 1960s and 1970s, I approach it instead through its deep and insightful critique as represented in a 2006 volume produced by the INCITE! Women of Color against Violence collective. The volume, called *Color of Violence: The INCITE! Anthology*, is a powerful testimony and critique of the pervasive racism of the battered women's movement as part of first-wave feminism, with its focus on white and middle-class women, on the one hand, and an indictment of the anti-DV movement as increasingly usurped by the state and thus deeply embedded in state-sponsored racism on the other.

One contributor, Ana Clarissa Rojas Durazo, describes and critiques the medicalization of domestic violence as one process of depoliticization of what started as a political movement:

> When institutionalized, "mainstream" or western medicine reconstitutes social problems as "diseases" or individual pathologies in need of medical intervention, we can call this medicalization. Medical intervention is increasingly deemed indispensable in eliminating the epidemic of domestic violence, and the "medical industrial complex" is beginning to shape how we think about domestic violence, as well as how we prevent—or intervene and treat—the "disease." Like criminalization, medicalization represents a deep threat to the movement, because it uproots the conceptualization of domestic violence as a social problem. Instead, it replaces the ideology and structures of social movements with the structures of (western) medicine, subsuming grassroots to state and capital interests.[11]

Rojas Durazo goes on to warn that women of color working against violence need to recognize that working within the structures of medicalization, because of "its unjust institutional structure, as well as its racist, classist, and sexist interests," cannot be disentangled from it.[12] Similarly, the editors of the volume in their introduction describe the broader history of state efforts to depoliticize the movement against gender violence. The first paragraphs of their introduction are reproduced here for the powerful formulation of the problem:

> Since the first domestic violence shelter in the United States opened in 1974, and the first rape crisis center opened in 1972, the mainstream antiviolence movement has been critical in breaking the silence around violence against women, and in providing essential services to survivors of sexual/domestic violence. Initially, the antiviolence movement prioritized a response to male violence based on grassroots political mobilization. However, as the antiviolence movement has gained greater prominence, domestic violence and rape crisis centers have also become increasingly professionalized, and as a result are often reluctant to address sexual and domestic violence within the larger context of institutionalized violence.
>
> In addition, rape crisis centers and shelters increasingly rely on state and federal sources for their funding. Consequently, their approaches toward eradicating violence focus on working *with* the state rather than working *against* state violence. For example, mainstream antiviolence advocates often demand longer prison sentences for batterers and sex offenders as a frontline approach to stopping violence against women. However, the criminal justice system has always been brutally oppressive toward communities of color, including women of color.... Thus, the strategy employed to stop violence has had the effect of increasing violence against women of color perpetrated by the state.
>
> Unfortunately, the strategy often engaged in communities of color to address state violence is advocating that women keep silent about sexual and domestic violence to maintain a unified front against racism. Racial justice organizing has generally focused on racism as it primarily affects men, and has often ignored the gendered forms of racism that women of color face.[13]

Emi Koyama, in "Disloyal to Feminism," describes the movement toward professionalization, which I already discussed in chapter 3 (in far more positive terms as did my interlocutor there), as a continued process of depoliticization, "fueled by patriarchal backlash and cooptation."[14] Such co-optation as patriarchal backlash can take the form of pushing protective patriarchy as an agenda. As I argued in chapter 1, domestic violence in particular, unlike the broader issue of gender-based violence, does not have to be cast as a feminist cause or a radical political critique and indictment of the state system as deeply patriarchal, as well as sexist and racist. It can and has flourished when framed as an issue of care for the family and the protection of those who are selectively represented as more vulnerable in American society; and it has allowed the state to both interfere and define acceptable victims.[15]

The critical assessment above, provided by the *INCITE!* anthology authors and editors,[16] helps situate organizations and service networks, not only of Muslim providers but also somewhat earlier ones dedicated to the needs of particular minority communities in the United States. In the introduction to *Domestic Violence in Asian American Communities: A Cultural Overview*, the editor, Tuyen D. Nguyen, explains the book as an attempt to break the silence on the issue of DV in this specific community. He explains this silence as a function of Asian culture(s), which has forced Asian Americans to maintain their families' reputation and hide problems, also leading to a lack of research in/on these communities. Nguyen uses the culture framework to explain both low reporting and a tendency to handle issues within families and communities (without appealing for outside support or intervention), as well as specific forms of violence.[17]

Body Evidence, a volume edited by Shamita Dasgupta, offers insight into "intimate violence against South Asian women in America," the subtitle of the book. Beyond providing a more nuanced picture of the experiences of intimate partner violence in South Asian communities, the volume also offers critical perspectives on the racist exclusion and domination of services by notions of inferior culture. Margaret Abraham has provided one of the most sustained engagements with domestic violence in a specific minority community in her *Speaking the Unspeakable: Marital Violence among South Asian Immigrants in the United States*. I will return to her two chapters on the dynamics of South Asian women's organizing against DV below. Abraham, too, is invested in a cultural explanation framework that occasionally maps onto religious dynamics as well but does not provide a sustained unpacking of her respondents or her own investment in culture as a foundation for her analysis.

I list these books here as a link in my chain of argument to come back to the level of service provider organizations. Part of the history of the DV movement is the emergence of organizational structures to support specific communities after recognizing that they had specific needs legally, culturally, and perhaps also politically, even though the radical political movement's rhetoric I celebrated above was largely absent from many of these organizations. This is not to assign blame but to recognize that many of the organizations worked within tight financial constraints, and their image and communal reputation were directly linked to their ability to provide any services at all and to do so in a long-term, sustainable, and accountable manner.

One such organization is what is now called the Asian Pacific Institute on Gender-Based Violence (API, formerly Asian & Pacific Islander Institute on Domestic Violence).[18] API began in the early 1980s as a shelter for Asian and Pacific Islander women in Los Angeles and developed into a network of such shelters in major metropolitan areas. In 1997, organizations in the network participated in a conference on Asian women and DV, and in 2000, API was formalized into

> a national resource center on domestic violence, sexual violence, trafficking, and other forms of gender-based violence in Asian and Pacific Islander communities. It serves a national network of advocates, community-based organizations, national and state programs, legal, health, and mental health professionals, researchers, policy advocates and activists from social justice organizations working to eliminate violence against women. It analyzes critical issues; provides consultation, technical assistance and training; conducts research; and engages in policy advocacy.[19]

Abraham, in her book mentioned above, focused her research on several South Asian organizations, including Sakhi for South Asian Women,[20] SEWAA (Service and Education for Women Against Abuse), now called Women Against Abuse,[21] Apna Ghar (Our Home),[22] and Maitri.[23]

API maintained a database, organized by state, of "120 programs in the country for API survivors: the majority are community-based-organizations serving API battered women; some are multi-service agencies for an API community, with a domestic violence program; and some are traditional, pan-ethnic agencies with a program for a specific, local Asian community. Activists, organizers, professionals, volunteer or paid staff, all attest to the strength of a deeply-committed grassroots leadership."[24] The directory contained a number of Arab American community organizations that, like their South Asian counterparts, were founded earlier and provided services to Muslims before specifically Muslim organizations were created around ideas of a Muslim community, rather than ethnic communities of immigrant background. Among these older organizations are Arab American Family Services in Illinois[25] and the Arab-American Family Support Center in New York.[26] I will defer my discussion of other religious organizations in the DV movement such as the FaithTrust Institute and a number of Christian and Jewish organizations to chapter 7, where I analyze their emergence in relation to their interactions and cooperation with Muslim organizations. This latter discussion accounts for yet another facet of the intersectional nature of DV service work. Suffice it here to restate that American Muslim organizations interface and cooperate but also compete with a variety of ethnic, religious, and secular (mainstream) organizations, while negotiating often competing visions of effective service work for victims and survivors.

Historically, explicitly Muslim organizations that participated in some form in the mainstream DV movement as formal organizations started to appear in the 1990s, as I have already argued in chapter 3, predated by informal networks of helpers and supporters, as well as mosque-based services, which I will discuss below. This historical development is not equal to the triumph of institutionalization over volunteer efforts but rather a complicated path of struggling to define the parameters of the work, the needs of victims, and the constraints of the system. Informal community efforts and the tireless work of dedicated individuals were much more difficult to trace and account for, especially when their efficacy as well as safety depended on their not being identified publicly as community activists against DV. Such work continued to happen in and around Muslim communities and families alongside more institutionalized efforts.

Providing (Muslim) Services

In what follows I introduce some of the dedicated Muslim service organizations, followed by a discussion of my work on Muslim shelters. I sketch the role of mosques and community centers as spaces where institutionalized service work took place and where some of the organizations originated but later became relatively independent. This section closes with some of the ways in which Muslim individuals as service providers outside Muslim institutions and organizations constitute both bridges to and guides within the mainstream. I frame my analysis around what it means to be a Muslim service provider and what impact identification as Muslim might have on organizations as well as individuals.

Muslim Service Organizations

FAITH (Foundation for Appropriate and Immediate Temporary Help), located in northern Virginia, started as a group of volunteers in ADAMS (All Dulles Area Muslim Society) in the 1990s and became an organization still associated with ADAMS in 1999. We have encountered the ADAMS Center before as well as its leader, Imam Mohamed Magid. It is necessary and important to credit the Muslim women volunteers assisting DV victims in need in the ADAMS community with having raised awareness in their community and in its leader, Imam Magid, rather than the other way around. FAITH provided a range of services and described itself in these terms on its website:

> FAITH assists low-income people with emergency and temporary assistance needed to address the consequences of a traumatic event or time in their life. In addition, FAITH's Self-Sufficiency Program offers individuals and families assistance with case management, housing, processing applications for rent, medical expenses, transportation, food, utilities, education, childcare and other forms of assistance.
>
> FAITH also promotes stable families by providing victims of domestic violence with crisis counseling, safety planning, legal representation, court advocacy, translation services, financial assistance and support from the moment they leave an abuser to the point where they are settled in a new situation. FAITH considers the needs of every person in a client's family and works to place each of them solidly on the path towards self-sufficiency.[27]

Noteworthy details in this self-description include the direct mention of domestic violence while leaving the range of needs open to others, including those in poverty and those who have experienced traumatic life events. It mentions a focus on stable families but also, and in the same sentence, makes clear a focus on leaving an abusive situation as necessary. This is a carefully crafted statement that does not identify victims or potential clients as women only but balances the focus on the family with an individualized focus on self-sufficiency.

FAITH did not operate a dedicated shelter but rather provided temporary and transitional housing in apartments around town; it also offered financial assistance to cover rent. Many of the other services are listed above. Importantly, FAITH was open to "all low-income people and victims of domestic abuse regardless of their faith, ethnicity, or gender." The organization operated a thrift shop in Herndon where some of the donations to the organization were sold in order to generate funds. The thrift store offered "cultural, modest, and Islamic clothing" and was thus unique in the area. Some mainstream organizations would send survivors to the thrift store to find clothing that fit their particular needs. The thrift store also offered job training for clients who wanted to build their résumé.

Funding for the organization came mostly from the local Muslim community and from Muslim organizations and businesses, including restaurants and halal food stores in the area. FAITH held fund-raising events in the community, encouraged Muslims to donate to the thrift store, and clearly indicated on its website that donations marked as *zakat*, Muslim charitable obligation, could be given to the organization. *Zakat* contributions were also tax-deductible, and for those Muslims concerned that such deduction would constitute a form of interest, FAITH suggested they donate that money to them as well. In one interview, I was told that some Muslims were willing to give *zakat* to the organization but did not want it to be known that they had supported a DV service organization with their charity. The leaders of the local Muslim community were important and instrumental in promoting the work of FAITH, thereby vouching for its reliability and Islamic authenticity.

FAITH had very good relations with other DV organizations and networks in the area including the Virginia coalition against DV, local shelters and service providers, and even law enforcement and regional elected officials. These relationships were a two-way street: at the inception of the formal organization in 1999, several of the volunteers who constituted the founding circle of FAITH had volunteered in a local shelter and in several other DV provider organizations in the area to get the necessary basic training and insights into frameworks and management. Theirs was a very professionalized as well as depoliticized notion of DV work as service and not as social transformation, let alone as a critique of capitalism, patriarchy, or racism. I was told that these training experiences also helped confirm the need for this Muslim organization: they observed that Muslim women were not accommodated in their religious needs, often out of ignorance rather than prejudice, and their cultural differences could not be acknowledged or taken into consideration. These observations strengthened FAITH as an organization that could not only meet those needs but also offer cultural (but not religious) sensitivity training to mainstream organizations, legal professionals, and law enforcement. The organization had received some funding from the Department of Justice and from the local government for specific aspects of their work.

Over time, FAITH also played a role in formulating a distinct Muslim perspective on domestic violence, as reflected in *What Islam Says about Domestic Violence* by Zainab Alwani and Salma Abugideiri, discussed in chapter 4. FAITH was an example of a very successful Muslim organization that for two decades had managed to not only survive but also grow the number of clients it served and the services it provided, while staying financially solvent and well supported in the community. There were professional staff members, including a manager and several caseworkers; however, many tasks in the organization were performed by community volunteers. FAITH had community support, was recognized as authentically Muslim through its association with ADAMS, and enjoyed good relations with mainstream providers and law enforcement. It navigated its commitments to being a Muslim organization dedicated to services for DV victims in the tense space of drawing on ethical Islamic frameworks against abuse while serving all members of the local community in need.

Karamah: Muslim Women Lawyers for Human Rights, both in its history and framework, represented a very different kind of organization.[28] It was founded in 1994 by Dr. Azizah al-Hibri, then law professor and specialist for Islamic law at the University of Richmond. Al-Hibri, unlike many others involved in Muslim DV work, also had long-term connections to feminist scholars and activists, including serving as the founding editor of *Hypatia: A Journal of Feminist Philosophy* in 1982. Karamah's mission was adjusted over the years and encompassed a vision of dignity for all and "a world in which all human beings, regardless of gender or other differences, enjoy their God-given right of dignity. We believe that through education, women will be empowered to transform archaic, culture-based interpretations of women's status in Islam, to the betterment of themselves and their communities." The organization was committed to a human rights–based framework in which women's rights were defined as part of human rights. There is, of course, a much longer history of women's organizations in Muslim contexts embracing a human rights framework. Not unlike Muslim feminists, the proponents of such frameworks have faced suspicion and criticism over adopting a "western" and thus not authentically Muslim ideology for their movements and organizations.[29]

The work of the organization, too, involved a variety of activities from providing education materials and new Islamic legal interpretations to offering leadership programs for Muslim women from all over the world. Domestic violence played a significant role in such efforts, based in part on the interest of Dr. al-Hibri in the topic. In 2003, al-Hibri published "An Islamic Perspective on Domestic Violence," an article that constituted the foundation for Karamah's anti-DV efforts. Based in Washington, D.C., Karamah enjoyed good relations with Muslim communities and organizations in the D.C. area as well as with policymakers and the Department of Justice (DOJ). While there had been calls for Karamah to offer legal services to Muslim clients, and there were many who approached Karamah for help and information over the years, it was not until 2014 that Karamah started offering such direct legal services. Uniquely positioned with a staff of lawyers to take on this task, Karamah set up points in the D.C. area where its lawyers could meet with clients in need. In addition, Karamah functioned as an access point for other organizations by creating and maintaining (at least at some point) a database for victims and survivors. When I checked the Karamah website in 2017, I could no longer find information on direct legal services.

Karamah did cooperate with the Peaceful Families Project (see chapter 3), with support from the DOJ, on producing training materials on addressing domestic violence in Muslim communities in 2008. Several trainings were held in various locations around the United States. In these trainings, the distinction between what constituted a cultural (and thus acceptable to the DOJ) framework for Muslim communities and what counted as religion came to the fore and led to some discussion. For several years and starting in 2012, Karamah organized a series of DV awareness events in mosques in the D.C. area titled "Love Like the Prophet: Ending Domestic Violence in Our Community," which offered information on DV, locally available services, and "Islamic perspectives" on this important issue. This initiative took place for several years during October, which has been designated as Domestic Violence Awareness Month since 1987 by the National Coalition against Domestic Violence.

The North-American Islamic Shelter for the Abused (NISA),[30] located in Palo Alto, California, was an organization that focused on education as well as direct services in California. On its website it stated: "Domestic Abuse is against the law. You have a right to be safe. Let us help you. You do not have to be Muslim to contact us, because this crime affects people of all faiths." NISA (which means women in Arabic) was a registered nonprofit organization and described its advocates and service providers as state certified and confidential. Services offered included a hotline, a shelter, support in applying for social services, counseling (including family counseling), referral to legal services, "Religious guidance/counseling through Islamic principles; Anger management classes; and Parenting classes." These last three were significant in establishing an Islamic framework for NISA's approach and in providing at least one kind of education for and thus engagement with perpetrators.

Many more organizations should be described here in detail for the important work they perform. In *Speaking the Unspeakable*, Margaret Abraham

analyzes the challenges of South Asian Women's organizations in "the existing political climate of anti-immigrant and racist sentiment" and recognizes
"the tension between the issues we seek to address and the tactics we choose."
She points, in a less strident critique than the *INCITE!* authors, to the difficulties of collective decision making as organizations grow and to the power
dynamic between members, founders, and paid staff. In the organizations she
studied, conflicts arose over decision making and strategy that were cast in
the language of oppressors and victims, thus mirroring the power and control
dynamic in abusive family situations. Abraham also identified individual and
collective accountability as a challenge, especially in situations where support
and services were offered to victims, providing them with a sense of security
that turned out to be false when organizations did not follow through.[31]

It is in the nature of service organizations to be locally focused, which in
turn exposes them to all the backlash and rejection from local Muslim communities while also allowing them access to the very same communities for
raising awareness and financial support. One of the enduring challenges of
Muslim (and other) organizations operating locally in a particular community
was that of safety, for clients as well as staff. Local volunteers as well as local
victims were sometimes difficult to protect from becoming known, the former
because word spread about whom to approach with DV issues in the community, and the latter when they were seen in the company of those activists.
Similarly, shelter locations were difficult to keep secret when they served a specific community and were located in close physical proximity.

Considering Muslim Shelters and Shelter for Muslims

When a victim comes to us, she has many needs. Maybe she is in the shelter, she doesn't have many clothes, or just the clothes on her back; she
doesn't have Islamic [*zabiha*] meat. Or she feels that the shelter staff don't
understand her.... Once a lady called me from another county, she had a
client who was not eating. She was at the domestic violence shelter but
refused to eat. She said, "We offered her everything that we have and she
is refusing. So can you talk to her?" And I said, "Yes, sure." So this client
said, "Really, I am very thankful to these ladies and that they are helping
me. But I am not going to cook in the same pots and pans where pork has
been cooked. But I don't want to give them hardship, so that's why I am
not eating." So I said, "No problem, I can tell them to give you separate
pots and pans." But she said, "No, I don't know if they used them for cook-

ing pork before." So I said, "Okay, I will send you pots and pans." She said, "Okay." So I sent her pots and pans and she was fine.

Stories like this one from one of the Muslim providers, Ghazala, appeared in many of my interviews. The issue of cooking in pots and pans that are not "contaminated" by previous use for pork may seem trivial but is of religious significance. For many Muslims, dietary restrictions and dress play an important role in asserting their religious identity as well as boundaries with other communities. In the context of trauma and the complete upheaval of all routines of life, the loss of belongings, and most comforts, the insistence on ritually clean cooking utensils is both a pillar to hold on to and an exercise of the agency that is severely limited by the domestic abuse and then again, at least potentially, by the shelter situation.

There are stories about women who are told to stop wearing hijab and who are encouraged to see their religion as part of the problem and walk away from it. There are also stories of women not being able to find modest clothing or a place to perform their daily prayers. And there are, less frequently, stories told about proselytizing and even mandatory Bible study in Christian shelters, as well as some about turning women into lesbians, as we saw in chapter 5. These stories seem to circulate among Muslim DV providers, religious leaders, and advocates and are likely known to victims and survivors as well. This general impression of the shelter system (in locations where DV shelters are even available) is often cited as a significant obstacle to Muslim women considering shelter even in potentially fatal DV crisis situations. Even when shelters do exist and victims are provided with information about them, and even when they are encouraged by imams or Muslim providers to seek shelter there, they are reluctant to go. Two strategies for addressing this problem have been to offer cultural sensitivity training to mainstream providers and to introduce Muslim providers to shelters and organizations in order to dispel some of these supposed myths so that they can encourage their clients to go there.

There is, however, a third option: the argument that Muslim women victims can only be fully accommodated in Muslim shelters. I do not know the exact number of Muslim women's shelters in the United States; this is in part due to the shifting landscape and the problem of funding, which I discuss further below. It is also due to the necessary secrecy surrounding shelters that goes beyond keeping the location itself secret. I visited two Muslim women's shelters in different locations in the United States and will participate in keeping their secret by keeping their description vague. There is one shelter,

Muslimat al-Nisaa, that is well known and publicized through the efforts of its founder, Asma Hanif, which I will discuss based on publicly available information.

The first important question for a Muslim shelter in the planning stages is whether it will be exclusive to Muslim women. If so, then the substantial funding necessary to furbish and then sustain a shelter will need to come from individual and community donations. DV organizations that limit their services to certain categories of victims, such as by religion, are not eligible for state and federal funding and thus have to rely on other sources for their financial survival. We have already seen in earlier chapters that Muslim communities are often reluctant to acknowledge DV in Muslim families and to recognize the widespread nature and devastating effect it has on the community. It is not difficult to imagine that communities that cannot accept that DV exists in their midst would be even more reluctant to invest funds that would effectively recognize it as a problem. Muslim providers did get funding from Muslim organizations and individuals, but I was frequently told that neither wanted to be publicly acknowledged as a donor. That may be a function of humility and an effort to give for the sake of God and not for public recognition, but there was also fear of stigma associated with the DV movement and perhaps by extension any association with feminism and gender justice.

Muslim shelters, or organizations whose services include a shelter, which are open to all, like we saw with NISA and FAITH, can apply for grants and funding on various levels and from philanthropic organizations and foundations. They then have to make a decision about how the setup of the shelter and its rules and routines will accommodate specific needs and limitations. The Peaceful Oasis Shelter, run by the Texas Muslim Women's Foundation, described the shelter in these terms: "Established in 2012, this shelter is the first and only family violence shelter in Texas addressing the specific language, faith, diet, social, and legal needs of Muslim women. With a diverse staff speaking more than 14 languages, the shelter is housed at an undisclosed location and welcomes women of Muslim and non-Muslim backgrounds."[32]

ICNA Relief, a branch of the Islamic Circle of North America, offered "Safe, Culturally Sensitive Temporary Housing for women age 18 years up to the age of 65 who are homeless, unmarried and/or legally separated and are residing in the USA legally." Women can, in some facilities, bring children with them but they "do not accept male children over the age of puberty; being the age of 10 due to Islamic guidelines." Even though ICNA Relief acknowledged that the women who approached them "have experienced emotional abuse as well as neglect and are underemployed or unable to obtain affordable housing," these sites of transitional housing "do not provide housing for victims of Domestic Violence who have just left an abusive situation due to safety concerns and the well-being of the victim. However; ICNA Relief does operate one Domestic Violence Shelter in S. California which is tailored to the unique needs of victims of violence which include safety precautions and counseling."[33] The existence of the program, which is a housing program exclusively for women, does seem to acknowledge the specific vulnerability of Muslim women and even emotional abuse in their lives but then makes a distinction between its forms of transitional housing and an actual DV shelter. In a similar and strategic move, Asma Hanif decided to describe her shelter in Baltimore as a shelter for homeless Muslim women rather than emphasize the fact that she almost exclusively took in women from acute DV crisis situations. She has openly acknowledged this move in several public presentations.

Muslimat al-Nisaa was founded by Asma Hanif and Maryam Funches after they had worked together at a health clinic for clients in need. Both were African American converts to Islam; Hanif was a trained nurse, and Funches was a well-known community activist. Formulating the need for a shelter exclusively for Muslim women, they started fund-raising in 2005 (a difficult and ongoing process), but by the time the shelter accepted its first occupant in 2007, Funches had passed away.[34] In a long feature on Hanif and the shelter in 2015, *Islamic Monthly* writer Salma Hasan Ali described the shelter: "Muslimat al-Nisaa is a multifamily dwelling on a quiet street in a residential area of Baltimore. It has eight bedrooms, five bathrooms, three kitchens and two living rooms. The bedrooms have bunk beds, and there is space for congregational prayer on the main floor. At full capacity, it can accommodate 50 women and children. Currently, there are 27 people living there."[35]

Searching for the shelter online revealed not only a significant number of articles about Hanif but also an impressive number of fund-raising events, campaigns, and appeals. When Hanif spoke at awareness events, she shared stories from the women in the shelter, with the intention to shock the audience into accepting DV in their midst, and then almost always appealed for financial support for the shelter. Hanif was a bit of a legend in the metro D.C. area: always dressed completely in purple, she was a registered nurse and frequently appeared at domestic violence awareness events and community functions. She staffed an information table with brochures and fund-raising flyers and sold plates with hand-painted calligraphy and pictures that the women in the shelter had made. In a *Washington Post* article in 2013, she told her life story to journalist Robert Samuels, sharing details about her upbringing in the South, her move to the Northeast, destitute and with her children, and how she took over an abandoned building and turned her life around. The article describes her soul-searching when her mother in North Carolina was slipping into dementia and she could not visit her because the shelter and its occupants depended on her. Hanif appreciated the public recognition and praise she had received but complained that she could not ever let go of her responsibilities and that there was no one she could turn to for care: "Asma Hanif, founder of Muslim women's shelter, finds herself in need of care."[36]

In March 2017, Imam Zaid Shakir, a prominent African American Muslim community leader, posted the following on his public Facebook page, with a picture of Hanif in her signature purple hijab:

> As Salaam Alaikum,
>
> As the founder of Muslimat Al Nisaa, the only known shelter in the country that exclusively serves Muslim women, Sr. Asma Hanif has devoted over a decade of her life to providing safety and stability for women in a place where they could comfortably practice their faith.
>
> Sr. Asma lives in the shelter with the women, allowing her to dedicate more of her resources to her work and be available for counseling and support. Her vision for her work is clear: "It started with my grandmother, but every time I find another person, maybe another category of individuals whom I can do something to help, then I add them. They become part of the project as well."
>
> I have known Asma for many years and wholeheartedly support her work and encourage you to support her as well by making a donation to this LaunchGood appeal.[37]

None of the supporters and writers of human-interest stories about the shelter seemed to find it problematic that its director lived in the same building and ran the organization by herself, with her children and community members assisting in a volunteer capacity. Only in private conversations did I hear concerns from other Muslim advocates and providers that there might be issues with Muslimat al-Nisaa's approach to and handling of shelter functions and clients' needs. One of my enduring concerns was the way in which Hanif represented her shelter (with its limited capacity) and its exclusiveness to Muslim women as the only acceptable form of shelter, both by perpetuating the stories I described above about problems with mainstream shelters and by warning advocates, leaders, and victims that mainstream services could not fulfill the specific needs of Muslim women.[38] She actively discouraged Muslim women from going to mainstream shelters and sent the same message to Muslim advocates, especially among community leaders.

During my day visit to one Muslim shelter, I was allowed to participate in a group counseling conversation, a lunch, and an afternoon prayer. Zahra, the staff person showing me around, had told me that I should wear a headscarf so that the women at the shelter would not think I was an outsider. I complied as she explained that all the occupants of the shelter were encouraged to wear hijab outside the shelter as well as inside. Outside, it was meant to protect them by identifying them as Muslim sisters (I have a hard time seeing how that would make them safer in the city), and inside it was meant to remind them that they are all Muslims. This applied also to occupants who did not wear hijab when they came to the shelter. In passing, Zahra praised one of the women who recently started wearing *niqab* in the shelter.

Earlier, she had explained to me that the shelter was in some upheaval on this particular day: one of the women had experienced a miscarriage during the night and was rushed to the hospital, accompanied by two other women. They had all returned from the hospital but the woman who miscarried was still in shock at the loss and their sudden departure had disrupted the regular routines of the shelter. Zahra said: "Routine is so important for these women, they need structure, and they need guidance, they don't know what to do." When the time came for *'asr* prayers, she went around the house to call the women. I got the feeling that participation was not really optional except for those women who were menstruating who were not allowed to pray. They had to explain, though, why they could not pray that day.

The lunch consisted of cold sandwiches two of the women had made in the kitchen. I felt bad about eating the food that was for the shelter occupants. They told me that they share what they have and hope that God will provide more. Most days, there was enough food for everyone. Also most days, there were fights about kitchen chores, cleaning, and food preferences. When one of the South Asian women cooked, the others complained that the food was too spicy and unfamiliar.

We sat down together in a circle for the counseling session. The counselor, who came to the shelter once every two weeks, was perceived as someone outside the shelter structure. I received permission to attend, but none of the shelter staff were present. The counselor went around and asked each woman how she was feeling that day. One said she was missing her husband and exclaimed that she should have never left to come to the shelter even if he was not always good to her. She loved him and it was unnatural for a Muslim woman to not be with her man. Another woman complained that she had not been sleeping because both of her children, one fourteen months and one six years old, had been sick with a cold. They slept in one room, so she would probably get sick as well and wake up as many times as they had the night before.

One woman's plan for getting out of the shelter was to get married again. She had lived at the shelter for six months and had gotten a divorce from her husband, so she was ready to move on. A friend "on the outside" had been helping her with finding a new husband in the local community. She said she missed love and she missed sex and the protection of a good husband. The other women nodded as she expressed in words something that I rarely saw acknowledged this openly in Muslim conversations: women's desire for sex.

Another woman launched into a monologue on how badly run the shelter was and that she was really tired of all the conflicts and the rules. She admitted that it was in the nature of a shelter, a place where people came in a state of crisis, with all their problems, and none of their belongings and routines, to be turbulent, despite all the efforts to establish routines. Women came and went, newcomers needed to be trained in shelter rules, older occupants went through cycles of denial and grief, and all of that took place in a really small space. The shelter should not admit more women, she said, but she was grateful that she had found a space here. That made her feel guilty for not wanting the same for her sisters in need.

The counselor offered an open ear and frequently interjected sentences on Allah's compassion and love for each of them and that they should try to find the same compassion and love for one another. She was patient, affirming, and open to whatever the women were willing to share in a group conversation. In the hour-long conversation, I did not see her criticize or advise the women once. The women trusted her and evidently also one another enough to say things out loud. I was surprised that they accepted my presence at the counseling session, but I was grateful for the opportunity and for their trust.

After nine hours, I left the shelter emotionally exhausted and overwhelmed by the depth of grief, pain, and sadness that permeated the space itself. The glimpses of life stories, not only stories of abuse, all deserve recognition, but they would stay at the shelter with the women and would, perhaps, leave with them for another chance at life.

My brief encounters with Muslim shelters as one form of DV services have left me with mixed thoughts and, admittedly, mixed feelings. In a world of danger, pain, injury, threat, and fear, shelters are islands for emergency and crisis situations and it is certainly better to have them, with all the problems they pose, than not to have them at all. And many of the problems described appear in a specific form in Muslim shelters but are also part of broader issues of institutionalizing care and services in specific ways, especially in DV shelters. In her "Disloyal to Feminism," Emi Koyama delivers a scathing indictment of the structural problems and resulting abuses in the shelter system. Koyama, who both lived in a shelter at one point and worked at several later in her life, writes: "After working at several domestic violence shelters in various capacities, I realize that my thinking has changed. While I still believe that there can be better rules, better trainings, and better volunteer screening procedures for domestic violence shelters than those currently employed, I now feel that these reforms do not fundamentally change the dynamic of power and control within the shelter system."[39]

The other reason for my skepticism about Muslim women's shelters may be illustrated with the story of Baitul Salaam in Atlanta. What started in 1997 during a conversation involving Hadayai Majeed and several other women evolved into a network of women volunteers and a set of initiatives and efforts that at its height included a Muslim women's shelter. I remember hearing about Baitul Salaam in the early stages of my research and how it was an important example of a shelter for Muslim women. There were frequent appeals for donations and signs of trouble with maintaining the high level of funding required to keep the shelter open. Twice the shelter had to close temporarily, and in 2008, Majeed made the difficult decision to close for good and transform Baitul Salaam into a DV service organization that took calls, connected women in need to other services, and operated a food bank and some clothing assistance and toy drives for the Islamic holidays. In 2016, Majeed announced on Facebook that she was phasing out her leadership of the organization and was looking for a successor.[40]

The trials and tribulations of Baitul Salaam illustrate the difficulties in focusing local community efforts on exclusive shelters. Of course, other DV service organizations face challenges of turnover, funding, single-personality organizational models, and the slow but steady erosion of enthusiasm that comes from seeing the denial of DV in communities on the one hand and the steady and never-ending stream of victims and survivors in need on the other. It is hard in such a situation to invest energy in new initiatives and projects that are both part of and distinct from mainstream DV structures and institutions and thus subject to all the applicable criticism and a host of additional dynamics from anti-Muslim hostility and racism in American society to protective patriarchy and the silencing of DV awareness voices.

On Mosques, DV Services, and Muslim Providers

It is prudent here to return to Muslim services that are not offered through dedicated organizations but are more closely linked to mosques and Muslim community centers. Initial DV services were often informal and were provided, mostly by women, to victims on an ad hoc basis. One of my interviewees described the home she grew up in as a kind of shelter even though she did not realize as a child why women and children who were not relatives would come to stay with them. Many advocates and service providers in this study first realized that DV existed in their communities through an encounter at the mosque or a conversation about a community member.

In the mosques where DV is acknowledged as a communal problem, some version of a committee, often called the social service committee, will be in charge of deciding on and offering limited services to victims. As discussed in chapter 5, imams are often called upon as first responders in crisis situations and will be expected to offer counseling and advice and, in the ideal-case scenario, will also have resources and service provider information to share with a victim in need. Some mosques utilize *zakat* money to support victims financially. There is usually an application process involved and financial assistance can sometimes be provided through this channel. The main problem with DV services through the mosque is the total lack of confidentiality and thus increased danger for victims. Even if an abuser is not a prominent figure or fixture in the community (which they sometimes are), speaking to the imam, receiving counseling, and applying formally for financial support are all actions that can publicize a victim's identity and thus increase her risk and the threat of further violence from the abuser.

Several of the organizations I encountered originated in a mosque context and some still received funding through the mosque from the local community but they had acquired separate institutional status and had also moved their physical space to be separate from the mosque. One interesting model was the Muslim Community Center Clinic in Silver Spring, Maryland. The Muslim Community Center (MCC) was founded in 1977 and played a prominent role in Montgomery County. With several community members being medical professionals, and over a period of over ten years, MCC constructed a dedicated clinic building on the grounds of the mosque and opened the MCC Clinic in 2003. The clinic, aside from providing health care for those in need, offered specific services for DV victims including a counselor and a caseworker with experience in mainstream DV work.[41] The doctors in the clinic also constituted a link to yet another way to approach Muslim DV services: the many individuals who identify as Muslim and recognize Islamic ethics as an important motivator for their anti-DV efforts who work in mainstream organizations and/or professions that link them to DV victims.

I spoke to Muslim lawyers who were approached by Muslim clients; Muslim nurses and medical doctors who encountered Muslim victims; and Muslim social workers, therapists, and counselors who were sought out by Muslims to fulfill their specific needs, to engage in cultural and religious translation with mainstream institutions, and to provide religious comfort and understanding in an overwhelming and potentially hostile system. Some of these Muslim lawyers, social workers, therapists, and nurses turned their concern for Muslim victims of DV into their professional focus—they started working for Muslim DV organizations in their professional capacity. Others combined their day job in the mainstream with volunteer and pro bono work in Muslim organizations, and yet others became bridges between Muslim service organizations, the mainstream, and DV victims. Each of their stories is worth telling and touched me deeply in the interviews and encounters I had with them. In what follows, I have selected passages speaking to some of the central questions and themes of this chapter. I have combined materials from different interviews into composite narratives. The quotes are taken from more than one interviewee in each "profile," not in order to create types of providers but to help obscure their identities. If I could publish all the interviews in full, the stories would be even more powerful and speak more loudly. As I protect the women who put their trust in me, I decided to select passages that speak to the role of religion as motivation for their work, that reflect on gender and feminism, and that tell of survivor experiences, burnout, and the pressure of professionalization.

Interviews with Muslim Providers

Ghazala

Ghazala was in her fifties, divorced and with grown children. She had been working with an organization that provided various services to DV victims for more than a decade when I met her. She was eager to explain the history of the organization to me and pointed out all the important people who were involved and in support. She never mentioned her own important role but insisted on speaking of "we" when she described the frameworks and inner workings of the organization. When she described herself in the beginning of the interview, she only mentioned that she had started working at the organization sometime after her divorce. Much later, in a discussion of fatality assessments and the difficulty of gauging the risk level in any given case, she said:

> There is verbal abuse but it can end in homicide or suicide. You have to be very careful when you are analyzing these cases because it is not only physical violence that can end in murder. It is a lot of responsibility to make these assessments and it is hard, you know? We carry this to our homes. These women are really in very bad situations when they come to us. Some of them are in danger but not willing to leave. So you cannot do anything except advise them and some of them ... there was one lady, she called me on and off for eight years, eight years, and I was working with her and finally she came out for a year or so and then she went back and she is still in contact with me. It is their life; their choices and we cannot make these choices for them.

Ghazala pointed to the significance of an individual caseworker in the life (or death) of a survivor—if she decided to leave her job at the organization, the woman she had been working with for over eight years might not call back at all. When I cautiously asked whether there had been cases that ended in homicide, she said: "Not yet, Alhamdulillah," and realizing the implications, she gave me a sad smile and said, "We have been lucky so far." I told her about another interview in which a service provider was asked what a "good" outcome for a case would be and she answered, "If the woman doesn't get killed, if she is in fact a survivor." Ghazala nodded and we moved on to a question I have asked each of my interviewees: "Why are you doing this work?"

Ghazala looked at me and said in a flat voice: "I am a survivor." She cleared her throat and continued:

> I feel good when I help women, and I feel connected to them. I feel when they are talking that I can understand and that I can feel what they are going through. One of our caseworkers was telling me that she has one client, she cannot pack her stuff, we have the housing ready for her and her husband is in jail, why can't she pack her stuff, her stuff is all over the floor. I told her, this is her life that is on the floor. She is closing one chapter and

opening a new one; it's not that easy when you are packing your home that you had with your husband and you are separating your things from his, it is a very, very hard thing to do. So for an advocate who never went through that, it is hard to understand. She thinks she is lazy.

I asked her if she tells her clients that she is a survivor herself. She said:

Yes, yes, I do; they feel it, and I also tell them sometimes, I have been through this. I used to be very open about this but I learned because I saw that many women responded to me but then I learned to be careful. There was one case, a horrific case, my God, her husband was beating her, dragging her by her hair to the next story of her house, her kids were watching all that, he was raping her. When her husband was in jail and she had a protective order and this lawyer called me to help explain to this client why she should separate from her husband and how it is going to affect her kids. She did not want to leave her husband and told her lawyer to do what she wanted him to do. She did not want the protective order and she wanted her husband to come home. She had never been independent and didn't think she could survive with her kids without her husband. So I told her my story, I am a single mom, and she was so surprised. But she stopped trusting me and was convinced that they had sent me to break up her family. So I learned that I have to be careful when and how I tell about myself.

Engaging in DV work as an advocate or a service provider and openly acknowledging survivor status can not only go either way as in Ghazala's story but can also be seen as a major obstacle to professionalization efforts. As Norma Jean Profitt has shown in her work on survivors of gender-based violence and their participation in feminist political activism, survivors of violence were a powerful source in feminist organizing against violence. She argues that

feminist social work theory and practice with survivors of woman abuse must recognize survivors' work for social change, and develop new, more inclusive models that provide opportunities for survivors to make sense of their experience, develop a critical consciousness, and belong to community as they undertake personal change and make explicit commitments to strive for a more just world.[42]

Professionalization can also cast survivors and their specific issues and challenges as an obstacle to the kind of systematizing and measurable service work that is its goal.

Several years after the interviews, I saw one of Ghazala's colleagues in the same organization at an event and heard that she had decided to quit her work at the organization. Her former coworker said that she had had health issues that she eventually recognized as signs of secondary trauma from working with DV victims every day, which potentially exacerbated her own personal trauma experience. She had agonized over the decision to leave and expressed deep guilt at abandoning her work. When I was conducting my ethnographic research, I created a snapshot of a particular moment/period of a few years in the life of the Muslim DV movement. People in the movement are familiar with compassion fatigue and burnout from research in the medical and social work fields (to which some of them belong), but it is still hard to continue one's own efforts when others seem to get so negatively affected that they need to leave as an act of self-preservation. I never heard anyone blame another advocate or provider for "moving on" but rather saw expressions of sadness and loss. As one of my interviewees said: "Even if you stop doing the work, the stories of the victims never leave you, never."

Samia

Samia was a trained lawyer, in her mid-thirties, and involved in DV cases both in her professional capacity as a family lawyer in a small firm and in her additional service as a pro bono lawyer for a Muslim organization. When she was training as a family lawyer, she dealt with many different aspects of family law but realized that domestic violence appeared at the nexus of divorce, child support and custody, immigration, housing, benefits, and Social Security. She described growing up in a loving and supportive Muslim family without any idea about domestic violence. It was in court that she first encountered the parents of a Muslim classmate in a divorce case and realized with great shock that DV was indeed an issue in her community, one she had never noticed before. Her own first "Muslim" case was a woman in an egregious abuse situation and she struggled in several ways: "It was hard but I had to recognize that there was a Muslim husband abusing his wife and the husband was also represented by a Muslim lawyer. It bothered me so much."

The years of working with Muslim DV victims took a toll on her, not only through burnout. She said:

I know it doesn't sound important, but all these DV cases have made it hard for me to get married. I hear about Muslim guys from my parents; I get introduced to someone; I meet someone, and all I can think is, what if he is an abuser? What if he will become one? How can I know? What is the likelihood? I have seen religious guys, who pray and who fast, and who go to the mosque all the time who beat their wives, who sexually assaulted women, and who do horrible things. How can I trust any of them?

When I began my research, I did not pay attention to whether the advocates and providers I was interviewing were married, unless it came up in conversation such as in survivor stories in which the interviewee was divorced. When Samia brought up this deep concern about finding a spouse I went back to look through earlier materials and realized that a significant number of the younger women in my project, those who started their involvement with DV work in their twenties, were not married even if they were now in their mid- to late thirties. In our interview, Samia also made a connection between her inability to find a spouse and her reputation in the community. Younger women advocates and service providers are, like their older counterparts, seen as troublemakers, bent on dragging their communities' dirty laundry into the open and breaking apart Muslim families. This "reputation," especially when associated with feminist ideas about gender equality, is a deal breaker for Muslim men. Samia said: "I think we are too strong for them, too independent. They are scared of professional women who know their rights." And with eyes tearing, she concluded: "And maybe that means I will be alone for the rest of my life."

Samia found comfort from her shaken perception of Muslim men in certain interpretations of the Qur'an, Hadith, and Islamic law regarding women and marriage. She was careful to distance herself from feminist talk of gender equality and instead insisted on calling it "gender equity." She saw the example of the Prophet Muhammad as central for understanding love, affection, and sex within marriage as a woman's (and a man's) right. Gender was an important category for her thinking about these issues, but it had to be applied from within "the sources," namely the Qur'an and Sunna. The values she found most important in the Qur'an were justice, mercy, compassion, truth, and the important principle to "do no harm." She rejected patriarchy as an attempt to put some human beings over others in society but also believed that God created men and women differently, for different and complementary tasks in society. Her personal Islamic framework was not quite one of protective patriarchy but it was also not quite a gender-egalitarian (feminist) project to achieve gender equality in all aspects of life. She said: "I do this work and I know, deep inside, that God wants me to do this work, because He brought me here—how else would I have become a Muslim lawyer working against domestic violence—here in my country, the United States, at this time of Islamophobia?"

Sarah

Sarah was in her early sixties when I met her in the quiet women's space of a mosque outside of prayer times. We sat in a corner on the floor and she patiently answered all my questions about her DV work in Muslim communities. She was a nurse and worked in the emergency room of a large urban hospital. It was there that she encountered Muslim victims of domestic violence. Many physician's offices and hospitals screen for DV, and she would recognize Muslim names in the forms and would try to connect to the women: "I saw them all the time and I wanted to help but I was also afraid to get involved. I didn't know what to do. So I started to look around for resources, for Muslim organizations, and there were only a few options, but at least I could offer them something. All I can do is give them all the information; I can't make decisions for them. It is hard sometimes, but I can't just say, 'Come with me; I will help you.' They have to decide."

She described the many injuries she saw inflicted on women and how it was especially hard when the same woman would be in the emergency room for a second or third time. She reflected on culture and the many different cultural ways of being Muslim. She thought about women's circumcision (FGC) and ideas about what even constitutes abuse. She said: "Sometimes all I can do is pray for them, pray that they find a way out. That someone helps them; that they tell someone." She reflected on her legal responsibility to report child abuse[43] but not the domestic abuse of women. That also meant for her that parents could get caught up in a system and culture that they did not understand and lose their kids or have immigration authorities get involved; she felt helpless because she could not prevent any of it.

She kept telling me that she was not very knowledgeable about religion but that she trusted a Muslim chaplain she knew and a nephew who studied Islamic law in Saudi Arabia. When people had questions about Islam, she would send them to the chaplain. She also asked her nephew a lot of questions, but in the end, she said, "I know in my heart that Allah is merciful and just and that He would not want women to be hurt in this way. Not even with a handkerchief.[44] I feel that in my heart."

Robina Niaz

Robina is the founder of Turning Point, a Muslim DV service organization in New York, founded in 2004. I include her here based on publicly available information about her life and work, both to honor someone who can be named and to connect her experiences and ideas to those of my interviewees.

Niaz, who is a well-known figure in the New York area, even if as a trouble-maker to some in Muslim communities, was featured as a CNN Hero in 2009. In the CNN article, she offered insight into her own life experience and her work with Turning Point. The short article encompasses many of the themes and issues I encountered in my interviews. She explained her view on domestic violence as not a specifically Muslim issue but with a Muslim solution:

> A devout Muslim, Niaz stresses that there is no evidence that domestic violence is more common among Muslim families. "Abuse happens everywhere," said Niaz. "It cuts across barriers of race, religion, culture." But, she said, Muslims are often reluctant to confront the issue. "There's a lot of denial," she said. "It makes it much harder for the victims of abuse to speak out."
>
> When Niaz launched her organization in 2004, it was the first resource of its kind in New York City. Today, her one-woman campaign has expanded into a multifaceted endeavor that is raising awareness about family violence and providing direct services to women in need.
>
> Niaz said she firmly believes that domestic violence goes against Islamic teachings, and considers it her religious duty to try to stop abuse from happening. The "Quran condemns abusive behavior of women," she said, noting that the prophet Mohammed was never known to have abused women. "Allah says, 'Stand up against injustice and bear witness, even if it's against your own kin.' So if I see injustice being done to women and children, I have to speak up. It's my duty."

She identified openly as a survivor of domestic abuse and had turned her own experience into her motivation and commitment to help others:

> Niaz's mission began after a difficult period in her own life. Born and raised in Pakistan, she had earned a master's degree in psychology and had a successful career in international affairs and marketing when she moved to the United States to marry in 1990. "It was a disastrous marriage," she said.
>
> As Niaz struggled to navigate the American legal system during her divorce, she said she appreciated how lucky she was to speak English and

have an education. She realized that many immigrant women without those advantages might be more likely to stay in marriages because they didn't know how to make the system work for them. "If this is how difficult it is for me, then what must other immigrant women go through?" she remembered thinking.

And 9/11 had a particular impact on her self-perception and the ways in which she perceived her work:

> After volunteering with South Asian victims of domestic violence, Niaz, who speaks five languages, got a job using those skills to advocate for immigrant women affected by family violence. But Niaz's focus changed on September 11, 2001. "I was no longer a Pakistani-American ... I looked at myself as a Muslim."
>
> Niaz said the backlash many Muslims experienced after the terror attacks made abuse victims more afraid to seek help; they feared being shunned for bringing negative attention to their community. "Women who were caught in abusive marriages were trapped even more," recalled Niaz.
>
> In 2004, Niaz used her savings to start Turning Point for Women and Families. Today, her work focuses on three main areas: providing direct services to abused women, raising awareness through outreach, and educating young women—an effort she hopes will empower future generations to speak out against abuse. Crisis intervention services are a critical element of Niaz's efforts. Through weekly counseling sessions, she and her team provide emotional support to the women while helping them with practical issues, such as finding homeless shelters, matrimonial lawyers, filing police reports or assisting with immigration issues. Niaz has helped more than 200 Muslim women. While most of Turning Point's clients are immigrants, the group helps women from every background. While Niaz has support from many people in New York's Muslim community, she acknowledges that not everyone appreciates her efforts. She keeps her office address confidential and takes precautions to ensure her safety. "There have been threats ... but that comes with this work," she said. "I know that God is protecting me because I'm doing the right thing."[45]

Muslim service providers in and beyond Muslim organizations and networks operate most directly at the intersection with mainstream and other religious service organizations as well as law enforcement and the criminal justice system. Their personal motivations for engaging in DV service work rely heavily on a religiously framed ethic of non-abuse that they put into practice every day. The following chapter links their work as well as that of Muslim advocates to the interreligious anti-DV movement and addresses in more detail how Muslim advocates and service providers have navigated the DV mainstream and the state.

7

Above and Beyond

MUSLIMS IN INTERFAITH AND
MAINSTREAM DV WORK (AND THE STATE)

Interreligious cooperation on a cause like domestic violence makes much more sense to me than interfaith dialogue. It does not erase the different histories of the different religious communities in the United States, nor does it usually account for the power differentials between Muslims, Jews, and Christians as minority/majority communities but there seems to be plenty of goodwill and sometimes even a dose of religious feminism in these circles.

THESE NOTES from an interfaith event leave quite a different impression from what can be discerned on the relationship between DV efforts and religious communities. Consider this summary of a chapter titled "Matters of Faith, History, and Society" from a comprehensive and widely used volume on domestic violence that has been published in updated editions since 1990:

> Historically, domestic violence was considered a normal part of some intimate relationships and a part of everyday life for some women. This historical context of violence against women is neither of a short time span nor of a sporadic one. It often has been explicitly stated in pronouncements and codified into numerous laws, becoming an endemic feature of most societies from the ancient world until very recent times. Religion, being a key component of, and justifying much of, social and legal attitudes towards women, has reinforced such history, although in modern times religion has shown that it can be part of the solution.[1]

This framing is representative of a common approach in scholarship on domestic violence that attempts to consider religion as significant for DV research and work while struggling to assess its place in society. This quote is from the 2012 edition of the book and incorporates considerations of Christianity, some Judaism, and notably several references to Islam in the context of the United States.

This chapter of the book was a struggle for me; throughout my research, I encountered Muslim DV advocates in both interfaith contexts and in their outreach to the DV mainstream as well as lawyers and law enforcement. Thus broader questions of religion and DV, on the one hand, and the looming presence of the state, on the other, regularly appeared in my conversations, readings, and observations. They took me beyond the Muslim community and family contexts that I was exploring and were a constant reminder that, of course, American Muslims are (and have been) a part of the fabric of American society, which impacted them in significant ways. American Muslim efforts against domestic violence were part of broader structures, part of broader struggles, and subject to the broader forces of the society they took part in. But how could I acknowledge these broader structures without either writing a book about religious efforts against domestic violence in the United States (perhaps a project for another decade!) or losing my focus on American Muslims as agents in the DV movement? This chapter then is an attempt to capture some of the intersections I encountered without allowing them to take over the focus of the book. The chapter on honor and domestic violence murders (in essence a chapter on media framing and representation) has already provided ways to think about the connections between what happens in Muslim communities and how they are affected by and, in turn, affect an "outside" that is never absent. In fact, the binary between inside and outside itself is misleading in that it assumes the possibility of demarcating and then policing a boundary between the two. Everyone is always simultaneously inside and outside many communities, structures, and systems; notions of identity, belonging, agency, and power shape our functioning and participating in all of them. As in previous chapters, I want to stay close to the ethnographic as well as textual contexts I have explored in this project. I touch upon the role of religion in society, in the public sphere, without being able to fully attend to theories of secularism, public religion, and the important links between patriarchy, religion, race, and capitalism. Perhaps somewhere in this chapter (and elsewhere in this book) lie some answers to two questions formulated by the authors of the quote above: "Why do we care about historical attitudes and precedents toward women or religion in what is now a secular society? Are religious doctrines and attitudes still important in the context of modern society?"[2]

My own questions are formulated somewhat differently and relate back to the ethic of non-abuse I have been weaving through the book: What happens to the religiously framed ethic of non-abuse beyond the religious community context in which it emerged and in which it makes the most sense as a reference point? How do Muslim DV advocates read the contexts beyond their communities? How can a religious ethic of non-abuse, which exists in other religiously framed efforts against DV as well, be addressed in secular contexts? Can religious advocates negotiate their religion with the state?

In what follows, I locate negotiations of these questions by Muslim DV advocates and their communities in three overlapping spheres: interfaith contexts, the mainstream DV movement, and finally the state. It appears, at first, that Muslim advocates are influenced by the structures, assumptions, and power dynamics of these three spheres, thus making their interaction with the interfaith DV movement, the mainstream DV system, and the state appear one-directional. And in many ways, the power dynamic is stacked in that direction. However, Muslim advocates, because they recognize these structures and their own exclusion from power, at least attempt to speak back to them from within their own religious and ethical frameworks. As was the case within Muslim communities, they negotiate questions of authority, critique, and interpretation in an ever-changing landscape of social justice, politics, and power. And as demonstrated throughout the book, the issue of domestic violence in Muslim families is deeply embedded in broader issues such as Islamophobia, racism, patriarchy, the state monopoly on violence, and the role of religion in a secular society.

The Interfaith Context

As I entered the exhibition hall at the People's Community Baptist Church in Silver Spring, Maryland, I was handed a purple brochure—the program for the thirteenth annual conference of the Interfaith Community Against Domestic Violence (IFCADV). The stated motto of the conference was printed on the top: "Creating a Society of Equality and Mutual Respect for All." The conference itself was titled "Domestic Violence: Legacy? Choice?: Faith Communities Respond to Abusers."

In wandering around the exhibition space and looking for Muslim representation, I encountered Mildred Muhammad and her organization, After the Trauma. This is where I bought her book, *Scared Silent*, discussed in chapter 2. Not far from her table, Nadia Janjua from Muslim Women in the Arts had set up several of her own works and some of the pieces that would later that spring be displayed at an art exhibit titled "Healing & Empowerment: Violence, Women & Art" that I attended for this project as well. Nadia was happy to see me and excited about the opportunity to represent Muslims at the conference and do her own part in raising awareness of Muslim efforts against domestic violence.

I had looked through the program online before registering for the conference and was a bit disappointed that there were no Muslim speakers listed. I had encountered other religious advocates against DV at some events the previous year—Jewish Women International offered support for a training event in Washington, D.C., and the FaithTrust Institute had come up several times in my discussions with Muslim advocates. I collected brochures from organizations and bought several books that day. There was representation from religious groups: the Domestic Violence Ministry of the People's Community Baptist Church (where the conference was held), whose motto is "Women empowering women"; End It Now: Adventists Say No to Violence, which was a campaign of the Women's Ministries of Seventh-Day Adventists; the Time to Fly Foundation, a faith-based response to domestic abuse whose motto was "No Excuse for Abuse"; and several others. There was a table with information from the Muslim Community Center (MCC) Medical Clinic in Silver Spring, which specifically addressed the MCC's stance on domestic violence and provided resources within and beyond the clinic itself. What was notable about this interreligious conference was the close connection of religious organizations and initiatives with others in the DV mainstream; local shelters, the Montgomery County Crisis Center, the Family Justice Center, the Montgomery County Commission for Women, and other mainstream agencies and resources were all represented at the conference.

IFCADV was founded by Maud E. Clarke "in 1999 as a committee after being asked to do training for clergy by her director at the Abused Persons Program in Montgomery County," which I learned from a fond farewell leaflet to Clarke, who was retiring from her position that year after the organization had grown "to be a full non-profit organization providing trainings and assistance to faith communities," including the annual conference.[3] IFCADV was "dedicated to engaging, educating, and energizing faith communities to respond to and prevent intimate partner abuse"; it defined intimate partner abuse in by now familiar ways but offered a specific link to religion:

> Intimate partner abuse affects thousands of people in Montgomery County, the state of Maryland, and the entire country each year. It happens to people of all religions, ages, races, economic levels, and educational backgrounds. Much of this abuse is against the law. All of the abuse is against the teachings of the world's major religions, which teach that violence in any form is wrong and that relationships between people should be respectful and peaceful.[4]

This powerful statement was formulated in this way to convince readers that all forms of DV are indeed not only morally and legally reprehensible but also, and more importantly, *against* religious teachings. The statement is powerful because it does not leave any room for "but" and "if" or distracting nuance in a brochure that is intended to convince its audience to increase awareness of DV, educate communities, and "empower congregations and their leadership to develop an active domestic abuse ministry."

Yet it is here that my academic training makes me skeptical of whether such powerful and unequivocal statements stand the test of community organizing, or of reality. Or perhaps, yet again, the nuance I search for and am trained to formulate can really only hinder the kind of work that is necessary on the community level. I pondered this question throughout my research and the writing of this book, and I perpetually wondered whether there could be a productive equilibrium between critical self-reflection and efficacy in this important endeavor.

The critique I formulated above should also be read in the complicated historical context of religious efforts against DV. It is worth emphasizing that there was a time when religion was assumed to only be a roadblock to efforts against domestic violence, a stance that was echoed in the quote at the beginning of this chapter. It is worth appreciating that religious approaches to DV have carved out some space, however small, in broader societal and even state efforts against DV in the United States. Montgomery County and IFCADV had an exceptional track record in establishing services and structures that were significantly less confusing to navigate than in other parts of the country *and* in incorporating religious communities, leaders, and organizations into those structures. IFCADV was a reflection of the need for localized and tailored initiatives against DV from within and addressed specifically to religious communities. Its inception in 1999 pushed forward religious efforts against DV that had started to emerge in the 1970s. While this is not the place to sketch a history of the religious movement against DV (which was initially Christian only), it will be helpful to explore one important initiative, the FaithTrust Institute, which has already been mentioned several times in previous chapters.

The FaithTrust Institute

Founded in 1977 by Marie Fortune, the institute described its mission as providing "faith communities and advocates with the tools and knowledge they need to address the faith and cultural issues related to abuse" and its vision of the world as one "where all persons are free from violence in relationships; faith is fundamental to ending violence; religious institutions create a climate in which abuse is not tolerated; faith communities become sanctuaries of safety, worthy of our trust; and all of us experience justice and healing in our communities."[5]

While I will say more about its history below, I want to first explore the way in which the institute represented itself on its website during the years of my active research. Its guiding principles represented a comprehensive as well as (to me) surprisingly nuanced list of ideas about the causes of sexual and domestic violence and the commitments to changing the current situation. It is worth reproducing them here in their entirety to discuss how they contain both a religious ethic of non-abuse and a clear appreciation for the broader frames of power and domination that DV is a part of. Importantly, the institute's leadership has, since its inception, acknowledged the connection between sexual and domestic abuse (which was almost always downplayed in the religious contexts I have studied) and has demonstrated its willingness to adopt gender-specific frameworks in its analysis of DV and sexual violence.

The institute's website states:

WE BELIEVE:

- Sexual and domestic violence violate the rights and dignity of all women, men and children. To the extent that any person is violated by sexual and domestic violence, the dignity and worth of all persons are diminished.
- Oppression is deeply ingrained in our society and all forms of oppression—including racism, sexism, classism, anti-Semitism,

ageism, heterosexism and oppression of the differently abled—increase
the suffering caused by sexual and domestic violence. Sexual and
domestic violence are often instruments of these forms of oppression.

- All those without power and privilege are the most vulnerable to and
  the most likely to be victimized by sexual and domestic violence.
- Ending sexual and domestic violence requires changing attitudes and
  practices of individuals, communities, and institutions.
- Organized religious communities have an ethical responsibility to play
  a major role in bringing about an end to sexual and domestic violence
  within their own communities and within society at large.

WE SERVE:

- Faith communities and institutions in supporting and advocating for
  victims of abuse and in calling perpetrators of abuse to account.
- Victims and survivors by utilizing education and training as the means
  to engage in the prevention of sexual and domestic violence, and
  address religious issues and spiritual needs of victims, survivors,
  offenders and their communities.

*FOUNDATIONAL PRINCIPLES for a Faithful Response to Sexual and
Domestic Violence:*

- Faith is fundamental to ending sexual and domestic violence regardless
  of our faith tradition.
- Tradition, sacred texts, doctrines, teachings and cultural values will be
  either a roadblock or a resource to ending violence against women.
- Healing goals are safety for victims, accountability for abusers, and
  restoration of relationship (if possible).
- Justice-making is the theological and ethical context for the response
  to the victim/survivor, the perpetrator, and the faith group or
  congregation.
- Taking sides means to not abandon the victim/survivor; to not accept
  the abuser's behavior; to seek justice for the victim/survivor and
  repentance for the abuser.
- To recognize and address gender based violence is part of our analysis
  and should be part of our strategy for response.
- The role of the faith leader is naming the unmentionable sins and
  promoting healing and justice.

It is no coincidence but rather a conscious choice of words to list a set of principles the institute leadership "believes" in as the opening for that list of principles. A framework that incorporates both the ethical notion of human dignity and a rights framework reminiscent of human rights and women's rights as human rights creates the foundation for an appeal both to religious sources and principles and the widely accepted, if also debated, notion of universal human rights. It also hinges on a universal understanding of religion. An ethical framing based on dignity opens the door for notions of justice, which are formulated later in the same list as "justice-making," a much more action-oriented form than abstract ideas.

Also, note that the first principle is both gender specific in its mention of women (first) and men and children second and third while also extending beyond a "violence against women" framework as found and debated in feminist and mainstream DV work. This is neither an exclusive way of framing the issue, which has been very powerful and important for bringing DV into societal awareness, nor a completely gender-neutral reframing of DV as nothing to do with gender dynamics in society. It is only later that the approach is made more specific: when gender-based violence is identified as "part of" both the analysis and the necessary responses.

The embeddedness of domestic and sexual violence in interconnected forms of oppression, and as expressions of such oppression, allows for a comprehensive analysis and critique of these broader structures without losing sight of the specific focus of the organization. And the calling out of "organized religious communities" both creates a framework that limits their conception of religion to recognizable religious institutions and community structures, for example, world religions or traditional religions, and simultaneously holds those same structured and recognized communities accountable in specific ways. The formulations in the list are also relatively neutral in their references to religion: elsewhere and in other organizations I have encountered much more obvious Christianity- (and Judaism-)centered approaches and word choices. The reference to "tradition, sacred texts, doctrines, teachings and cultural values" clearly attempts to move beyond a monotheistic or Judeo-Christian framework, while the language of faith as fundamental, even to faith traditions in the plural, assumes a unified framework for defining religion. Such definitions may well be the precondition for the specific framing of responses to DV as an ethical responsibility. The only angle that is absent from this list of principles is the legal angle, which is limiting in that it does not equip religious leaders and communities with the tools necessary to interact with the state as a structure for most efforts against domestic violence and as a structure that has the power to define what religion is and how it can function in its secular legal system.

Equally fascinating, and perhaps more than a little emblematic for the broader history of religiously framed efforts against DV, is the "Our History" section of the institute's website. It starts with its founder, Rev. Marie Fortune:

> It was 1976. Jimmy Carter was president and Rev. Dr. Marie M. Fortune was fresh out of seminary. Rev. Fortune had been ordained in the United Church of Christ to a "specialized ministry," a ministry outside the local church, to address sexual and domestic violence within the church. Although she had no idea what that would look like, her volunteer work at Seattle Rape Relief had made it clear that someone needed to initiate the conversation. She often received calls from women who, when they learned she was a pastor, would begin to explore their spiritual concerns: "Why did God let this happen? Do I have to forgive the rapist? Does God still love me?"[6]

Fortune was also serving a small rural church near Seattle and would try to talk about her volunteer work at Seattle Rape Relief only to learn that her congregants were uncomfortable discussing the issues. She also realized that the majority of Christian clergy at the time did not know of any resources for victims of sexual or domestic violence. "Fortune knew that most clergy had the best intentions, she shuddered to think what they did offer to those victims who had the courage to disclose."[7] Fortune made it her goal to convince sexual assault programs to consider religion on one hand while trying to open up space in church conversations on sexual assault on the other.

In laying out the landscape, one that was simultaneously formed by early feminist efforts to engage the state in regulating domestic abuse and opening the private sphere of family to legal oversight, there are also echoes of the common experiences of denial, of domestic and sexual violence by religious communities and their leaders, and the initial connections Fortune made between her work in sexual assault contexts and her religious training. There is the still prevalent and woeful lack of awareness, let alone training, in counseling and/or resource sharing with victims by religious leaders that appears in the narrative. Only a few years later, the emerging FaithTrust Institute began working with and was supported by the U.S. Department of Justice.

In 1979, as the initial project to train local clergy was drawing to a close, the US Department of Justice approached the group to develop a pilot project to initiate work in rural communities addressing domestic violence, using the churches as the base of organizing. This notion was based on a recognition that rural communities relied on churches as an institutional base for leadership. So with federal funding in place, training in five areas of the US began. From this effort, FaithTrust Institute's basic training model was developed—the same model we still use today. And the project worked. We began to see the possibilities of national work and the potential leadership in local communities and in national denominations.[8]

This description of the early funding and support from the DOJ is quite surprising considering how cautious the DOJ has been more recently in engaging with religious organizations, especially in the form of state funding. I will return to this issue, but I suspect that the DOJ reluctance about religion is partly a product of more recent (than 1979) historical developments in the relationship between the state and religious institutions in the United States and partly a bias toward Christian, especially mainline Protestant, organizations as opposed to Muslim-minority communities.[9] This is not an indictment of or accusation against the FaithTrust Institute but a genuine attempt to understand the wide range of experiences of different religious DV advocates over the years since the 1970s. In the later parts of the historical narrative, the institute points to what it sees as its greatest achievement, namely the broadening of the framework to different religious communities and traditions:

> Possibly the most exciting development in the past fifteen years has been the expansion of our interfaith work at FaithTrust Institute. With our support, strong leadership has emerged in Jewish communities to address both domestic violence in Jewish families and sexual abuse by rabbis. In many Muslim communities, men and women leaders are breaking silence about domestic violence and leading their communities to address this reality. The US Conference of Catholic Bishops continues to encourage parishes to address domestic violence, even as they struggle to respond to the need to make parishes themselves safe places, and Roman Catholics in these parishes take the lead. Evangelical Christians from many groups are pressing forward to name sexual and domestic violence as realities within their churches and to confront the misuse of scripture to justify these evils. Additionally, the Jains have begun to examine the issue of domestic

violence as something from which they are not immune and Buddhist teachers are raising the issue of abuse by spiritual teachers and seeking ways to hold their colleagues accountable.[10]

It is notable that the institute not only provided training to a wide variety of religious communities and organizations but also, over the years, developed specific resources to address the needs of different communities.[11] In producing these materials, including films such as *Garments for One Another*, the institute recognized the need for resources that address DV from within specific ethical and scriptural frameworks that are in turn legible to those whom its advocates are attempting to reach. *Garments* is a good example of how the institute has worked with leaders, scholars, and advocates in communities to facilitate the production of a resource that, as we have seen in previous chapters, is a powerful tool for creating awareness in Muslim communities.

FaithTrust Institute materials including books have joined a body of written materials, especially books that are worth highlighting (and many of which I bought at the IFCADV conference and from the institute). It is significant to explore the titles of such works, which provide resources to victims of domestic abuse from within their religious traditions and contexts. They often represent creative (and perhaps reformist) reengagements with sacred texts while also serving to convince (lay) readers that domestic abuse exists in their communities and can/needs to be addressed from within religious frameworks. There is Anne Weatherholt's *Breaking the Silence: The Church Responds to Domestic Violence*, a book by an Episcopal priest and DV advocate addressed to all denominations of Christianity. As early as 1987, Marie Fortune published a book called *Keeping the Faith: Guidance for Christian Women Facing Abuse*. In *No Place for Abuse: Biblical & Practical Resources to Counteract Domestic Violence*, Catherine Clark Kroeger and Nancy Nason-Clark develop a framework similar to those we have encountered from Muslim advocates: God does not condone injustice and oppression; men and women have different responsibilities in marriage but are equal; and the church has a responsibility to intervene. The book offers sometimes radically different but not explicitly feminist readings of biblical passages.[12]

Rabbi Abraham Twerski's 1996 volume, *The Shame Borne in Silence: Spouse Abuse in the Jewish Community*, was hailed as shattering "the myth that Jews do not abuse their spouses."[13] The book shares stories of abuse from Twerski's rabbinical practice and offers biblical resources and rabbinic wisdom for survivors and their supporters. A volume devoted to offering religious inspiration is Toby Landesman's *You Are Not Alone: Solace and Inspiration for Domestic Violence Survivors, Based on Jewish Wisdom*. It, too, was published by the FaithTrust Institute. *Sins of Omission: The Jewish Community's Reaction to Domestic Violence* by Carol Goodman Kaufman and *Shine the Light: Sexual Abuse and Healing in the Jewish Community* by Rachel Lev continue the theme of silence and darkness surrounding abuse in religious communities and the need to acknowledge it openly first in order to then be able to address the issue within and beyond these communities.

Marie Fortune was also the editor, from its founding in 1999 until its closing in 2008, of the *Journal of Religion and Abuse*.[14] The journal, which produced almost thirty issues over the nine years of its existence, contained academic articles as well as book reviews on all aspects of abuse, including but not limited to domestic and sexual abuse. The journal offered a wide range of articles, which approached issues of religion and abuse from theological to ethical, practical, and social scientific and historical perspectives. The majority of articles dealt with aspects of Christian communities and abuse, which is perhaps less an issue of bias and more a reflection of the size and numbers of Christians and Christian communities in this country. Notably, it was this journal that published Sharifa Alkhateeb's study of DV in Muslim communities in 1999, which was, at the time, hailed as the first significant study of Muslim communities and DV in the United States.[15] The articles of volume 4, issue 4 in 2002 were also published as a separate book with the title *Forgiveness and Abuse: Jewish and Christian Reflections* by Haworth Press.[16] The book and journal volume are significant for their focus on forgiveness, a central question for Jews and Christians in religious work against DV.

In her first editorial for the new journal, Fortune declared that the time had come for a journal dedicated to the topic and that the academic community owed it to survivors and victims as well as religious communities to take the issue seriously and give it the focused attention it deserved.[17] Almost ten years later, Fortune admitted that there was not enough quality research material in the form of article submissions to sustain the journal. She surmised that such research certainly existed but was too scattered throughout different disciplines and methodologies to be brought together in one journal. She implored scholars to continue research, as the urgency of the issues at hand had not decreased over time.[18] I have wondered whether the lack of support, in the form of submitting articles and buying the journal, was in part a function of discomfort in associating religion with abuse rather than as a resource against it. The inability to sustain the journal may also have been a reflection of the broader trend to draw boundaries between academic disciplines, with the bulk of scholarship on domestic violence produced in social work, criminology, and clinical as well as social psychology. Each of these fields has struggled with religion as a social force and with the role of religiously normative scholarship in its publications.

The FaithTrust Institute, in all its inclusion and its efforts to provide resources and training to diverse religious communities, has been led and advised primarily, if not exclusively, by Christians. It is hard to believe that this leadership structure would have had no impact on its approaches on the one hand while being a reflection of a broader Christian-centric narrative on the other. Not unlike the experiences of Muslim feminists, who have often been treated in religious feminist circles as relative latecomers to the conversation,[19] Muslim DV advocates have been allowed to participate but on terms that were determined before they joined the religious DV movement. Perhaps more troubling is the fact that even religious advocates against DV, and social justice activists more broadly, are as much the products of the societies and communities they emerge from as everyone else. In what follows, I want to recount in some detail three moments at the IFCADV conference in 2011 that illustrate this point.

Muslims and Interfaith Efforts against DV

During the lunch and awards session at the IFCADV conference in 2011, the organization gave one of their three annual awards, the Community Partner Award, to the Peaceful Families Project. The other two were the Board Leadership Award, given that year to Sister Andrea Cumberland for her service to IFCADV, and the Clergy Leadership Award, which honored the Reverend William C. Maisch. In the award description, PFP is praised for their awareness work in Muslim communities throughout the country, their creation of an edited volume (*Change from Within*), their cooperation with the FaithTrust Institute on the documentary, and their national gathering of imams to sign a proclamation against domestic violence. It states: "PFP is proud to have collaborated with IFCADV since its founding. The IFCADV was blessed to have Sharifa Alkhateeb as one of its first Conference Theme Speakers in 2002." Here was the full inclusion of a Muslim organization in interreligious DV efforts and even more than that, the honoring with a community award of only one organization that year, and that organization was a Muslim one. The "clergy panel" that followed the awards ceremony, however, did not include a

Muslim speaker, perhaps because the rather narrow notion of clergy did not quite work for Muslim notions of leadership but that is a generous reading. Even more notable was the fact that the entire conference that year did not include a Muslim speaker, on the main panel or in any of the workshop sessions. That this lack of representation spilled over into content became clear in at least two moments in one of the workshops I attended.[20]

Both parts of the workshop focused on faith leaders as first responders in many DV situations and aimed to equip them with the resources to carry out a lethality assessment. The workshop was based on the Lethality Assessment Program developed in Maryland, which the workshop leaders had adapted to the context of religious communities. Both were also involved with the Family Justice Center discussed in chapter 6. Notably, religious leaders in the county worked as ecumenical religious/spiritual advisors in the Family Justice Center and offered support to clients regardless of their specific religious community affiliation.

The rabbi had just introduced himself and described some of his work at the center, which included pastoral care for Christians, Jews, and Muslims; and he had explained that he did not like the term "victim" because in his view this term reduced a human being to a specific, even if prolonged, experience of abuse or violence. He advocated using the much longer "people who have been victimized" in order to get away from a sole victim identity. Rather suddenly, a woman who identified as a pastor decided that she needed to make a contribution to the conversation and said: "I have lived in both Israel and Indonesia and I have to say that I am happy to hear that something is being done about domestic violence in Muslim communities. When I was there, everything about domestic violence, that it existed and that we should do something about it, had to be kept secret otherwise it could be very dangerous."

While I do not deny that there is a lack of awareness and perhaps even secrecy around DV in Muslim communities (see all the chapters of this book), in that moment her comment struck me as exceptionalizing Muslims and singling them out for something that not only was equally prevalent in other religious (and non-religious) communities but had already been described as one of the main obstacles to ending DV in society. More problematic to me was the choice by all participants in the workshop and the rabbi to just let her comment stand in the room in order to validate and honor her experience rather than questioning the differential representation of Muslims and Islam it created. It left a bad taste in my mouth and made me apprehensive about the rest of the session.

Toward the end of the workshop, the rabbi refocused our attention on the important notion of spiritual care, for clients but also for religious leaders themselves. He described all forms of domestic abuse as also hurting our spiritual core and that spiritual healing, that is, a focus on the soul, was an important step after achieving a degree of physical safety. He described situations in which he, as an interfaith chaplain at the Family Justice Center, was asked about what Jesus wanted the person in question to do and, pointing to his yarmulke, said, "I always wear this and still there is so much need for spiritual guidance and direction. I will say Jesus is about love and this is not love. We have to try and use the spiritual language of the person we are speaking to." He then recounted a specific story: "I have met a Muslim woman, who seeing the yarmulke immediately got on the defensive and said that in her understanding *jihad* is not terrorism but it is a fight for justice. So later in our conversation, I think I said it calmly, but when I think about it afterward, I think it stuck in my throat a little, but I said, you need to move into a *jihad* here to make yourself safe."

What does one make of this story in which the idea that the notion of *jihad* is not limited to some form of terrorism is claimed by a Muslim woman who is a victim of domestic abuse? Why indeed would a rabbi who is an interfaith chaplain not be familiar with at least some of the long and deep debate about the notion of *jihad* as a struggle for justice?[21] How did his admission that he had a hard time even saying the word *jihad* affect his ability to meaningfully engage Muslim victims? After all, he used this story as an example of how to engage someone within the framework of their own religious language. This, arguably, requires a deeper investment in learning about other religious traditions and their efforts against domestic violence, complete with parallel struggles over authority and interpretation on the one hand and a willingness to acknowledge a deeply political bias on the other. Again, in that moment, no one objected to his narrative and its use for this training session. As often happened in these settings, where I wanted to be an observer but became a somewhat unwilling participant, I struggled whether to intervene. In the end, I did not. But the story stayed with me as an illustration of the power dynamic in interfaith work and the many obstacles to working meaningfully for a social justice issue with and within a community that has been maligned as outsiders who do not belong and have been reduced to terrorists and their sympathizers at every turn in the American media and political narrative.[22]

In my encounters with such interreligious efforts against DV, it became clear that Muslims were most often included on the other communities' terms and that there was and continues to be suspicion of Muslim organizations and a reluctance to engage. When Muslim advocates reached out, in search of support and willing to both learn from a longer history and make their own contribution to it, they had to meet the other religious advocates on those terms and be willing to patiently and continuously explain as well as defend their religion. The same cannot be said for Christians and Jews. There was no presence of other religious communities and advocates at the events I observed to draw any conclusions for religious communities such as Hindus or Buddhists. With these challenges in religious DV work in mind, we turn to what is in some way the next level and the next challenge: Muslim advocates working in/with/for mainstream DV efforts, which I define as located in the sphere between nonprofit organizations without a religious affiliation/ identification to social workers and various nonprofit coalitions, such as the state coalitions against DV, that exist in every U.S. state.

Muslims in the Mainstream DV Movement

In earlier chapters, I provided glimpses of the complicated landscape that constitutes the anti–domestic violence movement in the United States. Is it even possible or adequate to call it a movement? If it is a movement, who are the leaders, the movers, and what is the direction of this movement? There certainly was a movement historically to recognize what was described by terms such as "wife battering," "domestic violence," "domestic abuse," "violence against women," "intimate partner violence," and others. This movement campaigned to raise awareness and provide reliable empirical and theoretical frameworks for understanding the prevalence as well as the causes of this phenomenon, so ubiquitous in this society as to seem universal. An important dimension of the work in the movement was to affect legal changes that would protect victims and hold abusers accountable by criminalizing at least physical abuse and changing the ways in which law enforcement responded to domestic disturbance and abuse calls. This is the abode and responsibility of the state.

The second important dimension of the DV movement consisted of disparate, localized, and state-sponsored efforts to provide services to victims. Some were grassroots initiatives or personal efforts, others emerged from religious organizations that provided other social services, and yet others were philanthropic, were privately funded, and resulted in the emergence of nonprofit organizations. Yet other services were provided to victims and survivors through existing social service networks: for the homeless, for the unemployed, and in the form of food assistance, access to basic medical services, and not least child protective services. Eventually, screening for domestic violence also became linked to medical providers as first responders and to others who would come into contact with potential victims. Books like the aforementioned *Responding to Domestic Violence*[23] exist because the landscape/movement is complex, it has a specific history, and its parameters, theoretical frames, and empirical methods are debated among scholars and practitioners. And while scholars provide valuable data that in turn play an important role in policy debates and decisions, and not least funding, practitioners need to balance their theorizing on causes and remedies with the daily demands on them to do their work.

There is of course a link between this brief description of the "mainstream" and my earlier discussion of interreligious efforts against domestic violence. As pointed out above, religious organizations in the United States, congregations as well as more specialized organizations, have played an important role in providing social services to those in need and it is only logical that some of those services would have been offered to those affected by domestic abuse, even if that was not the primary or explicit purpose of such services. It is at the nexus between civil (and secular) society organizations and religion both as a concept and a social force that the deep tension between religious and non-religious frameworks comes into view, especially when triangulated with the secular state. Buzawa and colleagues' *Responding to Domestic Violence* offers a useful overview of the ways in which Christianity (mostly), as well as religious organizations such as churches, have historically influenced notions of marriage and family and with that provided a patriarchal framing for hierarchical structures in families.[24]

In this section, I am interested in the various ways in which Muslim advocates and service providers participate in the mainstream and how they negotiate their relationship to non-religious approaches. There is more than one way in which such interaction and participation take place, and I focus here on two distinct ways in which I have observed Muslims as agents participate: as individual (Muslim) advocates and service providers in non-religious organizations, and in their efforts to educate mainstream providers and advocates through explicitly Muslim frameworks and organizations. I argue that Muslim advocates and providers in either role are deeply affected by anti-Muslim prejudice and racism in their work and that coding religion *as* culture

becomes almost a precondition for either form of participation in the mainstream. I demonstrate these dynamics through several fieldwork encounters
and stories from my interviews.

Layers of Hijab

One spring weekend I attended training for social workers and other service
providers that was organized by a state coalition against domestic violence
and specifically focused on Jewish and Muslim communities. It was offered
through the FaithTrust Institute and brought together a woman advocate from
a Muslim DV awareness organization, Nusaiba, and a rabbi from a similar,
Jewish, organization, Rabbi Noah. The learning objectives according to the
program included:

- Increase effectiveness of preventing and responding to domestic
  violence in Jewish & Muslim communities
- Increase understanding of the role of faith and how religious teachings
  can be resources or roadblocks
- Learn best practices for working with these populations as faith leaders
  & DV advocates

As it turned out, the twenty or so people in attendance were all service providers in mainstream organizations who had expressed an interest in learning
more about the role of religion in domestic abuse as well as in DV awareness
and service work.

Imagine my surprise when I overheard a rather frantic conversation during the
lunch break. By then, Nusaiba and Noah had walked the participants through a
PowerPoint presentation and discussion called "DV 101: Religious Resources
& Roadblocks," which they had developed in cooperation with the FaithTrust
Institute. It stated many things that we have come across multiple times: that
religion can be a resource as well as a roadblock in DV work; that spiritual
abuse is a specific form of domestic abuse; the power and control dynamic in
abusive relationships (which included the Muslim power and control wheel as
a handout); and the existence of a religious mandate to help and intervene. The
presentation included clips from *Garments* and from the film for Jewish communities called *To Save a Life: Ending Domestic Violence in Jewish Families*.[25]

The rather intense debate, between one of the coalition leaders and the director of a local organization that was a member of the coalition, was a heated

exchange about whether it would be a problem for the coalition to justify this workshop: What would happen if participants complained about being taught religious content? Would that compromise the status of the coalition as a secular, expressly non-religious organization? Could complaints perhaps even jeopardize the state funding the coalition was receiving? My surprise came more from the fact that they were having this conversation now, a third of the day into the workshop, rather than when it was first organized. And what exactly did they think a workshop on DV in Jewish and Muslim communities would look like? It turned out they had expected presentations on the particular iterations of DV in those communities and, like many of the participants expressed in discussions, thought they would learn that religious communities would have higher rates of DV and specific problems that related to religion *as* a problem in DV work. They were, however, unprepared for a discussion of religious resources for intervention, healing, and care.

These assumptions permeate the limited literature on DV in religious communities and are especially prevalent in works on DV in Muslim communities. One article that is frequently cited in later works is by Nooria Faizi, then a JD candidate, and published in 2001. In her "Domestic Violence in the Muslim Community," Faizi presents a nuanced picture of the specific challenges faced by women in immigrant communities and tries to account for the complicated relationship between religious interpretation, patriarchal culture, and social norms. Based on anecdotal evidence, she describes the silence in communities, the inadequate training and preparation of religious leaders, and the challenges Muslim women face in navigating mainstream services. Hers is not an exceptionalist assessment of DV in Muslim communities but rather a plea to Muslim communities and their leaders as well as an attempt to explain specific challenges from an insider's perspective. It does suffer from the assumption that American Muslims are immigrants, completely erasing the presence and significance of African American Muslim communities in the United States. Even more concerning, however, is how Maura Finigan, also a JD candidate, in her 2010 article, translated Faizi's (and others') assessment into the following:

> Muslim-American women—rarely discussed in domestic violence scholarship—face domestic abuse risk factors not shared by the general population. Not only may these women be more likely to be physically abused than most, they are also subject to a variety of cultural factors, including sensitivity to attacks on their faith, mixed messages about batter-

ing in Islam, and limited knowledge of the American legal system. These factors seriously impede their ability to report domestic abuse. Some of these issues are common to all heavily immigrant populations and are not exclusively "Muslim" problems. However, the especially patriarchal culture surrounding the Islamic faith exacerbates many of these problems.[26]

Aside from the mistaken assumption that all or most American Muslims are immigrants or live in immigrant communities, this quote and the article as a whole perpetuate the notion that "Islam" and Muslim identity make Muslim victims of DV especially vulnerable, and it singles their religion out as *only* a roadblock. There is both anti-religious bias and specifically anti-Muslim bias embedded in this analysis. Neither, I would argue, has proven productive in mainstream approaches to working with Muslim victims or Muslim advocates and providers. Rather, such assumptions and attitudes might explain how training on DV in religious communities would need to confront bias and invest extra effort into convincing mainstream providers of the significance of religion *as a resource*.

Later in the training, Nusaiba and Rabbi Noah brought up the history of the FaithTrust Institute and the fact that the DOJ had in fact provided funding to the institute to create faith-based resources in mainstream work. Nusaiba emphasized the need and acceptability of bringing religion and spirituality into secular spaces precisely because they offer tools to victims and providers for doing what ultimately matters the most: addressing DV and offering meaningful care. Rabbi Noah added that providers needed to reflect on their own biases, including religious and anti-religious ones, in order to offer effective care; otherwise their own biases against a specific religion, their own investment in a religion, or their bias against all religion could all become roadblocks to providing services to victims. Nusaiba then pointed out that there is a distinction between religion and culture and that it is possible to challenge cultural norms and assumptions with religion. We have seen this very strategically employed distinction between religion and culture before; in this version, culture is the problem and religion is a possible solution.

Nusaiba then introduced an exercise for the group in which each participant received a copy of a woman's story of abuse. The exercise focused on helping participants visualize how specific circumstances in a battered woman's life limit her options. In the original exercise, developed by the Duluth Project and Ellen Penz, each time one of the limitations is read aloud by a participant, he or she then gets up and drapes a bedsheet over the volunteer who represents the woman in the story. After seven bedsheets have been draped over her, the exercise leader then asks: "Why do you put up with this? Why don't you just leave?" The person under the sheets indicates that she cannot move, demonstrating how all the sheets together prevent her from moving/leaving. In the second part of the exercise, participants each read a statement that represents a resource or some form of encouragement for the victim to leave the abusive situation. They then remove the sheets one by one until the victim herself removes the last one, representing her agency in leaving.

Nusaiba had brought a story that adapted this general framework to include some more specific experiences of Muslim women while also retaining features that appeared in the original story: witnessing abuse of her mother as a child; child sexual abuse (and fear of offending family honor); Islamic teachings on marriage and obedience; quitting school to become a housewife (financial dependence); the threat of deportation (immigration situation); her mother's refusal to support her (resulting in her discouragement from reporting to either community or law enforcement); and threats from the husband when she tried to leave once (as well as the presence of a gun). As we were reading the statements, I became worried about the impression this list would leave on the other participants. Would they be able to recognize these as particular to Muslim women while not simultaneously blaming Islam? Would the obstacles reinforce notions they already carried? Nusaiba was less concerned, in part because of much more experience with these types of trainings and in part because she believed that honesty was necessary in all her work—with less regard for how Muslim communities would look or how people perceived her religion. Her ethic of non-abuse here translated into her primary commitment to educating Muslims and non-Muslims so that DV in Muslim communities could be ended for good.

The second part of the story offered a possible corrective to the negative notion of Islam I was worried about: among the seven resources for leaving her abusive husband were Qur'anic teachings about the spiritual equality of men and women and God's hatred of oppression; a relative who had attended a workshop in her Muslim community on DV; a book with stories of abused Muslim women and their struggles that made her feel less alone; and several more Qur'anic references to justice and God's closeness to every human being. Only two of the seven were general points: that abused women are in danger of being killed by their abuser, and the victim witnessing the abuse of her children by her husband. The reading ended with a statement about remembering people and resources, within and beyond Muslim communities, and encouragement to find safety and freedom from abuse for herself and her children.

I found the exercise very uncomfortable not only because it involved physically draping these layers over Nusaiba, who represented the Muslim victim, which then prevented her from breathing or moving properly. Nusaiba had decided to replace the bedsheets with headscarves, so as we were piling the obstacles onto her, we were adding layers of hijab to her own headscarf already in place. I thought that the symbolism of headscarves impeding a Muslim woman's movement was extremely unfortunate, but Nusaiba, in a conversation later, challenged me by saying that she brought the headscarves because they were much smaller and lighter, thus allowing her to breathe under them, and that she had found it difficult to carry the bedsheets to workshops such as this one in her luggage. Would the exercise have left a different impression if the headscarves had been bedsheets?

Rabbi Noah then challenged all the participants who, in the debriefing of the exercise, had, like me, expressed discomfort at engaging in a physical activity that impeded another person's movement. He asked why we agreed to do it if we were worried about suffocating Nusaiba? Both Nusaiba and Rabbi Noah then explained that this discomfort needed to be taken seriously as our compliance to participate in the draping represented the fact that we are all involved in creating and maintaining obstacles and that we often follow rules in agencies, organizations, communities, and families because we do not want to interfere or create discord.

Nusaiba then returned to the last push factor, fear for children's safety, and emphasized how important this commitment to children is for Muslim women in particular. She then explained that "Eastern Muslims" tend to come from collectively oriented cultures that required not only tapping into concern for children over the woman's own safety but also recognizing extended families as resources rather than always part of the problem. She encouraged providers to look for supportive members of the family who also have authority (fathers, brothers, etc.) and argued that the mainstream focus on individuals needed to be adjusted in order to work effectively with Muslim women. This would require different levels of cultural competency and the ability to work with each individual client within a flexible framework. She said that it was not enough to know some passages from the Qur'an. In this part of her remarks, culture appeared very differently and not in opposition to religion. Instead, it was represented as a static system that mainstream providers needed to learn about in order to better understand and then work with Muslim clients. More room for interpretation was afforded with regard to religion—a theme that was followed up on later in the workshop by repeating that religion and culture cannot always be separated neatly but that anti-abuse interpretations of religious texts can constitute an important resource. She yielded her own religious authority to religious scholars and leaders by encouraging the participants to reach out to Muslim leaders in their vicinity, to build relationships with mosques and community centers, and to take advantage of some of the authoritative textual materials provided by FaithTrust and other publications.

There was a rather stark contrast during the workshop between Nusaiba's and Rabbi Noah's references to religious authority, both to define normative religious frameworks and to offer them as resources for mainstream providers. Nusaiba, an advocate and provider herself, most often spoke from her experiences, through stories and empirical evidence, and she pointed participants to others as religious authority figures. Rabbi Noah was both a religious authority figure and a provider, so he more easily and authoritatively spoke from biblical passages and rabbinic knowledge. His contributions to the workshop provided a basic introduction to Judaism, complete with history and an overview of relevant texts. Nusaiba on the other hand focused on DV in American Muslim communities, creating a very different framework while worrying the secular coalition organizers all the same.

The workshop ended the next day with a rather heated discussion about how to work with abusers. In this last segment, some of the participants had started opening up about their own work with Muslim clients and asked more specific questions as the workshop went on. Their questions were often puzzled, sounded prejudiced, and supported my impression that this type of workshop is absolutely necessary for providing Muslim women victims with better experiences in mainstream organizations. Basic knowledge of dietary restrictions and multiple meanings of modesty as well as more complex ideas about families, individuality, children, guilt and forgiveness, and not least religion as a source of support for victims would all help in making such services more accessible and welcoming to Muslim women. Nusaiba and the rabbi, for both their communities and faith traditions, patiently answered all the questions and attempted to provide as much nuance as possible.

Nusaiba had at some point specifically argued that "the coalition world," her term for the mainstream DV movement, needed to step away from solely pushing women to leave. There was surprise at her statement but also outrage. She explained that it was obvious from all of their work that women often cannot leave, that they will statistically leave seven or eight times and go back before they get away (if they do at all), and that services needed to include support for women in abusive relationships.[27] She added that this could include couple therapy. At this point, several participants became very upset and refused to even consider the possibility of couple or family therapy that included abusers. Nusaiba, with support from Rabbi Noah, argued that it was a complicated but not impossible option, especially when women do not access services on their own and thus fall completely through the cracks of service networks. If abuse came up in therapy, one way of reaching victims would be to encourage further couple therapy while working to ensure safety. One participant maintained that she would refuse couple therapy with an abuser because he would be able to manipulate both the victim and the therapist. She thought that there was an important difference in working with batterer groups as a therapist. Nusaiba agreed that batterer intervention was useful, even though there were even fewer resources than for victims to support such programs, but argued that studies existed to confirm that a family systems approach could, in some communities and situations, be more productive than the mainstream focus on the victim as an individual.

One of the organizers pointed out that the state coalition bylaws did not allow for family system approaches but that batterer-only programs could be supported. She mentioned that she had heard about clergy in the state that offered couple counseling and worried both about safety issues (for the victim) and whether such clergy actually had the necessary training for such counseling. Rabbi Noah responded that rabbis were being trained to recognize that they needed to refer those in need if they themselves lacked qualifications and that couple counseling was highly discouraged. He also said that as providers they needed to keep asking these difficult questions and continuously assess frameworks and policies in order to be effective in their work.

The final point of contention was the argument, made by both workshop leaders, that abusers can, under certain circumstances, be reformed and stop being abusers. While participants agreed that it was a learned behavior (there was no talk here of structural violence, patriarchy, and privilege), it was still foundational to the abuser and thus could not be changed through movement intervention. Nusaiba and Rabbi Noah instead argued that their theological perspective left reform and self-reform as possibilities because God has the power to change everything, including abusive behaviors in a person. People can never be beyond redemption in either Judaism or Islam. They saw a need to recognize perpetrators as people and not as irredeemably and essentially bad. But the potential for redemption could only be actualized if communities took responsibility for holding abusers accountable and prevented further abuse of their victims. Religious notions of redemption and transformation hinged, according to both, on convincing the abuser that God was not condoning their behaviors and that they should expect punishment for wrongdoing in the eyes of God. It was in this conversation that I noted the most profound disconnect between the mainstream providers and the two representatives of the religious DV movement.

The workshop demonstrated both shared spaces and overlapping experiences, on the one hand, and deep disconnects and prejudices (against religious approaches), on the other. Religion and cultures appeared in yet another iteration but only in discussions of Islam, not in the remarks about Judaism. Clearly then, Judaism, while perhaps unfamiliar in its details and practices, does not elicit the same coding as a foreign and unknowable religion in mainstream DV work. American Jews were never represented as immigrants or not belonging here while Muslims were defined through immigrant communities and experiences and foreign cultures.

Islam, DV, and Mainstream Social Work

What could possibly go wrong when a Muslim advocate presents at a conference on social work and is invited to speak on a panel titled "Culturally Competent Responses to Gender-Based Violence," which is part of a larger thread of the conference "International Social Work and Human Rights"? I attended such as panel and want to share here some of my observations about the dynamics. The panel was on a dreary spring afternoon, at a conference with many concurrent panels, and attended by both scholars and practitioners of social work. Consequently, presentations contained both research elements and training components, for the latter of which social workers could earn continuing education credits.

Rabia, the Muslim advocate from an awareness organization, was paired with two other women speakers, both, like her, women of color.[28] One, Janice, was an African woman and expert on human trafficking and the other, Maria, was a Latina activist who had worked in various organizations against gender-based violence. Maria's presentation focused on the need for culturally sensitive services for Latina women and argued that there were specific needs in Latino communities including language services, recognition of culture-specific forms of violence like physical harm from machetes rather than guns, forced abortions, and marital rape, and addressing threats of human trafficking and immigration status abuse. Maria referenced Catholicism as both a roadblock and a resource but focused her remarks on a generalized Latina culture. To be fair, part of the challenge for her and the other presenters was the fact that they each had about twenty minutes to make complex points and arguments and get across basic and necessary information. The time pressure created an added need to further generalize, but Maria's presentation set the stage for Rabia's in that she presented Latino culture as different from and foreign to the United States and used it as an explanatory framework for specific abusive behaviors, rather than as a roadblock/resource construction that is negotiated by victims, abusers, and communities.

Rabia warned the audience of her own generalizations in her presentation and downplayed her authority and expertise before proceeding to distinguish between the ethnic and cultural diversity of Muslims in many different (foreign) and unifying Islamic beliefs in one God, the Prophet Muhammad, and the Day of Judgment. She explained that she would focus on Muslims as a faith community rather than the different cultural iterations in the Muslim community. She offered the now familiar presentation of Islam as a resource versus a roadblock and offered it as an argument for engaging religion because "going through the justice system, as we all know, does not mean getting justice. In these situations, a religious notion of justice can provide at least comfort to the victim." She then advocated for a distinction between lived culture and religious teachings and suggested that social workers needed to work at the intersection of the two to realize that there was no one kind of Muslim.

She then aimed to dispel misconceptions of Islam and made the following unequivocal claims: There is nothing in Islam that allows violence. Gender equality is inherent to Islam as a part of justice. Men and women, husbands and wives are mutual protectors of each other. The objective of marriage is tranquility. Cultural values among Muslims were somewhat more variable than these absolute principles but included patriarchy (which she did not mean in a critical feminist sense as a problem), collectivism, family honor, complementary gender roles, and the supreme value placed on intact families. These, she realized, were the opposite of the push toward individuation found in mainstream therapy.

Janice presented from her experiences in several organizations working against human trafficking. She emphasized the high level of physical and psychological abuse victims of trafficking experience and discussed challenges to intervention in countries other than the United States, especially in relation to cultural expectations and norms, as well as attitudes toward social work and therapy intervention. She echoed a point both Rabia and Maria had made earlier about cultural prejudice against counseling and therapy in response to abuse and trauma. Rabia specifically was asked about arranged marriages. The questions for all three presenters reinforced the general impression their panel had created: issues of gender-based violence could and should be linked to foreign cultures and countries and thus did not represent systemic "American" issues but could be addressed by American solutions. I was troubled by the emphasis on the foreignness of Latinos and Muslims as not belonging here and having uniquely different cultures that needed to be explained, which coded them as essentially other. Many in the audience were white social workers, most of them white women, and there was a palpable sense of skepticism about the presenters' authority and whether they could offer insight beyond representing "their culture." The question of authority, however, was brought home for me when a man from the audience approached Rabia after the panel ended. He greeted her with "Assalamu Alaykum" and proceeded to share his opinion on Islam and domestic violence with her, complete with verses from the Qur'an, references to the Sunna, and the names of several medieval Muslim scholars to consult. Rabia was, as always, very polite and thanked him for his input, while I stood in disbelief at the familiar challenge to the religious authority of Muslim women advocates even in this mainstream setting.

Muslims in the Mainstream

It is safe to assume that there are more Muslims working in the mainstream DV movement than in Muslim-identified organizations. They are lawyers, social workers, shelter volunteers, advocates, therapists, and even police officers; like their non-Muslim counterparts in the movement, more than a few are survivors of abuse. Whether they have made domestic violence their cause because they have experienced trauma and abuse or whether they act on an ethic of non-abuse that is a commitment to reducing violence and trauma in society born from different sources, they participate in the structures, complications, and challenges not only of the movement but of society at large. The DV movement in its entanglement in society and the state is a reflection of the broader debates and issues I have brought up repeatedly in this chapter. They have to grapple with structural racism and sexism and with the ambivalent relationship between secular society and the state.

In interviewing Muslims who worked in the mainstream DV movement in some capacity it was I who fixed their identity category as Muslim when, of course, they could very well also have identified in other ways. I was interested to find out whether their Muslimness was in any way significant for their involvement in the DV movement. By asking them to identify as Muslim, I foregrounded that facet of their identity even if they might not have done so themselves. Some of these interview partners I met organically through the networks I was exploring, especially those who worked both in the mainstream movement and in Muslim organizations (often as a volunteer in one and professionally in the other) or those who had work experience in both. It was here that the overlap and link between some Muslim DV organizations and those that cater to specific ethnic groups (typically identified as of immigrant background) became most apparent.

These facets of the DV movement, namely those serving specific marginalized communities, emerge from a history of that marginalization. Like their Muslim, Jewish, and Christian counterparts, they were created in response to what was recognized as specific needs, usually from within the communities themselves, through grassroots efforts. There were large ones like the Asian Pacific Institute on Gender-Based Violence (APIGBV, or API), already discussed in chapter 6, which was a resource center for all Asian and Pacific Islander Americans. APIGBV played a significant role in providing resources for those among Asian Americans who are also Muslims, including a directory of agencies that provide "culturally specific" programs and services.[29] The listings included indicators for whether a specific organization catered to Muslims (as well as people in other categories such as refugee, immigrant, etc.), and the institute had clearly wrestled with the tension that is produced by a culture-centered approach to gender-based violence:

> Culture defines the spaces within which power is expressed, where gender relations are negotiated and gender roles re-defined. Cultural contexts are critical to the analysis of gender-based violence and are always applicable, since everyone has culture, not just people of color or from specific identity groups (such as LGBTQI). Asian, Native Hawaiian and Pacific Islander advocates maintain a delicate balance: engaging communities in internal critiques of their own culture, without rejecting or blaming it.
>
> Cultural explanations of gender violence are a contested terrain because they are either used to excuse individual actions or to engage in racial stereotyping. When outsiders (e.g., police), or insiders (e.g., community

members or family) link violence with culture, they obscure institutional responsibility and community accountability. Culture is often responsible for *how* the problem of violence against women is viewed and addressed: e.g., believing that women from a particular culture are passive and don't seek help; or that speaking out about abuse—not perpetrating it—shames the family.[30]

Many more locally focused organizations including service providers catered to specific communities, like the South Asian organizations discussed by Margaret Abraham in *Speaking the Unspeakable,* also discussed in chapter 6. Others, for Arab Americans for example, have experienced similar tensions between culture talk and marking immigrant communities as essentially different and foreign. At the same time, the services that they provided demonstrated the continued need for specialized attention to the linguistic exclusion of immigrant victims and the difficulties in navigating (let alone trusting) the U.S. court system and state social services. Louise Cainkar has carried out valuable research on Arab American communities and organizations that also attended to the significant overlap as well as tension between identifying victims, families, and communities as Arab, Muslim, immigrant, and so forth.[31] Perhaps, then, the conference panel I discussed above was more representative of an important dimension of mainstream DV work than my discussion of it would allow. Here again, important questions are raised about the politics of critique and when critique is a productive tool for holding one another accountable rather than leading to the deconstruction and then impossibility of grassroots political activism and service. I return here to the important notion of "responsible critique" as introduced in chapter 1 through Rochelle Terman and the equally significant and earlier notion of "multiple critique" I was introduced to in the writings of miriam cooke.[32] The advocates and service providers in the mainstream I interviewed brought much-needed nuance and a wide range of perspectives to my project: in what follows I reflect on some of the interviews in more depth.

Samina

Samina was in her mid-thirties when I interviewed her and was working for a mainstream DV organization as a caseworker. She had legal training and many years of experience as a professional in various DV organizations including Muslim ones. She had many important reflections on the complicated politics of the Muslim DV movement and admitted at one point that she had left the

Muslim organization she had worked for and moved to a mainstream one to avoid certain issues, including the continuous quest to perform a particular kind of religious authenticity (related to her not wearing hijab) and accepting that she had no authority to engage in textual interpretation. She also struggled with her own commitments to both human rights and feminist critiques of patriarchy, finding that both were making it difficult for her to interact with Muslim coworkers as well as clients. She narrated this struggle as a continuous internal debate about how she could and should relate to Islam.

When we discussed her work as a Muslim in her current organization, I assumed that religion would play less of a role than in a Muslim organization. Samina corrected me and said:

> Having said that, I think there is also huge interest. Even where I work here, people know about my background and it's always brought up. We have come to this point, and I am thankful to people like Azizah al-Hibri and others. They had the tough time where in their mainstream jobs they couldn't talk about their approaches from a faith-based perspective. Because of the work they and other minority women have done, now it is much more safe to be the Muslim woman and speak from that position. So I think it's changing and in some cases it has become an additional qualification, you know?

She also pointed me to others, some of whom, as she pointed out, would not see themselves as even involved in DV work, like several nurses and physicians and a number of family lawyers she knew. They came across DV in their work all the time but did not exclusively focus on it or participate actively in advocacy work defined round DV. Her comment points to the blurry boundaries of what I have called the DV movement and more specifically the Muslim DV movement. If people do not see themselves as part of it, how can we define it?

Samina discussed what she described as different ways of dealing with religion she had observed in her surroundings and among Muslim colleagues. She admitted that she had ignored the rising tension between her human rights and women's rights commitments and what she saw as Islamic norms without seeing a range of different interpretations. She focused on the positive aspects of God's love but would stay away from confronting misogynist Hadith.

> The truth is the literature and the scholarship is full of really hateful things against women. What are you going to do when you get outside of your comfort zone? Either you are going to retreat from your faith or you just

carry on being blind. But if you want to take a leadership position in your community on these issues, you need to surround yourself with it; talk about all of it openly. I did this in a leadership program, and so I felt safe with these Muslim women who are all feminists, and I could confront it all with them and not lose my faith.

But there were limits to what could be questioned; Samina would only confront Hadith and Islamic legal literature but drew the line at the Qur'an. She acknowledged that Muslim survivors might need a different approach and that the action of the woman in South Africa, as told by Sa'diyya Shaikh in her "*Tafsir* of Praxis," who cut out the verse on wife beating from the Qur'an she gave to an agnostic friend, was not available to her.[33] Rather, she could buy into a Qur'anic ethical framework that could then be used to question certain Hadith and other examples of Islamic legal literature. This framework would center on justice and nonviolence in dealing with other people. "It is about confronting all the things that I am afraid of, all the things that might make me lose my faith. This makes sense to me as a woman, but where does that leave me as a Muslim?"

Ruqayya

Ruqayya was in her late twenties, from an Arab and South Asian background, and working as a psychologist in a research context. She had interned in several mainstream DV shelters over the course of her training and was interested in intimate partner violence in different marginalized communities. She recounted stories of Muslim clients she had encountered in her shelter work and recognized the importance of training mainstream service providers about the specific needs of Muslim victims of DV. She also recalled that her Muslim clients, who were assigned to her randomly rather than by design, were usually grateful to be working with a Muslim caseworker or counselor. It was less a matter of providing them with religious frameworks as resources (which she said would not have been accepted by the organizations she worked for) and more about insider knowledge that she as a fellow Muslim was assumed to have about Muslim family and community dynamics.

Ruqayya described herself as a progressive feminist *and* a Muslim and insisted that these were not mutually exclusive even if some members of Muslim communities would not accept that. She had grown up in what she said was an open-minded Muslim family, which did not mean that there was no power hierarchy but she credited the possibility of questioning pretty much everything in her childhood with creating the opportunities she had to explore marital relationships, power dynamics, and social psychology as a tool to research them.

Religion was not central to what she would offer Muslim clients as resources, but it played an important role in her research interests and even more so in her personal motivation for doing research on marriage and violence. She also recognized how she negotiated questions of power distribution, religion, and equality in her own marriage. She felt that it was necessary to distinguish religion from culture and described her "cultural" experiences in different communities as full of gender inequality and oppressive expectations for women. But then she also argued that there was no such thing as religion without culture and that it was impossible to distinguish them from each other. Her example was the Qur'an:

> So, the Qur'an is the word of God. But the moment a human hears or reads the word it is no longer the word of God—it becomes human and we change it, so then it becomes prone to human error. I realized that interpretation of the Qur'an is always a product of culture. There is no religion that is not marked by humans. Once we touch a thing, it becomes non-Divine.

She also developed an argument that adds a fascinating dimension to the many places where I encountered Q 4:34 in my project. I had asked whether there was a passage in the Qur'an that was important to her:

> The classic one that jumps out is 4:34. Is that beating or is it not beating? Is it beating lightly with a feather and what does that mean? Does the one have more over the other, and what does that mean for the relationship between the two genders, you know? Have you heard of the Rorschach inkblot test where you fold a piece of paper and you have to say what you see? To me that is what 4:34 is; here is a really ambiguous phrase, what do you make of it? It says more about the individual and the society than about the verse itself or about God.... I tried to avoid making my own decision about what it means but now I think it does not mean beating. If you take the Qur'an in context there are so many themes of peace and equality there, it cannot mean to beat.[34]

In essence, Ruqayya made one's interpretation of Q 4:34 a litmus test for that person's broader ethical commitment to justice and equality as ethical values derived from God's revelation. This appeal to justice, equality, and non-abuse echoes the reflections of others I spoke to in the course of this project. It is also reflected in some academic writing on the topic, as in the article by Nooria Faizi already mentioned. Faizi quotes Q 30:21, the verse on marital tranquility, love, and mercy, as the introduction to her article in a legal journal and goes on to describe an ideal Islamic marriage model in which stability allows for spiritual growth of all family members. She argues, "Violence shatters the very security Islam is supposed to maintain in the home."[35] After offering policy recommendations for mainstream providers and Muslim communities and leaders, Faizi concludes:

> Islam is a faith that calls for justice and forbids evil and oppression. A good Muslim wants a Muslim brother or sister to have what she would want for herself. Violence towards fellow humans is condemned, while mercy and goodwill are prescribed.... If the cries remain unheard, it can only lead to the breakdown of the Muslim family unit and the Muslim community, and with that comes the breakdown of the true Muslim identity.[36]

Muslim DV Work and the State

"The State" as a counterpart, player, and certainly also as hovering above Muslim and non-Muslim efforts against domestic violence has appeared frequently in these pages. Its omnipresence makes it perhaps especially difficult to analyze in a book with this specific focus. In what follows, I have selected two arenas in which the state looms large: Islamophobia as racism and surveillance of Muslims, and the ever-present role of state funding (or the lack thereof) for Muslim DV efforts. I discuss them based on various aspects of my research, realizing that much more could be said to account for the entanglement of this third sphere with the other two discussed in this chapter.

Islamophobia Is Racism Is State Surveillance: Feminism and Colonialism

There is a robust literature on the production of anti-Muslim sentiment, hate crimes, and the nature of Islamophobia as racism.[37] I have contributed to literature on anti-Muslim hostility myself, with an interest in its gendered dimensions and the ways in which Muslim women are on the "center stage" as purported victims of Islam and Muslim men, while also being targeted as an embodied threat to the United States.[38] And, as explained in chapter 2, I have come to favor the term "anti-Muslim hostility" over "Islamophobia."

There is a long history of marking Muslims, especially Muslim men, as violent, threatening, and in opposition to the state: Edward Curtis and Sylvester Johnson have chronicled the role of the FBI in both surveilling and infiltrating Black Muslim organizations in the first half of the twentieth century.[39] Curtis writes:

> Though Islamophobia has deep roots in American culture and US society, its vitality in those domains is a result, at least in part, of the state repression of political dissent organized around Islamic symbols and themes. Long before 9/11, the US government was concerned about the possibility that Muslims on American soil would challenge the political status quo. Beginning in the 1930s, this fear resulted in formal government surveillance and prosecution of African American Muslim civil and religious organizations and their members.[40]

After a careful analysis of this history, Curtis concludes that the "Black Muslim Scare" of the early twentieth century was resurrected through redirected government attention to (and fear of) Brown Muslims: "Focusing on the doctrinal differences between black and brown, pre- and post-9/11 Muslims, however, covers up a critical link between our age and that of the Black Muslim Scare.... Expressions of Islam that make radical critiques of the United States will be suppressed, even if they do not pose a direct security threat to the nation-state."[41]

It is not difficult to see a connection between the construction of a dangerous group of Muslims, mostly men, who might pose a threat of some kind, not only to the state but also to American society at large. It is also not difficult to see how easily such a construction would connect to representations of Muslim men as inherently violent, including toward women and children in their own families and communities. This suspicion toward all Muslim men as potential abusers has been discussed in its relation to media representations in chapter 2. Here I will only add that societal perceptions of Muslims, which are not accidental or originating in the no-man's-land of "the media," are intentionally produced by what has been termed the Islamophobia industry, which in turn is connected to both various levels of government and media outlets. There is intentionality in this production of the violent Muslim, which is then used to justify not only government surveillance and disciplining of Muslims but also policies that support Muslim women, as victims of domestic abuse, only on the condition that they distance themselves from their religion and their religious communities.

This embeddedness of (mostly male) Muslim bodies in state perceptions and policies, historically as much as today, is compounded when we consider the important role that feminist theory and the feminist activist movement have played in the creation of the DV movement. It is now widely acknowledged that early European feminists actively participated in colonization projects including the colonial theft of Muslim lands and the domination of Muslim-majority societies.[42] More broadly, questions of gender roles and the status of women in Muslim societies were constructed as a litmus test for the potential of Muslims to be truly modern by European standards. The supposed backwardness of Muslim societies in their treatment of women was utilized as one important justification for why Muslims needed to be colonized and "civilized." A similar rhetoric has been employed, much more recently, in the many military campaigns the United States has engaged in over the past several decades.[43]

It must be rather difficult to disentangle negative attitudes toward Islam as *especially* misogynist from state and civil society efforts against DV. These attitudes toward Islam transcend the more general suspicion, in much of mainstream secular feminism, of religion as inherently patriarchal and are thus a more formidable obstacle to working with Muslim advocates and communities. This has many consequences: from suspicion and fear toward law enforcement[44] even in a domestic crisis situation to biased treatment in court and victim blaming. Muslims, as advocates, providers, and victims, are never disconnected from negative perceptions of their religion and communities, and are even affected by them if they themselves do not foreground being Muslim as their defining identity. The willingness of different government agencies to fund DV efforts in Muslim communities, through Muslim and non-Muslim organizations in turn, is deeply entangled in this web of perceptions, ideas, and policies.

To Fund or Not to Fund

We have already seen in the brief discussion about the state coalition workshop that there is deep tension about how to account for religion in mainstream DV work. The funding structures of the DV movement are complex, and each organization perpetually depends on either private funding or support generated through grants on all levels of the state and various foundations to survive. Some Muslim DV organizations I researched did not want to get entangled in the time- and energy-consuming process of applying for grants and jumping through the myriad hoops of paperwork, accounting, and reporting. They often relied on community funding, including Muslim charity (*zakat*), fund-raising events, and Muslim organizations that would support them. Ultimately, the survival of any organization depended primarily on its ability to generate economic support. Even those who relied on volunteer work for offering services needed some funding for overhead, and, of course, direct financial support for victims was impossible without cash flow.[45]

Once an organization decided to apply for state-level grants, a number of conditions came into focus, chief among them that services needed to be made available to all victims in need. Thus public grants made it more difficult if not impossible to provide services exclusively to Muslim victims. In at least one Muslim DV organization, I was told that they had repeatedly applied for public funding and had received it without any issues raised about their project of raising awareness of DV specifically in Muslim communities and training (Muslim) religious leaders. I wagered that the response would have been different if the funds had been intended for direct services.

In another story, where the funding came from the Department of Justice (DOJ), the situation was more complicated. There was clearly support in the DOJ on various levels for funding the development of a curriculum to both raise awareness in Muslim communities and provide training for mainstream service providers, law enforcement, and lawyers. The organization receiving the grant utilized the funds to create a comprehensive curriculum and then wanted to demonstrate its effectiveness in a training workshop. The DOJ provided support for the workshop and even sent an observer to the training. It was here that the limits of state support for religiously framed efforts against domestic violence became clear. There was no problem with discussing DV in Muslim communities and offering what had to be called "cultural" rather than religious sensitivity training. However, the curriculum also included a component that introduced (as we have seen multiple times before) religious resources, including passages from the Qur'an and selected Hadith, to the participants. At that point, the DOJ observer requested that the workshop leaders clearly demarcate this component of the curriculum as *not* funded by the DOJ.

Complicated funding structures, decreases in available government funding for DV work, and the ongoing backlash against anti-DV policies in their framing as anti-patriarchal have all affected the mainstream DV movement in profound ways. Muslim advocates and providers struggled together with and, more so than others, in a climate of economic disengagement of the state from all levels of social projects and support for the most vulnerable in society. It was both naïve and dangerous to assume that civil society, here in the form of private funding and philanthropy, can or should step in where the state refused its responsibility.

The work of Muslims in the DV movement cannot be understood only within their own communities but rather needs to be considered as part of broader structures, processes, and systems. They were keenly aware of the ways in which Muslims and Islam are perceived by the public and the state, and they continuously had to negotiate how they wanted to engage with them. Beyond being deeply affected by the relationship of the American state with religion and religious communities, on the one hand, and feminist critiques of patriarchal systems and hierarchies, on the other, Muslim advocates and providers actively and intentionally participated in shaping the DV movement and the many ways in which U.S. society addressed this important societal ill.

8

Looking Back and the Road Ahead

GENDER-BASED VIOLENCE, ACTIVISM, AND CRITIQUE

FOR YEARS BEFORE I started this project, I had listened to a song by Tracy Chapman, "Behind the Wall" (1988), and I often thought about its lyrics while researching and writing this book. It vividly describes so much of what I found during my explorations of the Muslim landscape of efforts against domestic violence: hearing the screams of the victims, recognizing that the police might not interfere, especially in marginalized communities, and fearing the worst outcome, death, in a domestic violence situation.

The song is also a constant reminder of the fact that domestic violence is a widespread and urgent issue in all of American society and that Muslim efforts against domestic violence are embedded in larger issues of patriarchy, misogyny, racism, and state control. In this concluding chapter, I want to look back at the central arguments I have developed throughout the book, as is customary in conclusions. In the second part of the chapter, I share a set of notes that look ahead and beyond the boundaries of American Muslim efforts against domestic violence. These notes emerged from the research itself, in particular a meeting of Muslim DV activists and their supporters during the last year of my fieldwork. The event, at the time, proved a powerful culminating moment for my research and supported my main findings, but it also created openings for further questions and research avenues. From it, I derived a set of reflections on the relationship between scholarship and activism, revisiting my thoughts in chapter 1 on power dynamics in researching activism, and, lastly, a broader set of ideas about oppression, violence, and the role of religion in social change.

Looking Back

American Muslim efforts against domestic violence have a long history, partly institutionalized and partly informal, that intersects with the broader history of such efforts in the United States. It is precisely the embeddedness of specifically Muslim efforts against DV, historically and in the present, in the wider structures of institutional, political, legal, and social struggles against DV, that makes this project an important contribution to our understanding of religious communities in the United States, to the relationship between religion and politics, and to the role of feminism both as an idea and as a movement in societal transformation. American Muslim efforts against domestic violence demonstrate powerfully that Muslim communities in the United States are indeed American, both in their affirmation of American values and in their resistance against oppressive and exclusionary laws and practices. In other words, critiques of anti-Muslim hostility, racism, and marginalization through cultural and religious domination are as much an expression of American-ness as the necessary engagement with American structures, institutions, and levels of government. Thus one conclusion from this project is that Muslim advocates against domestic violence are no more than a specific example for American advocacy against DV.

However, they are also set apart by their reference to their Muslim identity (and construction of Islam) as a powerful resource for this struggle to end DV in Muslim communities and American society. They reject the use of "Islam" as a roadblock to fighting DV and insist that their religion offers them powerful arguments against any form of domestic abuse. I have argued that Islam as a resource against DV requires a specific construction of what this "Islam" is, and the process of constructing an Islam against domestic violence does not begin with scriptural sources but rather originates in an ethic of non-abuse, a deep-seated sense, born from witnessing and/or experiencing domestic abuse, that Muslim individuals respond to by engaging in advocacy and service work in the DV field. This ethic of non-abuse is then conceptually linked to Islam and supported by marshaling Qur'anic as well as prophetic proof texts for the prohibition of domestic violence as the will of God as represented authoritatively in the practice of the Prophet Muhammad. I emphasize that the ethic of non-abuse is practiced before it is discursively formulated, thereby questioning the common privileging of discourse/ideas/mind over practice/actions/body. Once the ethic of non-abuse has been discursively supported, a process that is debated, is challenged, and has proponents arrive at different conclu-

sions and marshaling different texts and interpretations, discourse and practice in the form of activism and justification for such activism enter an interdependent relationship in which they mutually reinforce each other.

That "Islam" is categorically opposed to domestic violence requires exegetical struggles with a particular passage in the Qur'an, 4:34, as well as the
development of ideal Islamic marriage models that emphasize tranquility,
love, and mercy as the foundations of marriage and family. Such marriage
models tend to accept gender hierarchies as God-given or at least as not a
problem that may cause domestic violence in the form of abuse of the hierarchy for domination and control. It is here that the issue of gender justice, in
pro-feminist Muslim terms, appears as a conceptual and practical challenge
in Muslim anti-DV. Rather than considering any kind of gender or marital
hierarchy as potentially abusive and harmful, proponents of the ideal Islamic
marriage model most often embraced rely on what I have called protective or
benevolent patriarchy, a model in which it is precisely the leadership status of
the husband/father in the family that obligates him to protect and maintain
his female spouse(s) and children. Any abuse of this leadership position is a
breach of the ethic of non-abuse based on protective patriarchy. Protective patriarchy becomes a powerful tool for reaching those Muslims who reject gender justice and gender equality as Islamic norms and/or are invested in other
types of patriarchal privilege even though they do not support domestic abuse
in any form.

Muslim feminist engagements with "Islam" as grounded in an egalitarian
notion of gender justice as social justice, which they also claim to be the will
of God, have relied on Qur'anic exegesis, engagement with the prophetic example, and reform efforts in Islamic law while recognizing domestic violence
as one symptom of patriarchy. Patriarchy in turn is rejected as essentially hierarchical and unjust. In and beyond Muslim efforts against domestic violence,
the struggle over how to end it revolves around questions of religious authority and influence on Muslim communities, in and beyond mosques and
community centers. Recognition, or the lack thereof, as a religious authority
figure is both gendered, with male authority being naturalized, and depends
on whether particular interpretations and exegetical claims align with existing
"mainstream" consensus.

Muslim feminists share their critique of patriarchy with other, including
secular, feminists, who in turn have profoundly influenced mainstream anti-
DV efforts in the United States. In a climate of increasing anti-Muslim hostility
as well as the marginalization of religious efforts against domestic abuse, it is

common to find Muslim efforts dismissed and marginalized in the DV mainstream, while Muslim advocates who identify as feminists or with feminist critiques of patriarchy as the cause for DV find themselves alienated and silenced in Muslim community contexts.

The specific debate about domestic violence in Muslim communities and the efforts to raise awareness, provide services, and ultimately end it are reflections of broader trends of several kinds:

- They are a microcosm of changing practices *and* discourses connected to gender and sexuality in Muslim communities (and Muslim societies globally).
- They provide blueprints for contemporary Muslim engagements with Islam as an ongoing process of construction—through the Qur'an as scripture, the Sunna as a normative source of guidance, and communal debate and consensus—with the goal of creating a relatively stable Islamic tradition.
- They bring to the fore issues of authority, community formation, exegesis, and practice with tangible consequences in the lives of Muslims.

In the end, this book is part of such trends and aims explicitly to tell the multiple stories of Muslim efforts against DV, to explore the people who engage in these efforts in their motivations and practices, and to simultaneously raise awareness of DV in and beyond Muslim communities. This book required me to focus on certain aspects, certain people, and certain stories, so that I could complete it, even though there were always more interviews and event notes, more research ideas, and more organizations and initiatives. It also gives me hope that I see Muslim efforts against DV continue all around me and that this project is only a glimpse of what has been happening. In what follows, I tell of one last event and the many openings it provided to think about Muslim efforts against domestic abuse as one of many social justice issues.

Muslim Efforts against Domestic Violence: A Review

The event, organized by a group of advocates in a large metropolitan area, had, notably, been publicized by several other organizations involved in efforts against DV in Muslim communities but also other community organizations. It brought together advocates and service providers with researchers and was

intended to both take stock of the existing landscape and plan for ways forward including better networking and organizing and a potential shift in
strategy in working with other nonprofits, law enforcement, and the state. I
had been invited to present some of my findings and thus had a first opportunity to summarize my research and to share it with the people who, I hoped,
would find it useful for their own work.

Other speakers reflected, in similar ways, on their own work and that of
their organizations and confirmed many of my findings. Their assessment included concerns about funding problems, the complicated roles of religion
and culture in DV work, the urgent need to raise awareness in communities,
the necessary negotiations with (often white) feminist frameworks, and the
constant threat of burnout of advocates and service providers.

There was, among the women in the room, also a clear generational difference: older advocates, honored for their long years of service and experience,
spoke more often about meeting communities where they are, negotiating
with patriarchal frameworks, and relying on male authority figures including
religious scholars and leaders but also male community members with significant influence. These older women described the history of their efforts
before and during the institutionalization of Muslim DV work and reflected
on the many obstacles they had faced during those years. They also described
recent shifts in their strategy from directly raising awareness of domestic violence to focusing on "healthy Islamic marriage," not only through communal
awareness events but also through Muslim couple dinners in which participants would discuss conflict resolution strategies as well as express feelings
through "love language" and forms of equality and joint decision making in
Muslim marriages. Advocates insisted that Islam was significant as a framework for declaring DV unacceptable to Muslims and that the religious arguments against DV were useful in their work.

Younger activists related their frustration with the need to acquire legitimacy in Muslim communities through wearing hijab and their experiences
of being dismissed or ignored by male leaders and scholars, especially when
they were not married. They also pointed to the limitations of an approach
to Muslim communities that only recognizes mosques and community centers as communities. There was a longer discussion on how to reach younger
Muslims and those who are "unmosqued"—including reaching into third
spaces, such as the Ta'leef Collective[1] and a group called Third Space, led by
Suhaib Webb.[2] Some of the younger advocates, however, went further and
poignantly asked whether Islam was in fact central or helpful to their work.

They recognized that Islam could provide a set of supporting resources for victims and survivors but were less convinced that the centering of "Islamic arguments" was equally useful in convincing perpetrators or communities and families that stayed silent in the face of such abuse.

This discussion was also only the second time that I heard advocates discuss issues of intimate partner violence outside of marriage. One advocate pointed out that it was important and necessary to address sexual violence including dating violence experienced especially by younger Muslims and that it was almost impossible to discuss such issues in communal contexts where even acknowledging that Muslims might have premarital sex was taboo. Another advocate added that there was no room at all to address IPV in same-sex relationships because those, too, were considered outside the realm of "Islamically acceptable" forms of relationships, especially the framework of marriage as the only licit way to have sex.[3] Here, Islamic frameworks effectively prevented any meaningful engagement with questions surrounding IPV.

A representative from an organization that provided resources to Asian women made a rather interesting point: she said she recognized many of the central points and arguments as well as problems, even though in her context religion did not play any role. Attitudes toward shame, silence, marital issues, and abuse manifested as cultural problems in her context, with no reference to religion, despite the fact that, of course, the clients of her organization could also belong to religious communities. Another advocate, also from an organization focused on Asian women, added that she was impressed and a little bit jealous to hear of Muslim (as well as Christian and Jewish) religious frameworks when neither Hindu nor Sikh communities seemed to have developed parallel religious tools and arguments against domestic violence. These two contributions raised questions about the place of Islam as an American religion but also about the public nature of Muslim communities as opposed to the privatization of other religions based on the Protestant model.

The most important part of the conversation was initiated by one of the organizers, Noura, who challenged the group to think beyond both Muslim communities and frameworks limited to domestic abuse. She consistently used the term "gender-based violence" (GBV), which she argued was a necessary corrective to the exclusive focus on violence within family contexts. While the term "gender-based violence" has been in use since the 1990s, most often coterminous with violence against women, more recently, activists have embraced the term as more open to addressing the ways in which patriarchal hierarchies and gender binaries impact people of all genders. This makes it, among other things, possible to consider anti-LGBTQI hate crimes and discrimination, alongside domestic and intimate partner violence, child sexual abuse, human trafficking, and sexual assault.[4]

Noura also explicitly linked domestic violence work, which she argued, like I have, could be supporting patriarchal notions of family very much in line with social conservative ideals in American society, to different forms of state violence inflicted on Muslim families and communities and on people of color more broadly. She especially singled out the U.S. government's Countering Violent Extremism (CVE) program, which was created in 2011 under the Obama presidency and aimed to surveil extremist groups both in the United States and abroad in order to prevent violent attacks on U.S. soil.[5] With its almost exclusive focus on Muslim communities in the United States, she argued, it constituted a government-funded surveillance and infiltration program that threatened the safety and inclusion of Muslim Americans and marked them, yet again, as permanently other and as inherently dangerous. In essence, CVE represented the most obvious form of government-sponsored anti-Muslim hostility and actively supported the securitization of Muslims in line with a long history of securitizing those who challenge and critique the U.S. government. Sahar Aziz, a legal scholar, has criticized CVE in similar terms: "Despite the Obama administration's lofty rhetoric, this article argues that CVE programs are fundamentally flawed for three reasons: they are counterproductive, unnecessary, and a waste of government resources. Government programs seeking to build community resilience are most effective when administered by social service agencies with the requisite expertise, not law enforcement agencies."[6]

Noura pointed out that CVE programs had split Muslim communities over their involvement or their refusal to participate, with the latter putting those communities, leaders, and activists in acute danger because refusal to participate in CVE, and even critiques of the program, would be taken by the Department of Homeland Security as indications of extremist inclinations and thus reason to be surveilled. In other words, Muslims could not win either way, and radical activists, like herself, were in double jeopardy and increased danger for their work as it linked gender-based violence to state violence.[7]

Noura also repeated the earlier question of another advocate as to how important Islam was for advocacy work on gender-based violence. This was the central question I was left with at the end of the event. Possible responses to this question depend on the positionality of the person answering the question. As a scholar studying American Muslim efforts against domestic violence

I had already accepted that those efforts were significant and worthy of study—I had not formulated a vision for what such efforts should look like but was instead capturing what they did look like in practice. I found Noura's question challenging but also see it now as an indication for the expanding circles of Muslim DV work that extend beyond both Muslim communities and frameworks on the one hand and domestic violence on the other. The deep introspection leading to new strategies for future activist work embodied in this event inspired me to further develop my own ideas about gender justice as social justice and Muslim social justice work in an age of political erosion and attack.

Scholarship, Activism, and Power

I want to return to the question I raised in chapter 1 regarding the relationship between scholarship and activism. I self-identify as an engaged scholar, that is, as someone who sees the purpose of my scholarship as inherently political and intended to produce change in society. This inherent link between analysis and activist practice is central to the feminist project and methodology, both of which I embrace. Sa'diyya Shaikh has usefully defined her notion of feminism along similar lines:

> My definition of the term "feminism" includes the three critical components of awareness, activism, and vision. "Feminism" refers to a critical awareness of the structures of marginalization of women in society; it engages in activities directed at transforming gender power relations to strive, according to its vision, for a society that facilitates the development of human wholeness based on principles of gender justice, equality, and freedom from structures of oppression.[8]

Feminist scholars share this commitment to changing society toward justice, equality, and freedom from oppression with those in academic fields such as critical race studies, African American studies, Black diaspora studies, and ethnic studies. These scholars also embrace similar theoretical frameworks, based on the intersections between race, gender, and class, which interrogate power dynamics, modes of oppression and domination, and notions of change. The vision that Shaikh describes is perhaps more complicated to formulate in intersectional scholarly and activist work because the societal change at the heart of such projects can have more than one direction. Notions of societal change tend to assume a shared vision for the direction of such change—a forward-pointing progress narrative that takes certain notions of justice and equality for granted. In studying activist movements and their visions, it has become clear to me, especially in the context of Muslim efforts against domestic violence, that there can be more than one vision for how to end it and what advocates are actually working for. My concern then is one of judgment. Is my only option as a feminist scholar and activist to judge Muslim DV work built around protective patriarchy as fundamentally flawed?

A few years ago, I presented on this project to a group of scholars in women and gender studies. When I introduced my argument that anti-DV projects based on protective patriarchy and Islam as a resource for ending DV appear to be potentially more effective because they meet more people in Muslim communities at their convictions, I was accused of not being a real feminist and of excusing patriarchal violence. This encounter has stayed with me as an illustration of the difficulties of political and ethical self-positioning and the need for constant self-reflection on the politics of feminist and leftist work, scholarly and activist alike. I want to bring back here Rochelle Terman's reminder of the importance of both double critique and, most importantly, responsible critique.

Questions and Answers

One dimension of responsible critique is linked to the power dynamic in ethnographic research, on Muslim Americans, and on violence in Muslim communities. Throughout the project, I asked questions addressed to advocates, leaders, and service providers, and they had, at the outset, some power to decide whether they wanted to answer my questions. Unlike with CVE, I did not interpret the refusal of some to participate in my research as suspicious or problematic but rather as a reflection of the issues of surveillance, lack of trust in researchers, and perhaps also a deep skepticism about the utility of an academic study that would not yield the kind of quantitative data they most needed or general doubt of the utility of academic research for that matter.

Those who did generously give of their time, and who invested their trust in me, must have realized that I would not only ask them questions and collect their answers, as well as observe them in a variety of events, but also, eventually, develop an analysis of these materials. I have often wondered what they expected the outcome of this project to be. I have promised some of them to share my findings with them, as I did in the event described above, but the question of the purpose of my study as a tool for further activism in some ways remains. I have expressed hope that it would prove useful for their own self-reflection, in addition to highlighting their important work, with a deep sense of appreciation on my part.

The analysis as critique embedded in the dilemma of institutional power dynamics becomes perhaps most complicated in instances where I did indeed offer assessments that were also critical of the efforts I have studied. A powerful example is my continued concern about Muslim-only shelters, which I see as inherently problematic in their exclusionary policies and practices, in their discouragement of mainstream shelters, and, importantly as well, in their financial burden on Muslim communities that, I believe, should invest in other service and transitional housing models instead. Similarly, my analysis of "Islamic" arguments against domestic violence through exegetical relativism has the potential to weaken the authority of both the advocate interpreters and the Qur'an itself. Is a deconstruction of these approaches even ethical?

And on the broadest scale possible, how does grassroots activism of the kind described and analyzed in this book stack up against the recognition that domestic abuse is part of a system of marginalization and oppression that, once recognized as permeating the structures of our collective lives, can only be addressed (or ended) by dismantling the very system that enables it? What is the relationship between grassroots activism, focused on a specific cause, and political critiques of the system? And who am I to teach activists how to see the world and engage with it? One aspect of the above may need to be reformulated; as Beth Ritchie has argued, the "anti-violence movement" in the United States achieved mainstream legitimization as it "softened the radical politics of the work and ultimately betrayed the visions of the early grassroots feminist, anti-racist activism."[9] Later she continues:

> The anti-violence movement is a loosely organized collectivity that challenges individual behaviors, cultural values, accepted norms, public policies, and laws that lead to abuse of women. In contrast to agencies that are more focused on providing services and support to individual women who have been harmed, the work that I am referring to when I use the term "anti-violence movement" includes those groups or social actors that are making demands on the existing social order to be different; more oriented towards social justice than social services.[10]

While Ritchie completely discounts the role of religious organizations and communities in this anti-violence movement, I think it possible to situate Muslim efforts against domestic violence in broader circles of both oppression and resistance.[11] To be fair, Ritchie does so in a particular tradition of feminist and anti-racist, anti-violence work that has rarely intersected with either religious feminists or religious communities that are also committed to anti-violence, so this is not an indictment of her important and radical insights as anti-religious but perhaps rather another piece of the complicated puzzle as to why religion is so often discounted in both feminist analysis and anti–domestic violence work.

I think of domestic violence as overlapping but not identical with sexual violence, intimate partner violence, marital violence, relationship violence, and broader structures of gender-based violence. There are both individual perpetrators as in cases of domestic violence but also broader structures such as in human trafficking. Gender-based violence based on patriarchal power structures overlaps and runs parallel to racist violence and discrimination with both implicating the state as an important perpetrator. The picture gets further complicated when domestic violence occurs, is studied, and is addressed in marginalized communities. Muslims in the United States, in all their diversity, constitute one of these marginalized communities and are at the center of hostile government and public discourse as well as state policies including surveillance, infiltration, and a long history of marking Muslim bodies as foreign, other, and not belonging in the United States. In addition to race and gender, systems of violent marginalization are also linked to class structures, especially poverty. Muslim women who are victims of domestic violence are in the crucible of these axes of exclusion, discrimination, and violence. Both Muslim victims and advocates against their abuse are required to navigate these systems and structures as they attempt to survive and support.

On Purpose, Ethics, and Justice

One axis of my analysis has focused on the relationship between the ethic of non-abuse and an exegetical framework that vehemently insists that domestic abuse is incompatible with Islam, with Islamic values, and with God's will. In the tradition of Sa'diyya Shaikh's notion of a *tafsir* of praxis, and my own description of woman-led prayer as embodied *tafsir*, it defines these exegetical frameworks, grounded in the Qur'an and the Sunna, as a *tafsir of purpose*. I find this notion useful in recognizing both the hermeneutical potential and the limitations of this *tafsir* for the purpose of arguing against domestic violence. It is intrinsically linked, in an interdependent way, to the ethic of non-abuse.

The ethic of non-abuse, which is at the center of my explorations and reflections in this project, has generated a specific exegetical discourse in which the Qur'an and the Sunna, but not Islamic law, are deployed to create an authoritative response to domestic violence: an unequivocal no to any form of abuse. I am inclined to argue that the stability of this framework, often flavored by protective patriarchy, can but does not necessarily extend as a method to other issues in contemporary Muslim community discourse. In other words, it is specific to the issue of domestic violence. It may be tempting to try to extend its exegetical logic to other issues, such as same-sex marriage, racism, or women's leadership, but it does not transfer in an easy way. We see then that a set of ethical commitments, born from experiences of suffering, witnessed or lived, can produce a discourse that aims to diminish such suffering (and end it for good), but the strategies and methods employed to produce that discourse might not be easily transferable to other forms of suffering and injustice.

However, Noura and the other younger activists at the event I described above may point toward that very possibility. If they continue to connect their specific grassroots practices on domestic violence in Muslim communities to broader questions of social justice, including in support for the Black Lives Matter movement, in anti-racism work in Muslim communities, through LGBTQI inclusion and acceptance, in continued critique of patriarchy and misogyny, in a radical critique of systems of capitalist exploitation, white supremacy, colonialism, and even in environmental protection and conservation, then the ethic of non-abuse can become a broader ethic of social justice.

Alongside progressive Muslim intellectuals and activists, I would argue that, within "Islam" as a religious tradition, there are sources, tools, and models that can constitute the foundation and inspiration for Muslims to participate in the creation of a better, more just world for all of humanity. The Qur'an speaks of justice as related to acts, compelling Muslims to recognize justice not only as a value emanating from the divine but as a mandate to recognize injustice and act to replace it with justice:

> We sent Our Messengers with clear signs and sent down with them the Book and the Measure in order to establish justice among the people. (Qur'an 57:25)

> O you who believe, be upright for God, and [be] bearers of witness with justice! (Qur'an 5:8)

O you who believe! Stand out firmly for justice, as witnesses to Allah, even if it be against yourselves, your parents, and your relatives, or whether it is against the rich or the poor (Qur'an 4:135)

And the Prophet Muhammad is reported to have said: "Whosoever of you sees an evil, let him change it with his hand; and if he is not able to do so, then [let him change it] with his tongue; and if he is not able to do so, then with his heart—and that is the weakest of faith."

Both Muslim intellectuals who critique racism as an evil and those who identify misogyny as unjust have drawn on Qur'anic notions of justice as divine command, including Farid Esack, Amina Wadud, Sherman Jackson, and Kecia Ali. Their work may provide more than one guiding light for the road ahead.

Farid Esack

The Qur'an postulates the idea of a universe created with justice as its basis. The natural order, according to the Qur'an, is one rooted in justice and deviation from it is disorder. The status quo in a particular social order, irrespective of how long it has survived or how stable it has become, does not enjoy intrinsic legitimacy in Islam.... In the Qur'anic paradigm, justice and the natural order based on it are values to be upheld, while socio-political stability per-se is not. When confronted with this disturbance in the natural order through the systematic erosion of human rights (or threats to the ecosystem), the Qur'an imposes an obligation in the faithful to challenge such a system until it is eliminated and the order once again restored to its natural state of justice.[12]

Amina Wadud

The gender *jihad* is a struggle to establish gender justice in Muslim thought and practice. At the simplest level, gender justice is gender mainstreaming— the inclusion of women in *all* aspects of Muslim practice, performance, policy construction, and in both political and religious leadership.... As a Muslim woman living and working with other Muslim women worldwide, I have encountered enough to understand how many seek to find their identity and full voice through continued struggle in the gender *jihad*, whether consciously or coincidentally.... Hear our song, and when the words become familiar, sing along, for ours has too often been the silence that sustained and nurtured the background.[13]

Sherman Jackson

As for *black* theodicy, as a unique and specific genre of theodicy, it focuses on the problem of evil in the more specific context of the historical communal suffering of Blackamericans. It begins by asking how an all-good, all-powerful God could sponsor or allow moral evil that is as grand and sustained as the evil of American slavery.... It goes on to ask ... if and how Blackamericans can work to liberate themselves from such evil without calling into question God's all-goodness and all-powerfulness. Black theodicy, in other words, seeks not only to explain how or why God sponsors or allows Black suffering but to do so in a manner that justifies the effort to overturn this suffering in light of the theological presumption that it could only exist by the power and will of an omnipotent and omnibenevolent God.[14]

Kecia Ali

Those Muslims who strive for gender equality, considering it an essential component of justice, must address the central issue: what is justice? on what basis does one know it? Is something good because God says so? ... If one wants to consider certain moral standards as absolutes—such as the injustice of slavery—one must accept that God sometimes tolerates injustice. However, in a universe with human free will, allowing injustice is not the same as being the cause of it; God repeatedly rejects responsibility for injustice in Qur'anic passages declaring that God does not wrong or oppress people in any way, but rather people do wrong "to their own selves." This assertion is freeing, in that God does not demand that Muslims act contrary to the dictates of their conscience. However, it also implies a much more significant responsibility for the individual human being to make ethical judgments and take moral actions.[15]

A Muslim ethic of social justice is not only formulated in the above quotes from leading Muslim intellectuals (all of whom are also activists) but more importantly already being practiced in many forms: in Muslim participation in the Black Lives Matter movement; in antiwar protests; in Muslim LGBTQI communities and their supporters; in environmental awareness and preservation efforts; in decolonial struggles; at protests against deportation from the United States; and in Muslim awareness work on sexual abuse and sexual harassment. Advocates and activists are recognizing the challenging issues facing our planet and our communities and they are responding, as Muslims, to the call.

Understanding Domestic Violence

THE FOLLOWING DESCRIPTION of who is included in the "domestic" part of domestic violence was inserted into the 1994 Violence Against Women Act in 2005, thus representing the official government definition:

> The term "domestic violence" includes felony or misdemeanor crimes of violence committed by a current or former spouse of the victim, by a person with whom the victim shares a child in common, by a person who is cohabitating with or has cohabitated with the victim as a spouse, by a person similarly situated to a spouse of the victim under the domestic or family violence laws of the jurisdiction receiving grant monies, or by any other person against an adult or youth victim who is protected from that person's acts under the domestic or family violence laws of the jurisdiction.[1]

The violence prevention programs of the Centers for Disease Control and Prevention (CDC) include elder abuse, child abuse and neglect, sexual violence, youth violence, and a specific category addressing intimate partner violence (IPV). This is the CDC definition of IPV:

> Intimate partner violence (IPV) is a serious, preventable public health problem that affects millions of Americans. The term "intimate partner violence" describes physical violence, sexual violence, stalking and psychological aggression (including coercive acts) by a current or former intimate partner.
>
> An intimate partner is a person with whom one has a close personal relationship that can be characterized by the following: Emotional connectedness, regular contact, ongoing physical contact and/or sexual behavior, identity as a couple, familiarity and knowledge about each other's lives.

The relationship need not involve all of these dimensions. Examples of intimate partners include current or former spouses, boyfriends or girlfriends, dating partners, or sexual partners. IPV can occur between heterosexual or same-sex couples and does not require sexual intimacy.

IPV can vary in frequency and severity. It occurs on a continuum, ranging from one episode that might or might not have lasting impact to chronic and severe episodes over a period of years.[2]

Both of the above definitions seem to struggle with how to define the relationship between victims and perpetrators, the boundaries of what constitutes the family, and the distinction between adult members of a family who are in a specific relationship. The CDC definition of domestic violence would include child abuse as well as elder abuse, which is why the term "intimate partner violence" was created.

In the secondary literature, some authors seem to use DV and IPV synonymously while others perceive DV as a broader category than IPV. Both struggle with the boundaries of family units beyond state-sanctioned marriage and the many ways in which people can be involved in familial relations and units.

These government approaches and definitions play an important role in how funding for prevention and services is allocated and distributed. In addition, there are legal definitions that serve to define acts of domestic violence in terms that can be both acted upon by law enforcement and prosecuted by the court system.

Power and Control; Cycles of Abuse

Nonprofit organizations that raise awareness of DV and those who provide services to victims and survivors can differ in their approach to domestic violence by foregrounding some of its relational aspects and dimensions over others. The following definition provides clear parameters for identifying domestic abuse: "Domestic violence is a pattern of assaultive and coercive behaviors, including physical, sexual, and psychological attacks, as well as economic coercion, that adults or adolescents use against their intimate partners."[3]

In the 1980s, the Domestic Abuse Intervention Programs (DAIP) in Duluth, Minnesota, developed a comprehensive model for identifying and addressing various forms of domestic abuse. The result was the Duluth power and control wheel, which has been in use across the United States for several decades. Over the years, advocates have developed further nuanced wheels for different communities and populations that recognize that power and control dynamics are embedded in social and political structures that can play out differently in those different populations. However, these adjusted power and control wheels, based on the original Duluth wheel, have retained the focus on DV dynamics as expressed in coercive power and control by one partner over the other.[4]

The Duluth wheel is framed by a thick black circle that reads "VIOLENCE" in capital letters on the top and bottom and "physical" twice on the left and "sexual" twice on the right side of the circle. The center of circle reads "POWER AND CONTROL." While physical and sexual violence form the outer ring of the wheel, the segments inside can be present as important other dimensions of how an abuser establishes control, including "male privilege; economic abuse; using children; minimizing, denying, and blaming; isolation; emotional abuse; intimidation; and coercion and threats." In each segment, there are more detailed explanations of the abusive behaviors associated with the broader category. For example, the segment titled "Intimidation" lists the following behaviors: "Making her afraid by using looks, actions and gestures. Smashing things. Destroying her property. Abusing pets. Displaying weapons."[5] The power and control wheel highlights the interconnected forms of abuse that DV victims experience, not all of which would immediately be identified as part of the larger issue of DV. Because domestic abuse is often a spiral rather than a flat cycle, these forms of establishing control often precede the infliction of physical and sexual violence. In a significant number of cases, abusive relationships end with the ultimate assertion of control when the perpetrator kills the victim.

Scholars and practitioners who have observed and studied abusive relationships have also identified a typical but not universal pattern in abusive relationships, namely cycles of abuse that are repeated over and over, even though as the violence escalates in a spiral pattern, the making-up and calm stages can disappear.

Incident

- Any type of abuse occurs (physical/sexual/emotional)

Tension Building

- Abuser starts to get angry
- Abuse may begin

- There is a breakdown of communication
- Victim feels the need to keep the abuser calm
- Tension becomes too much
- Victim feels like they are "walking on eggshells"

Making-Up

- Abuser may apologize for abuse
- Abuser may promise it will never happen again
- Abuser may blame the victim for causing the abuse
- Abuser may deny abuse took place or say it was not as bad as the victim claims

Calm

- Abuser acts like the abuse never happened
- Physical abuse may not be taking place
- Promises made during "making-up" may be met
- Victim may hope that the abuse is over
- Abuser may give gifts to victim.[6]

Such cycles of abuse can occur over the span of a few hours to a few years, the latter indicating that once a pattern of abuse has been established, the likelihood of it disappearing without intervention is minimal. The power and control wheel and the cycle of abuse are tools that are used to help train advocates and service providers, but they also play, in various iterations, an important role in helping victims recognize their own relationship or family situation as abusive.

NOTES

Chapter 1. Shifting Landscapes and a Missing Map:
Studying Muslim Efforts against Domestic Violence

1. Warsan Shire is a Somali British poet. The poem is called "what they did yesterday afternoon" and does not seem to have been published in a conventional printed collection of poetry. For more on Shire, see Malak Gharib, "Beyonce's 'Lemonade' Turns a Somali-Brit Poet into a Global Star," NPR, April 27, 2016, https://www.npr.org/sections/goatsandsoda/2016/04/27/475872852/beyonces-lemonade-turns-a-somali-brit-poet-into-a-global-star.

2. Kahf, "The Muslim in the Mirror," 135.

3. See, for example, Dragiewicz, "Patriarchy Reasserted"; and Boba and Lilley, "Violence Against Women Act (VAWA) Funding." The very existence of a journal called *Violence Against Women* demonstrates the significance of feminist scholars and activists in the movement, and its creation in 1995 shows the impact of VAWA.

4. Kimberlé Crenshaw developed the concept of intersectionality in the early 1990s. Contrary to how it is now often understood, intersectionality for her was not only the consideration of gender, race, class, and other factors as influential for power differentials in society. Rather, her analysis of structural, political, and representational intersections between race and gender carried forward the need to recognize and criticize racism and sexism as systemic and interconnected issues in need of change. See Crenshaw, "Mapping the Margins."

5. Here are some of the numbers in NCADV's fact sheet:

- In the United States, an average of 20 people are physically abused by intimate partners every minute. This equates to more than 10 million abuse victims annually.
- 1 in 3 women and 1 in 4 men have been physically abused by an intimate partner.
- 1 in 5 women and 1 in 7 men have been severely physically abused by an intimate partner.
- 1 in 7 women and 1 in 18 men have been stalked. Stalking causes the target to fear she/he or someone close to her/him will be harmed or killed.
- On a typical day, domestic violence hotlines nationwide receive approximately 20,800 calls.
- The presence of a gun in a domestic violence situation increases the risk of homicide by 500%.
- Intimate partner violence is most common among women between the ages of 18–24.
- 19% of intimate partner violence involves a weapon.

- 1 in 3 female murder victims and 1 in 20 male murder victims are killed by intimate partners.
- 72% of all murder-suicides are perpetrated by intimate partners.
- 94% of murder-suicide victims are female.

See the entire fact sheet from 2015 here: https://ncadv.org/assets/2497/domestic_violence .pdf. The second bullet point statistic indicates that women are more likely to experience domestic abuse than men but that physical abuse of men is also widespread. This fact has been used in the backlash against feminist frameworks that emphasize violence against women. Such statistics are produced by the Centers for Disease Control and Prevention, a government body; see https://www.cdc.gov/violenceprevention/nisvs/summaryreports.html. https://ncadv .org/about-us.

6. Similar and parallel to the construction of the notion of the "Muslim world" as explored in Cemil Aydin's work, the notion of Islam as a religion can be linked to European colonialism, the invention of world religions including hierarchies between religions, and notions of civilization and culture. Muslims have participated and continue to participate in this construction, albeit not as equals, in order to demonstrate that they "have religion" and as a tool of resistance. See Aydin, *The Idea of the Muslim World*; Masuzawa, *The Invention of World Religions*.

7. There is a long and complex debate about the relationship and, indeed, interconnectedness of Islam and feminism. While I share the concern of some gender justice activists that identifying as a feminist might also support the colonial co-optation of feminism to undermine Muslim societies and communities, I ultimately see my position in line with what Fatima Seedat has called translucence. She explains: "To pay heed to an anticolonial critique of Islamic feminism is to replace the apparent transparency between the intellectual paradigms of the West and non-West with a translucence that maintains distance even as it affirms the historical imbrications and connections between Islam and feminism. If the convergence of Islam and feminism is to be such translucence, then we must be mindful of the multiple forms of this convergence and open to the multiple ways of doing equality work that they allow for. To claim a necessary single convergence precludes other convergences and other ways of being Muslim and feminist." Seedat, "Islam, Feminism, and Islamic Feminism," 44.

8. Wadud, *Inside the Gender Jihad*, 10, emphasis in the original.

9. Their works, even if not listed in the notes that follow, have been influential in writing this book and are part of the bibliography.

10. Ali, "Timeless Texts and Modern Morals."

11. Wadud, *Qur'an and Woman*, 76. This page number is in the 1999 edition, published in the United States. The book was originally published in Malaysia in 1992.

12. Wadud, *Inside the Gender Jihad*, 203.

13. Wadud, *Inside the Gender Jihad*, 204.

14. Bauer, " 'Traditional' Exegeses of Qur'an 4:34"; Ali, " 'The Best of You Will Not Strike' "; Chaudhry, "The Problems of Conscience and Hermeneutics"; Silvers, " 'In the Book We Have Left Nothing Out.' "

15. Silvers, " 'In the Book We Have Left Nothing Out,' " 177.

16. Chaudhry, *Domestic Violence*, 197.

17. Chaudhry, *Domestic Violence*, 197.

18. Chaudhry, *Domestic Violence*, 210.

19. Shaikh, "A *Tafsir* of Praxis," 80.

20. Mahmood, *Politics of Piety*, 10.

21. Hidayatullah, *Feminist Edges of the Qur'an*, 151.

22. See Spivak, "Criticism, Feminism, and the Institution." Spivak has since distanced herself from this notion, but I find it an eminently useful tool for analysis and activism. See Spivak, "An Interview with Gayatri Spivak."

23. See, for example, Karim, *American Muslim Women*; Jackson, *Islam and the Blackamerican*; and the work of the Muslim Anti-Racism Collaborative, www.muslimarc.org.

24. Though I know of self-identified Shi'a Muslim organizations addressing DV, I did not encounter any of the advocates in the networks I explored. The marginalization of Shi'a perspectives is a continuous issue in the study of American Muslims and in Islamic studies in general.

25. See Mamdani, *Good Muslim, Bad Muslim*; Ernst, *Islamophobia in America*; Ali et al., "Fear Inc."; and a public syllabus called "Islamophobia Is Racism" (2017), which I helped create: https://islamophobiaisracism.wordpress.com/.

26. Foucault, *Power/Knowledge*; Said, *Orientalism*.

27. Hammer, "Gender Matters."

28. Lila Abu Lughod has been an important influence on my own scholarship in many ways: as an anthropologist who pioneered a new way to study Muslim women in the 1990s, as a scholar who takes explicitly political positions, and as a writer whose work I have always admired. See, for example, Abu Lughod, "Do Muslim Women Really Need Saving?" and *Do Muslim Women Need Saving?*

29. See the video here: https://www.youtube.com/watch?v=UjnFbe7D9pY.

30. Abu Lughod and Mikdashi, "Tradition and the Anti-Politics Machine."

31. Nafar, Nafar, and Jrery (DAM), "DAM Responds."

32. Abu Lughod and Mikdashi, "Honoring Solidarity during Contentious Debates."

33. "In an age of Islamophobia, how does one engage in a feminist critique of women's status in Muslim contexts without providing ideological fuel for undesired political ambitions? When the US invokes the oppression of Muslim women to justify war, how do we practice feminist solidarity without strengthening orientalism and imperialism?" Terman, "Islamophobia, Feminism, and the Politics of Critique," 2.

34. Terman, "Islamophobia, Feminism, and the Politics of Critique," 24. Terman's double critique reminds me of the earlier work of miriam cooke in an article titled "Multiple Critique."

35. See Hammer, *American Muslim Women*. They rightly assumed that I support woman-led prayer in Muslim communities and saw this support as indicative of my broader identification as a feminist. For some, this broke their trust in my work, and for others it enhanced it.

Chapter 2. Murder, Honor, and Culture:
Mediatized Debates on Muslims and Domestic Violence

1. There is a very useful German word, *Dunkelziffer*, which literally means "dark number," that captures the much larger number of unreported cases by describing them as being in the dark, unknown.

2. Excerpted from Domestic Violence Statistics page, website of the Domestic Abuse Shelter of the Florida Keys, http://www.domesticabuseshelter.org/infodomesticviolence.htm.

3. See, for example, http://www.huffingtonpost.com/2014/10/23/domestic-violence-statistics_n_5959776.html.

4. Between February 2009 and 2018 I read countless news pieces about domestic violence murders, of Muslim women and others, and an equally large number of pieces that focus on "honor violence." My terror at having to read descriptions of injury and murder has never abated, and perhaps it should not, lest I become immune to the pain and suffering they represent.

5. Dragiewicz, *Equality with a Vengeance*, 5.

6. http://www.vosizneias.com/27373/2009/02/13/new-york-police-prominent-ny-muslim-man-charged-with-beheading-his-wife/.

7. In many of the news reports Aasiya Zubair was identified as Aasiya Hassan or Aasiya Zubair Hassan. Muslim activists and others started referring to her as Aasiya Zubair, in an attempt to disconnect her name from that of her killer and husband, Muzzammil Hassan. I follow this reasoning and refer to her as Aasiya Zubair throughout.

8. Fred O. Williams and Gene Warner, "Man Charged in Beheading of Wife: Police Probe Killing of Woman Married to Orchard Park Businessman," *Buffalo News*, February 14, 2009.

9. See, for some of the media coverage, Liz Robbins, "Upstate Man Charged with Beheading His Estranged Wife," *New York Times*, February 18, 2009; Joshua Rhett Miller, "Muslim Television Channel Founder Charged with Beheading His Wife," Fox News, February 16, 2009, https://www.foxnews.com/story/muslim-television-channel-founder-charged-with-beheading-his-wife; Sandra Tan, Gene Warner, and Fred O. Williams, "A History of Abuse Preceded Orchard Park Beheading," *Buffalo News*, February 22, 2009.

10. I discuss anti-Muslim hostility in its gendered dimensions further below and provide additional citations from the vast literature on this important topic. See here Ernst, *Islamophobia in America*; Lean, *The Islamophobia Industry*; and Love, *Islamophobia and Racism in America*.

11. http://www.danielpipes.org/blog/2009/02/bridges-tv-a-wifes-beheading-and-honor-murder.

12. Chesler, "Are Honor Killings Simply Domestic Violence?" *Middle East Quarterly* 16:2 (2009), https://www.meforum.org/articles/2009/are-honor-killings-simply-domestic-violence.

13. Joshua Rhett Miller, "Beheading in New York Appears to Be Honor Killing, Experts Say," Fox News, February 17, 2009, http://www.foxnews.com/story/2009/02/17/beheading-in-new-york-appears-to-be-honor-killing-experts-say.html.

14. http://pamelageller.com/2009/02/beheading-in-new-york-honor-killing.html/.

15. NOW is described on its website as "the largest organization of feminist activists in the United States, with hundreds of thousands of contributing members and more than 500 local and campus affiliates in all 50 states and the District of Columbia." www.now.org/about/.

16. As quoted in Fred O. Williams, "Possibility of 'Honor Killing' Mulled in Orchard Park Slaying," *Buffalo News*, February 17, 2009. See also http://www.nydailynews.com/news/muslim-tv-mogul-muzzammil-hassan-alleged-beheading-wife-aasiya-hassan-honor-killing-article-1.393494; Carolyn Thompson, "NY Man Accused of Beheading Claims He Was Battered," ABC News, January 22, 2010, http://www.sandiegouniontribune.com/sdut-ny-man-accused-of-beheading-claims-he-was-battered-2010jan22-story.html.

17. See Williams, "Possibility of 'Honor Killing' Mulled in Orchard Park Slaying." When I accessed the piece in 2016, the title had been changed to "Muslim Influence Speculated in Slaying," *Buffalo News*, February 17, 2009.

18. Suzanne Tomkins, "Stereotypes Mustn't Hide the Facts of Domestic Violence," *Buffalo News*, February 19, 2009.

19. Matt Gryta, "Orchard Park Slaying Highlighted in Discussion of Domestic Violence," *Buffalo News*, February 21, 2009.

20. Tan, Warner, and Williams, "A History of Abuse Preceded Orchard Park Beheading."

21. Eric Gorski, "Gruesome Killing Poses Another Test for US Muslims," Associated Press, February 21, 2009, reposted https://www.winnipegfreepress.com/world/null-40028052.html.

22. Maki Becker, "Bizarre Nature of Hassan Case Rivets Region," *Buffalo News*, February 6, 2011.

23. "New York TV Exec Gets 25 Years to Life for Wife's Beheading," CNN, March 9, 2011, http://www.cnn.com/2011/CRIME/03/09/new.york.beheading/.

24. Remla Parthasarathy, "Hassan Case Reflects Basic Truths about Abusers," *Buffalo News*, February 12, 2011.

25. Sandra Tan, "Raw Emotions Still Felt after Hassan Trial," *Buffalo News*, February 12, 2011.

26. For an example of such a move regarding a different topic, namely women leading prayers and being community leaders, see my *American Muslim Women*, where I discuss the strategies of the organizers of the woman-led Friday prayer in 2005 of simultaneously generating communal debate and changing media perceptions of Muslim women.

27. Hussein Rashid, "Domestic Violence Has Nothing to Do with Religion," February 18, 2009, http://religiondispatches.org/domestic-violence-has-nothing-to-do-with-religion.

28. Rashid, "Domestic Violence Has Nothing to Do with Religion."

29. http://www.peacefulfamilies.org/pressrelease090214.html.

30. Imam Mohamed Hagmagid Ali, "Responding to the Killing of Aasiya Hassan: An Open Letter to the Leaders of American Muslim Communities," February 17, 2009. The letter was posted on the ISNA website but is no longer there; see https://dawudwalid.wordpress.com/2009/02/17/isnas-response-to-the-murder-of-aasiya-zubair-hassan-domestic-violence/.

31. Asma T. Uddin, "Moving beyond the Slogans," www.altmuslim.com.

32. Wajahat Ali, posted here, http://www.beliefnet.com/columnists/cityofbrass/2009/02/american-muslims-call-for-swif.html, and on the sites of several other Muslim organizations and individuals on February 18, 2009.

33. Shirin Sadeghi, "Guilty: The Decapitation of Aasiya Zubair," *Huffington Post*, February 9, 2011, https://www.huffingtonpost.com/shirin-sadeghi/guilty-the-decapitation-o_b_821121.html.

34. Abdul Malik Mujahid, "9 Things You Can Do in Memory of Sister Aasiya Zubair," https://www.soundvision.com/article/9-things-you-can-do-in-memory-of-sister-aasiya-zubair.

35. Hammer, "Center Stage" and "Muslim Women, Anti-Muslim Hostility."

36. See Jasbir Puar's groundbreaking book, *Terrorist Assemblages*.

37. It is so tired a trope that the literature about hijab is beyond reference in a note at this point. However, talking about hijab has retained its power to delineate types and shades of right-wing as well as progressive (and secular) feminist discourses and thus should not be underestimated, however overanalyzed it might be.

38. See the article by Terman, already discussed in chapter 1, "Islamophobia, Feminism, and the Politics of Critique."

39. Ali et al., "Fear Inc."; Duss et al., "Fear Inc.2.0."

40. See this video posted by the American Program Bureau, an organization that represents public speakers, on January 6, 2015, https://www.youtube.com/watch?v=5Kam_sS8FzY. The web address of After the Trauma was no longer accessible in February 2016.

41. Cannon, 23 Days of Terror.

42. Albarus, The Making of Lee Boyd Malvo.

43. Censer, On the Trail of the DC Sniper.

44. On IMDB, this is how the film is described: "An abandoned boy is lured to America and drawn into the shadow of a dangerous father figure. Inspired by the real life events that led to the 2002 Beltway sniper attacks." http://www.imdb.com/title/tt2027064/.

45. Elijah Muhammad was the long-time leader of the Nation of Islam from 1934 until his death in 1975. The NOI was then led by one of his sons, Warith Deen Mohammed (d. 2008), who transformed it considerably and also changed its name several times. In 1981, Louis Farrakhan (b. 1933) decided to revive the original Nation of Islam and has been its leader ever since.

46. Albarus, The Making of Lee Boyd Malvo, 94–99.

47. In 2007, Kathleen McKinley on Newsbusters (intent on exposing liberal media bias) accused CNN of "ignoring radical Islam" in the story of the DC sniper. http://www.newsbusters.org/blogs/kathleen-mckinley/2007/10/19/cnn-ignores-radical-islam-story-washington-d-c-snipers.

48. http://www.danielpipes.org/blog/2003/08/the-beltway-snipers-motives; http://michellemalkin.com/2006/05/25/the-jihadi-snipers-revisited/.

49. http://www.finalcall.com/artman/publish/National_News_2/Minister_Louis_Farrakhan_addresses_sniper_arrest_2285.shtml.

50. Curtis, "The Black Muslim Scare," 99.

51. Curtis, "The Black Muslim Scare," 102.

52. Parthasarathy, "Identifying and Depicting Culture." Notably the article was part of a special issue of the Buffalo Journal of Gender, Law & Social Policy on domestic violence.

53. Parthasarathy, "Identifying and Depicting Culture," 89.

54. Parthasarathy, "Identifying and Depicting Culture," 86.

55. See the discussion of Uma Narayan, who coined the phrase, and Zareena Grewal below.

56. Ali, Heretic and The Caged Virgin.

57. AHA Foundation, http://www.theahafoundation.org/about-us/.

58. Chesler and Bloom, "Hindu vs. Muslim Honor Killings," Middle East Quarterly 19:3 (2012), https://www.meforum.org/articles/2012/hindu-vs-muslim-honor-killings.

59. Chesler and Bloom, "Hindu vs. Muslim Honor Killings," 52.

60. Lasson, "Bloodstains on a 'Code of Honor.'"

61. My examples here are two texts: Helba et al., "Report on Exploratory Study into Honor Violence (2015) Produced for the U.S. Department of Justice"; and Kulczycki and Windle, "Honor Killings."

62. Kulczycki and Windle, "Honor Killings," 1459.

63. Peter Gray, "'Honor' Killings and Political Correctness," March 15, 2012, http://theamericanmuslim.org/tam.php/features/articles/honor-killings-and-political-correctness.

64. Narayan, *Dislocating Cultures*, 85.

65. Narayan, *Dislocating Cultures*, 82–208.

66. Grewal, "Death by Culture," 14.

67. Quoted in Grewal, "Death by Culture," 13. See Razack, "A Violent Culture or Cultural-ized Violence?"

68. Sev'er and Yurdakul, "Culture of Honor, Culture of Change," 964.

69. Sev'er and Yurdakul, "Culture of Honor, Culture of Change," 994.

70. Baker, Gregware, and Cassidy, "Family Killing Fields," 164.

71. Baker, Gregware, and Cassidy, "Family Killing Fields," 180.

72. Shalhoub-Kevorkian and Daher-Nashif, "Femicide and Colonization," 295.

73. Shalhoub-Kevorkian and Daher-Nashif, "Femicide and Colonization," 296–97.

74. Welchman and Hossain, *"Honour."* 4.

75. Gill, "Reconfiguring 'Honour'-Based Violence," 219.

76. Volpp, "On Culture, Difference, and Domestic Violence," 395. See also Volpp, "Feminism versus Multiculturalism," which is useful in furthering the discussions in this chapter.

77. Parthasarathy, "Identifying and Depicting Culture," 93.

78. I mean by exegetical relativism the possibility of generating so many divergent interpretations of a text, here the Qur'an, without attaching ethical judgment to such interpretations that the authority of the Qur'an itself is potentially undermined. This is not an argument against diverse interpretations themselves but the potential slippery slope that they create.

Chapter 3. Need to Know: Educating Muslim Communities about Domestic Violence

1. This is also the place for a basic demographic note, important for how I deal with statistics. Estimates of the number of Muslims in the United States range from 1.2 to 12 million and are thus almost meaningless in measuring any other statistical values. If we do not know how many Muslims there are, then how can we say that a given percentage of them are married, college educated, or, most problematically of all, sorted into a variety of racial and ethnic categories? See, for example, this estimate, at 3.3 million: Besheer Mohamed, "A New Estimate of the US Population," January 6, 2016, http://www.pewresearch.org/fact-tank/2016/01/06/a-new-estimate-of-the-u-s-muslim-population/.

2. In 2009, the then Asian & Pacific Islander Institute on Domestic Violence, in cooperation with the Peaceful Families Project, produced a resource list containing most of the organizations I knew of at the time. The pdf was still available on the PFP website in 2018 but had not been updated: https://www.peacefulfamilies.org/uploads/1/1/0/5/110506531/apiidvdirectory.pdf.

3. http://www.faithtrustinstitute.org/. The FaithTrust Institute is discussed in more detail in chapter 7.

4. PFP described itself on its website in these words: "The Peaceful Families Project (PFP) is a national organization with international reach that recognizes domestic violence is a form of oppression that affects people of all faiths. Our mission is to work towards ending all types of abuse in Muslim families by increasing awareness regarding the dynamics of domestic violence. We believe that a better understanding of religious and cultural values can be used as a

resource to prevent domestic violence, and that religion and culture should never be used to justify abusive behavior. Through education and training, we seek to promote attitudes and beliefs that emphasize justice, freedom from oppression, and family harmony." PFP's objectives include: to work toward ending all types of abuse, including emotional, spiritual, physical, and sexual abuse in Muslim families; to facilitate domestic violence awareness workshops in cities across the United States for Muslim leaders and communities; to provide cultural sensitivity trainings for service providers and professionals; to conduct research regarding domestic violence in Muslim families; and to develop and disseminate educational resources regarding abuse in Muslim communities. http://www.peacefulfamilies.org/mission.html.

5. Alkhateeb, "Ending Domestic Violence in Muslim Families."

6. Abugideiri, "A Tribute to Sharifa Alkhateeb," 1. *Hawwa* is an academic journal dedicated to scholarship on women and gender in the Middle East and the Islamic world. In 2001, Hibba Abugideiri published an article on Muslim women's leadership, based on Hagar as a historical model for Muslim women, in which Alkhateeb appears as the new type of Muslim woman leader for American communities. See Abugideiri, "Hagar."

7. See news release of United Muslim Relief, http://umrelief.org/umr-welcomes-peaceful-families-project/.

8. Project Sakinah Newsletter, July 2015, http://projectsakinah.org/newsletters/Issue031.html.

9. The project chose as its name the Arabic word *sakina*, which means calm, tranquility, peace but also refers to the tranquility that comes from the presence of God. PS chose this name in reference to the Qur'anic verse instructing humans to live in tranquility together in their marriage (Q 30:21).

10. http://projectsakinah.org/Project-Sakinah/Who-We-Are.

11. "Huma," http://projectsakinah.org/Resources/Hear-Our-Stories/Huma.

12. Abid announced this in an email to subscribers of the Project Sakinah email list on October 15, 2014. Her blog can be found here: http://zerqaabid.blogspot.com/.

13. Anas Coburn, Project Sakinah, DV awareness event in Raleigh, NC, December 14, 2012.

14. I have also carried out research on marriage in American Muslim communities in both discourse and practice and argue elsewhere that talk of a Muslim marriage crisis is a reflection of pronounced discomfort with shifting gender roles and how this shift affects marriageability, selection of spouses, and life planning. For a brief overview, see my "Marriage in American Muslim Communities."

15. I use the term "Islamic law" to refer to Muslim jurisprudence, a complex, historically diverse, and ultimately human endeavor of producing legal interpretation that then has to be applied in specific contexts. The technical term for this Muslim jurisprudential tradition is *fiqh*. Muslim scholars distinguish *fiqh* from *shari'a*, which has come to be the stand-in for Islamic law, emphasizing its otherness and threat in the U.S. context. *Shari'a* refers to direct divine guidance, which is to be found and then interpreted and applied from within the Qur'an and the prophetic example.

16. The United States recognized the significance of immigration law as a tool in fighting various forms of abuse and created the U visa category: "The U nonimmigrant status (U visa) is set aside for victims of certain crimes who have suffered mental or physical abuse and are helpful to law enforcement or government officials in the investigation or prosecution of crim-

inal activity. Congress created the U nonimmigrant visa with the passage of the Victims of Trafficking and Violence Protection Act (including the Battered Immigrant Women's Protection Act) in October 2000. The legislation was intended to strengthen the ability of law enforcement agencies to investigate and prosecute cases of domestic violence, sexual assault, trafficking of aliens and other crimes, while also protecting victims of crimes who have suffered substantial mental or physical abuse due to the crime and are willing to help law enforcement authorities in the investigation or prosecution of the criminal activity." https://www .uscis.gov/humanitarian/victims-human-trafficking-other-crimes/victims-criminal-activity -u-nonimmigrant-status/victims-criminal-activity-u-nonimmigrant-status.

17. The U.S. court system has penalized abused women for not leaving an abusive relationship and thus failing to protect their children from abuse. One such case is that of Kelly Savage, who is serving a life sentence for the death of her son, who was murdered by his father. She was convicted because she did not leave her abusive husband in time to save her oldest child. See Jessica Pishko, "Serving Life for Surviving Abuse," *The Atlantic*, January 26, 2015, https://www .theatlantic.com/national/archive/2015/01/serving-life-for-surviving-abuse/384826/. For a more thorough treatment of this issue and its impact on women of color, see the important work of Beth Ritchie: *Compelled to Crime* and *Arrested Justice*.

18. *Kufr* means unbelief in Arabic.

19. *Shirk* means to associate something with God, thereby violating the mandate of absolute monotheism (*tawhid*).

20. This is a commonly cited translation of Q 30:21 by Abdullah Yusuf Ali: "And among His Signs is this that He created for you mates from among yourselves that ye may dwell in tranquility with them and He has put love and mercy between your (hearts); verily in that are Signs for those who reflect." Abdullah Yusuf Ali, *An English Translation of the Holy Qur'an* (Chicago: Lushena Books, n.d.), 338.

21. I state her argument here without further discussion even though I think it is one of the most dangerous arguments for Muslim-only services in the Muslim DV movement.

22. See Gray, *Men Are from Mars, Women Are from Venus*.

23. Arabic for "forbidden."

24. Arabic for "brother."

25. Chaudhry, *Domestic Violence*. She writes: "Since justice was a central value of Islam, and hitting wives was blatantly unjust, it was impossible for me to imagine an Islamic tradition in which no one challenged the right of husbands to hit their wives. Yet this is exactly what I found. Not a single pre-colonial Islamic jurist or exegete interpreted Q. 4:34 in a way that forbids husbands from hitting their wives" (8). Chaudhry chronicles the detailed debates especially among jurists about the extent of the violence permitted and whether the three steps needed to be followed.

26. See the epigraph to this chapter from my research notes.

27. Shaikh, "A *Tafsir* of Praxis."

28. There is a large collection of such statements online, especially on YouTube.

29. As I already explained, attending DV events in communal settings can raise suspicion that women are unrecognized victims of DV, which in turn can lead to both communal shaming (of the victim) and pressure on victims to not come forward, and, most dangerously, a feeling of exposure on the part of a perpetrator can escalate existing abuse.

30. Chaudhry, *Domestic Violence*, especially 135–95. Chaudhry formulates four different types of approaches to 4:34 and physical disciplining of wives: traditionalist, neotraditionalist, progressive, and reformist. I depart from her analysis with a focus on the Qur'an and 4:34 in that the videos I analyzed do not all center on the Qur'an and/or 4:34.

31. Posted in 2009 by Zaytuna College, the video had over eighty thousand views in 2017. https://www.youtube.com/watch?v=BDEKJDgXO-U.

32. *Jahiliyya* is often translated as "ignorance" and designates the age before the Prophet Muhammad was sent with God's revelation. The insertion of the word "patriarchal" here is interesting in that he seems to mean this as a negative term even though he supports what I have called protective patriarchy in his teachings, including in this very sermon.

33. Chaudhry, *Domestic Violence*, 170.

34. Posted in 2011 by Islam on Demand, with 1,220 views in 2017. https://www.youtube.com/watch?v=PHnlpl_nv5U.

Chapter 4. Need to Teach: Countering Oppression, Ending Injustice, and Preventing Harm

1. From a piece by Jennifer Mohamed (a pseudonym); see Mohamed, "A Survivor's Story."

2. FaithTrust Institute, *Garments for One Another*; Abugideiri, *Garments for One Another (Study Guide)*. The FaithTrust Institute produced this documentary with the support of the Peaceful Families Project. PFP facilitated access to survivors, religious scholars, and advocates and consulted on the structure and arguments made in the film. There were discussions along the way about exposure of survivors and advocates and related issues about confidentiality including interviewees who later asked to be removed from the film. They echo my concerns in this book and are one of the reasons I paid such close attention to the issue.

3. The three parts each have several chapters:
    1. Understanding Domestic Violence
       Introduction
       Who Abuses?
       Why People Ask, "But What Did She Do?"
       What Prevents Her from Leaving
    2. Islamic Perspective on Domestic Violence
       Verse 4:34—When the Qur'an Is Abused
       What It Means When He Says, "I'm Sorry"
       Is Divorce an Option?
       What about the Children?
       The Muslim Marriage Ideal
    3. What We Can Do to End Domestic Violence
       Seeking Shelter, Finding Safety
       What Imams & Leaders Can Do
       What Communities Can Do
       Journey to Healing

4. The book, first published in 2003, was produced as a resource for advocates and providers working with Muslim families. The project was coordinated by Ambreen Ahmed, then di-

rector of FAITH (Foundation for Appropriate and Immediate Temporary Help), a Muslim service provider organization in northern Virginia.

5. This resource was produced in 2008, with funding from the DOJ, primarily by Karamah: Muslim Women Lawyers for Human Rights. The folder lists APIDV (Asian & Pacific Islander Institute on Domestic Violence, now called the Asian & Pacific Islander Institute on Gender-Based Violence, https://www.api-gbv.org/), Diversity Wealth (www.diversitywealth.com), FaithTrust Institute, and PFP as having provided copyrighted materials for this resource.

6. The National Network to End Domestic Violence (NNEDV) is a U.S. umbrella organization that brings together all fifty-six state and U.S. territories' anti-DV coalitions, listed here: http://nnedv.org/resources/coalitions.html. The state coalitions in turn bring together advocacy groups and service providers in their state, which then lobby for state legislation, can apply for federal and state funding, and apply political pressure to address DV issues.

7. Alkhateeb and Abugideiri, *Change from Within*; see especially Kalam, "My Story"; Williams, "Toasted Cheese Sandwiches"; Hope, "Broken Wings No More"; and Mohamed, "A Survivor's Story."

8. http://projectsakinah.org/Project-Sakinah.

9. http://projectsakinah.org/Resources/Hear-Our-Stories/Anonymous-Survivor.

10. American Medical Association, "American Medical Association Diagnostic and Treatment Guidelines on Domestic Violence," https://www.nlm.nih.gov/exhibition/confronting violence/materials/OB11102.pdf, 42.

11. Quoted in Robert McAfee, *Unexpected News: Reading the Bible with Third World Eyes* (Louisville: Westminster John Knox, 1984), 19.

12. See, for example, Miranda Kennedy, "The Un-Mosquing of American Muslims," *The Atlantic*, October 18, 2015, https://www.theatlantic.com/politics/archive/2015/10/the-un-mos quing-of-american-muslims/411103/. The article makes an interesting connection between unmosquing, especially of women, and their status as divorcees.

13. Many DV organizations also have an escape button on their website, so that a victim searching for information and resources can leave the site quickly and not be discovered by her abuser. Such use of technology has become necessary because abusers effectively use technological means to stalk and control their victims. See Jamie Francisco, "Domestic Abuse Website Offers Escape Link," *Chicago Tribune*, August 7, 2006, http://articles.chicagotribune.com /2006-08-07/news/0608070085_1_domestic-abuse-domestic-violence-agencies-web-sites.

14. There is an extensive literature on this topic; see, for example, Adams, Boscarino, and Figley, "Compassion Fatigue and Psychological Distress"; and Conrad and Kellar-Guenther, "Compassion Fatigue, Burnout."

15. I have an academic colleague who worked on a study about domestic violence in Muslim communities and developed PTSD because of the continuous exposure to the trauma of victims and survivors.

16. As I was writing this chapter, I watched an AlJazeera Plus video on/with Suhaib Webb, who was described in the video as the Snapchat imam because he issued fatwas and connected with young Muslims via social media. Here is what he said about culture: "One of our major legal axioms is *al-urf al-muhkam*, which means 'culture is a decider.' And that really gave a lot of license for interpretation in the sense of how culture flows through the religion. Religion doesn't necessarily try to close a culture down. Islam doesn't care about how you do it, it cares

about the message, not necessarily the packaging." https://www.facebook.com/ajplusenglish
/videos/750147418460101/.

17. Abugideiri and Alwani, *What Islam Says*, 38.

18. The translation of Q 4:1 on the slide read: "O mankind! Reverence your Guardian-Lord,
Who created you from a single person, created, of like nature its mate, and from them both
scattered countless men and women. Fear Allah, through Whom you demand your mutual
rights, and (reverence) the wombs that bore you, for Allah ever watches over you."

19. On the next slide, Abugideiri quotes excerpts from the Qur'an again, Q 49:13, "We created you from a single (pair) of a male & a female ... that you may know each other ... the most
honored of you in the sight of Allah is the most righteous"; and Q 9:71, "The believers, men &
women, are protectors, one of another, they enjoin what is just & forbid what is evil."

20. Abugideiri and Alwani, *What Islam Says*, 27, emphasis in the original.

21. Q 4:19, "nor should you treat them with harshness ... on the contrary, live with them on
a footing of kindness and equity"; Q 2:187, "they are your garments and you are their garments";
and Q 42:38, "[The believers are those who] conduct their affairs by mutual consultation."

22. I discuss some scholarly interpretations of Q 4:34 in chapter 1 and have written about Q
4:34 elsewhere as well: see Hammer, "To Work for Change" and "Men Are the Protectors of
Women."

23. Abugideiri and Alwani, *What Islam Says*, 33–36.

24. Q 4:35, "If you fear a breach between them both, appoint two arbiters, one from his
family, and the other from hers; if they wish for peace, Allah will cause their reconciliation; for
Allah has full knowledge and is acquainted with all things."

25. Q 2:229, "the husbands should either retain their wives on equitable terms or let them
go with kindness"; Q 65:6, "Let the women live (in iddah) in the same style as you ... annoy
them not, so as to restrict them."

26. Hammer, "To Work for Change," 109.

27. Bonita McGee (MANADV, Muslim Advocacy Network against Domestic Violence),
2012. Among the resources listed were Wadud, *Inside the Gender Jihad* and *Qur'an and Woman*;
Ali, *Sexual Ethics and Islam*; Barlas, *"Believing Women in Islam"*; and Barazangi, *Women's Identity
and the Qur'an*.

28. Hammer, *American Muslim Women*.

Chapter 5. To Lead and to Know: Religious Leaders and Scholars in the Work against Domestic Violence

1. See these and other endorsement videos for Project Sakinah, recorded in 2011 when the
organization went public and requested the support of scholars, leaders, and activists: http://
projectsakinah.org/Resources/Videos/Activism-and-Endorsements.

2. Other videos on the same page show two members of the *nasheed* group Native Deen, an
organizer against DV and self-identified survivor, and the editor of a Muslim women's magazine endorsing the message that PS deserves support from Muslim communities.

3. See the discussion of the speeches of Mohamed Magid and Hamza Yusuf in chapter 3.

4. A good deal of academic literature focuses on community building among American
Muslims; see, for example, Ihsan Bagby, "The American Mosque 2001," Council on American-

Islamic Relations (CAIR), 2012, https://www.cair.com/images/pdf/The-American-Mosque -2011-part-1.pdf. See also Bukhari et al., *Muslims' Place in the American Public Square*; Kahera, *Deconstructing the American Mosque*; and a more recent and very important study of leadership and authority negotiations, Grewal, *Islam Is a Foreign Country*.

5. Unpublished study by Maryam Al-Zoubi; the summary is based on a conversation with the author.

6. See Levitt and Ware, " 'Anything with Two Heads Is a Monster.' " The authors cite several studies of Christian leaders in the United States as well as materials developed for pastoral care settings to support their argument. "The perspective of religious leaders is particularly important as they have been found to be among the first persons to whom women report marital abuse, but often they are not trained to address IPV or to intervene effectively when presented with IPV. Inappropriate responses to initial disclosures of abuse from leaders can encourage women to remain in abusive relationships despite serious risks to their physical and mental health" (1170–71); IPV is intimate partner violence.

7. As in the other chapters, the names of the imams are pseudonyms to protect confidentiality. This interview took place in the fall of 2012.

8. He made reference here to Q 4:1, "O mankind! Fear you Guardian Lord, Who created you from a single Person, created out of it, his mate, and from them twain (like seeds) countless men and women."

9. Q 30:21 without direct reference.

10. The issue of polygamy, in both its implications for Muslim women and its legal challenges in a context that does not allow it (i.e., the United States), is complicated. For a thorough discussion and deep ethnographic study, see Majeed, *Polygyny*. It is certainly the case that polygynous practices in U.S. Muslim communities have the potential to become abusive precisely because they are illegal and thus women have no recourse to legal protections, however flawed they may be for women and communities of color.

11. Imam Khaled is African American and Imam Salman is originally from Africa; both men were in their mid-fifties when I first met them.

12. Imam Amir, who is South Asian and in his fifties, spent the most time on the topic—he had been involved in DV work as a frontline provider and only reluctantly, he told me, referred women to mainstream shelters. He would have preferred not to do so if there had been more Muslim-run shelters and service providers in order to avoid these risks. I was struck by how convinced he was of his charge that living in a women's shelter without men put Muslim women at risk of becoming gay.

13. The Arabic word "Allah" starts with alif, the first letter of the Arabic alphabet, and Allah is the One and the first, always, he said.

14. Imam Khaled was even more specific when he explained that there is great conviction in African American communities that the American state is out to destroy Black families but that he does not believe that to be the case. From the extensive literature in this topic, see Beth Ritchie's powerful critique of the criminal justice system and its treatment of Black women, *Arrested Justice*; see also Brunson, "Police Don't Like Black People."

15. Imam Ismail is of Syrian background and has spent more than half of his fifty years in the United States. He served as both an imam and a prison chaplain.

16. See the important book by Molly Dragiewicz, *Equality with a Vengeance*.

17. See the debate about woman-led prayer I chronicle in *American Muslim Women*.

18. *Taqwa* means God-consciousness and is, in Muslim feminist theology, often singled out as the only attribute of human beings that distinguishes them from one another—rather than gendered attributes. See Wadud, *Inside the Gender Jihad*.

19. Abugideiri, "Hagar," 88.

20. Abugideiri, "Hagar," 89.

21. Kandiyoti wrote in 1988: "Women strategize within a set of concrete constraints, which I identify as patriarchal bargains. Different forms of patriarchy present women with distinct 'rules of the game' and call for different strategies to maximize security and optimize life options with varying potential for active or passive resistance in the face of oppression" ("Bargaining with Patriarchy," 274). In 1998, she revisited her original analysis and cautioned that models of power and hierarchy derived from economic and class analysis would not always be helpful in analyzing gender dynamics; Kandiyoti, "Gender, Power, and Contestation." Saba Mahmood would later, in 2006, further question the link that feminist theorists had created between agency and resistance. See Mahmood, *Politics of Piety*.

22. Traditional practices focus on memorizing the text (and/or sound) of the Qur'an with the correct recitation technique. The purpose is *not* to be able to analyze the text, interpret its meaning, or approach it thematically by bringing together certain passages for the purpose of reinterpretation. See Nelson, *The Art of Reciting the Qur'an*; Ware, *The Walking Qur'an*.

23. See chapter 2.

24. The training events culminated in a ceremonial signing of a declaration in which the imams committed themselves to working against domestic violence in their communities. The signatures were displayed at the organization's office together with a photograph of the imams in attendance. The protection of their identities is thus relative, but I avoid identifying information in my narrative, such as age or country of origin of the participating imams.

25. Facebook announcement for PFP/UMR Imam training, April 16/17, 2016, in Alexandria, VA. https://www.facebook.com/events/1683679355255223/.

26. This bears mentioning both within the context of who the religious leaders of Muslim communities are and what connections can be made between background (including native language), "Islamic training," and degrees of religious authenticity and authority. The reverse argument would be that foreign-born leaders are not as familiar with the circumstances and laws affecting their communities and do not have the same connections to the generations that were born in the United States. The link between "foreign" training and religious authority has been beautifully explored and discussed in Zareena Grewal, *Islam Is a Foreign Country*.

27. See chapter 1. Also, for example, Johnson, "Domestic Violence." Johnson confirms that the physical violence that is most often identified as domestic violence is indeed primarily perpetrated by men. He then criticizes other authors who argue to the contrary because of ideological intentions and/or failure to assess the statistical evidence correctly.

28. I have already noted that there is significant backlash against the VAWA model; see, for example, Cook, *Abused Men*. Dragiewicz explores this backlash in *Equality with a Vengeance*. Such patriarchal backlash sometimes embraces protective patriarchy but at other times is rather a longing for the time when men were without question in control of society.

29. There is an extensive literature on women who kill their abusers and how such taking of life has been and/or should be treated in the criminal justice system. See one debate between

Joshua Dressler and Joan Krause: Dressler, "Battered Women and Sleeping Abusers"; and Krause, "Distorted Reflections." See also the case of Marissa Alexander, who was sentenced to twenty years in prison for shooting at her abusive husband even though he was not even injured: http://justiceformarissa.blogspot.com/ and http://www.alternet.org/civil-liberties/21 -year-old-woman-faces-decades-prison-trying-escape-her-abuser.

Imam Salim interjected here that sometimes a woman would resort to this kind of violence because she felt trapped and because an imam she approached refused or failed to approve a divorce in cases of abuse. Karima added that what looks like neglect of the husband, including refusing sex and household chores, might be her only means of resistance.

30. This typology is partly based on Johnson, *A Typology of Domestic Violence*.

31. Yet again, there is a sizable literature on this topic; see, for example, Holt, Buckley, and Whelan, "The Impact of Exposure"; and Dube et al., "Exposure to Abuse."

32. While not developed further, there was an opening here for thinking more carefully about perpetrators, which was taken up in other contexts.

33. The name of the survivor is provided in the film, but at screenings the producers and trainers at PFP always encouraged confidentiality, so I do not disclose the name.

34. I admit to wondering whether it is not quite often the case that the wives of religious leaders provide counseling and services—which would make them invisible leaders in their own right. This pattern of women as de facto authorities in religious communities can be found elsewhere in American history and other religious communities; Evelyn Higginbotham, for example, in her *Righteous Discontent*, traces the many roles Black Baptist women played in providing social services as well as resistance to racism and how complex their struggles against patriarchal theology and for women's authority and leadership were.

35. See Buzawa and Buzawa, *Domestic Violence*. Radha Iyengar has argued that mandatory arrest laws increase the likelihood of intimate partner homicide: Iyengar, "Does the Certainty of Arrest Reduce Domestic Violence?" There was, in the 1990s, a debate about mandatory arrest policies, the criminalization of violent domestic abuse, and the uneasy relationship of feminist victim advocates to state power in the form of the police and the criminal justice system; see Ruttenberg, "A Feminist Critique." Scholars have debated both the effectiveness of domestic violence laws as punishment as well as deterrent and the ways in which women in marginalized communities are differently and disproportionately negatively affected by mandatory arrests. See Sokoloff and Dupont, "Domestic Violence at the Intersection"; and Wachholz and Miedema, "Risk, Fear, Harm."

36. She described passive suicide as not eating at all, waiting to die, putting herself in harm's way.

37. See a longer discussion of DV, divorce, Islamic law, and the American legal system in Hammer, "Men Are the Protectors of Women."

38. The basic rules for divorce in Islamic law appear in two chapters of the Qur'an: 2:228–42, 65:2–7. See Imam Salim's discussion of the rules in this section.

39. Zainab Alwani is a professor of Islamic studies at Howard University in Washington, DC, and the coauthor of *What Islam Says about Domestic Violence* (with Salma Abugideiri), http://www.zainabalwani.com/. She is, of course, not the only Muslim woman scholar who has written about DV, but I witnessed her presenting at several DV-related events and she enjoys mainstream credibility, which many pro-feminist Muslim scholars do not have. Ingrid

Mattson, former president of ISNA and professor of Islamic studies at Huron University College in Canada, is another woman scholar who, especially during her tenure as ISNA's leader, supported the organization's effort to raise awareness of domestic violence in Muslim communities; see http://ingridmattson.org/about/.

40. Kecia Ali has discussed the foundational link between the dowry offered to the bride/wife and the husband's right to sex in Islamic conceptions of marriage. See Ali, *Sexual Ethics and Islam* and *Marriage and Slavery in Early Islam*. Ali's discussion of sexual ethics and her demand for a rethinking of consent in marriage point to two important conversations for contemporary Muslims, one about marital rape (and the lack of consent) and the other related to domestic violence situations in which forced sex or forced sexual practices constitute specific forms of domestic and marital abuse. It was striking to me that sexual abuse rarely appeared in my research, mainly because Muslim advocates and service providers, as well as imams, were reluctant to broach the subject. On marital rape as an Islamic legal question, see the important book by Hina Azam, *Sexual Violation*.

41. This, too, is potentially complicated as marriage and divorce law is regulated on the level of each state, and such state laws vary widely in the United States. In order to advise couples and families on civil divorce, providers as well as imams would require at least some knowledge of marriage law in their state and others if they were approached for advice from out of state.

42. See also Grewal, *Islam Is a Foreign Country*.

Chapter 6. To Support and Defend: Providing Services to Muslim Victims and Survivors

1. Coy, Kelly, and Foord, "Roads to Nowhere?"

2. Coy, Kelly, and Foord, "Map of Gaps." See a brief discussion of its findings by Marianna Tortell, "Violence against Women in the UK: A Map of Gaps," *Open Democracy*, November 23, 2009, https://www.opendemocracy.net/5050/marianna-tortell/violence-against-women-in-uk-map-of-gaps.

3. Circuit court: http://www.montgomerycountymd.gov/circuitcourt/Court/FamilyDivision/Domestic_Violence/dv.html; sheriff's office: http://www.montgomerycountymd.gov/sheriff/sections/domvioinfo/domestic-violence-directory.html; Abused Persons Program: http://www.montgomerycountymd.gov/HHS.Program/Program.aspx?id=BHCS/BHCSAbusedPerson-p207.html; Family Justice Center: http://www.montgomerycountymd.gov/fjc/; Maryland Network against Domestic Violence: http://mnadv.org/.

4. See works, from the 1990s especially, such as Daniels, *Feminists Negotiate the State* and Fineman and Mykitiuk, *The Public Nature of Private Violence*, for discussions of feminist approaches to domestic violence including the important step to argue that while taking place in the domestic context, DV was not to be treated as private and thus outside the purview of state control. Elizabeth Pleck has traced efforts to address family violence to the very beginnings of U.S. history; see her *Domestic Tyranny*.

5. DV statistics are highly politicized and have been interpreted in a variety of ways. Government statistics tend to interpret data to demonstrate that legislation has had the desired effect. See, for example, this DOJ report on non-fatal DV data from 2003 to 2012, published in 2014: https://www.bjs.gov/content/pub/pdf/ndv0312.pdf. The report indicates falling rates of

non-fatal DV in accordance with a decrease in other violent crime but shows that DV accounts for 21 percent of all violent crime. It also confirms that the overwhelming majority of DV victims (76 percent) are women and that reporting rates are especially low for this type of crime.

6. Fineman, preface to *The Public Nature of Private Violence*, xii.

7. Caroline Bettinger-Lopez et al., *Domestic Violence in the United States*, 2011, https://www.reproductiverights.org/sites/crr.civicactions.net/files/newsletter/DV%20in%20the%20US_Br%20Paper%20to%20SR%20on%20VAW.pdf.

8. http://www.montgomerycountymd.gov/fjc/.

9. There may be many reasons a woman has for not leaving an abusive relationship. According to Peace from DV, a DV organization serving southwestern Pennsylvania, reasons may include:

- Religious or cultural beliefs
- Economic dependency
- Isolation from support systems
- Shame of everyone knowing
- Hesitation to involve other agencies (i.e., police)
- She has children
- Unaware of help available to her
- Blames herself, outsiders blame her
- Denies or minimizes the abuse
- Abuser makes promises to change
- Abuser is not always abusive
- Does not want to be alone
- LOVES her partner
- FEAR! Abuser may threaten her, her friends or family

Simply leaving does not stop the abuse. Statistics show that leaving often escalates the situation. Safety planning is vital at this point. Please see the safety planning page of our website for assistance (http://www.peacefromdv.org/why-does-she-stay/).

10. In some states, women can be penalized by the criminal justice system for exposing their children to abuse because they do not leave. I mentioned Kelly Savage in chapter 3. Similarly, a violent response to a violent domestic abuser might put the original victim in jail rather than the original abuser. The case of Marissa Alexander, which I mentioned in chapter 5, is a poignant reminder of this legal dynamic.

11. Rojas Durazo, "Medical Violence," 180.

12. Rojas Durazo, "Medical Violence," 181.

13. Smith et al., "The Color of Violence: Introduction," 1.

14. Koyama, "Disloyal to Feminism," 209.

15. Several chapters in *Color of Violence* directly address the exclusion of queer victims of abuse, prostitutes, poor women, and women with substance abuse issues and/or experiences of homelessness and chronic illness. Shelters in particular, as Koyama shows, are run on templates of efficiency and manageability rather than accountability and care—leading to multiple forms of re-victimization. Koyama, "Disloyal to Feminism."

16. Another important volume is the 2005 collection edited by Natalie Sokoloff, *Domestic Violence at the Margins*.

17. Nguyen, "Overview: Asian American Communities and Domestic Violence," in *Domestic Violence in Asian American Communities*, 1–12.

18. See http://www.api-gbv.org/.

19. http://www.api-gbv.org/about.php/#ourHistory.

20. http://www.sakhi.org/, "Uniting Survivors, Communities and Institutions to Eradicate Domestic Violence & Form Healthy Communities."

21. http://www.womenagainstabuse.org/education-resources/learn-about-abuse/domestic-violence-in-philadelphia.

22. http://www.apnaghar.org/, "Apna Ghar provides holistic services and conducts outreach and advocacy across immigrant communities to end gender violence."

23. http://maitri.org/, "Helping women help themselves."

24. http://www.api-gbv.org/resources/programs-serving-apis.php.

25. http://arabamericanfamilyservices.org/, "Enhancing and Empowering the Lives of the Arab-American Community."

26. http://www.aafscny.org/.

27. https://faithus.org/about-us/who-we-are/.

28. www.karamah.org.

29. See Ahmed, *Women and Gender in Islam*. One interesting organization in this regard is Musawah, an international Muslim women's organization that advocates for "equality and justice in the Muslim family" by supporting grassroots movements for legal change. Musawah embraced explicitly feminist frameworks and listed its activities as based on four pillars: Islam, human rights, constitutional rights (in each country), and lived experience. See www.musawah.org; Mir-Hosseini, Al-Sharmani, and Rumminger, *Men in Charge?*; and Musawah, *Women's Stories, Women's Lives*.

30. http://www.asknisa.org/index.html.

31. Abraham, *Speaking the Unspeakable*, 174–96.

32. http://tmwf.org/family-violence/.

33. http://icnarelief.org/site2/index.php/programsummary/womenshelter.

34. Super User, "Reflections on the life of Maryam Funches," *Muslim Link*, January 26, 2007, http://www.muslimlinkpaper.com/index.php/editors-desk/4-community-news/764-Reflections%20on%20the%20Life%20of%20Maryam%20Funches.html.

35. Salma Hasan Ali, "Asma, Please Help Me," *Islamic Monthly*, October 25, 2015, http://theislamicmonthly.com/asma-please-help-me/; Lorena Ruiz, "Meet Asma Hanif, Nurse to Muslim Women in Need," March 30, 2013, in which Hanif was recognized by Melissa Harris-Perry as a "Foot Soldier," http://www.msnbc.com/melissa-harris-perry/meet-asma-hanif-nurse-muslim-women-nee. Hanif has appeared in a variety of media, both local and national: Jamie Tarabay, "Muslim Women's Shelter Provides Refuge, Support," NPR, January 1, 2010, http://www.npr.org/templates/story/story.php?storyId=120752667; Abu Ibrahim, "Positively Muslim in the West: Sister Asma Hanif," *Muslim Matters*, September 7, 2012, http://muslimmatters.org/2012/09/07/positively-muslim-in-the-west-sister-asma-hanif/; Bilal Mahmoud, "Dua for Sister Asma Hanif," *Oppressed Peoples Online*, January 19, 2017, http://oppressedpeoplesonlineword.ning.com/profiles/blogs/dua-for-sister-asma-hanif; Engy Abdelkader, "Religious Profiles: Another Amazing American Muslim Woman," *Huffington Post*, February 2, 2015, http://www.huffingtonpost.com/engy-abdelkader/religious-profiles-anothe_b_6572260.html.

36. Robert Samuels, "Asma Hanif, Founder of Muslim Women's Shelter, Finds Herself in Need of Care," *Washington Post*, April 19, 2013, https://www.washingtonpost.com/local/asma-hanif-founder-of-muslim-womens-shelter-finds-herself-in-need-of-care/2013/04/19/63973ace-a086-11e2-be47-b44febada3a8_story.html.

37. https://www.facebook.com/imamzaidshakir/?hc_ref=PAGES_TIMELINE&fref=nf.

38. I have only found one complaint about Muslimat al-Nisaa online, in the form of a review of the organization as a nonprofit, posted on April 17, 2015: "This woman, Asma Hanif collects thousands of dollars from donors and mosques nationwide. Herself and her children are well supported, however, the women 'she serves' are treated like animals. But only the ones that she can benefit from, whether monetarily or service wise. The house contains expired hygiene products and food is provided on sporadic basis. The women must buy any meat other than lamb donated almost a decade prior. The board consists of all family members and Ms Hanif calls the shelter 'her house.' She illegally collects money from the women while terrifying them through her volunteers. Some of those volunteers are used to communicate threats so that Ms Hanif can run from direct involvement. Her volunteers refuse to stand up for the rights of women. Lamb and rice is not sufficient meals for children. She refuses to purchase the women new underwear, hygiene products, transportation passes, medication, lawyer fees. I ask you … where is this money going? Paying rent and utilities for 'her house' is not appropriate dispersement of tax exempt funds. I request that the proper authorities do an audit and gain insight into this tax shelter and free ride for the Hanifs to dissuade future organizations from doing the same. Children should not be abused when they are trying to stabilize their life, women should not fear someone who designated herself as a trailblazer for the homeless and hungry, while contributing to this very population. I appeal to the public to direct your charity of financial means, time, and good intentions to an organization that meets the image they project and do not hide and lie to the public." https://greatnonprofits.org/org/muslimat-al-nisaa.

39. Koyama, "Disloyal to Feminism," 209–10. Other studies of DV shelters tend to tell similar stories and point to similar issues. See, for example, Plesset, *Sheltering Women*; and Mann, "Emotionality and Social Activism."

40. In 2014, Majeed wrote on the website of Baitul Salaam: "It is now almost 18 years later and the road for us as a domestic violence awareness organization has been peppered with temporary setbacks (closing of the shelter project twice), minimal to almost no support from those we thought would be on the front lines with us (many of our sisters especially our professional sisters), and subtle to overt backlash. We have learned from it all to stand firm in our belief in Allah and to trust Allah for all of our personal and organizational needs. We also have gained the respect and true loyalty of a committed and very diverse local and national support base. With the help of Allah we have made it to a benchmark in our history as an organization. We are at the place we oft times thought we would not make. With humility and pride we can look back at assisting just over 1,500 women and children through the shelter program (closed in 2008). We can look back at answering over 10,000 (conservative estimate) telephone calls yearly." http://www.baitulsalaam.org/?page_id=16.

41. http://www.mccclinic.org/.

42. Profitt, *Women Survivors*, 20.

43. See http://www.cphins.com/nurses-and-mandatory-reporting-laws/.

44. This refers to a particular interpretation of Q 4:34 that a husband should only hit his wife with a handkerchief or toothpick and not cause her any injury.

45. CNN Heroes, "Her 'Duty' Is to Help Muslim Women Heal after Abuse," CNN, September 25, 2009, http://www.cnn.com/2009/LIVING/09/24/cnnheroes.robina.niaz/index.html?iref=nextin.

Chapter 7. Above and Beyond: Muslims in Interfaith and Mainstream DV Work (and the State)

1. Buzawa, Buzawa, and Stark, *Responding to Domestic Violence*, 80.

2. Buzawa, Buzawa, and Stark, *Responding to Domestic Violence*, 53.

3. IFCADV, "A Fond Farewell," March 2011.

4. IFCADV information brochure.

5. http://www.faithtrustinstitute.org/about-us/guiding-principles.

6. http://www.faithtrustinstitute.org/about-us/history.

7. http://www.faithtrustinstitute.org/about-us/history.

8. http://www.faithtrustinstitute.org/about-us/history.

9. Gil Anidjar has argued that secularism is Christianity: "And Christianity turned against itself in a complex and ambivalent series of parallel movements, continuous gestures and rituals, reformist and counterreformist, or revolutionary and not so revolutionary upheavals and reversals while slowly coming to name that to which it ultimately claimed to oppose itself: religion. Munchausen-like, it attempted to liberate itself, to extricate itself from its own conditions; it *judged* itself no longer Christian, no longer religious. Christianity (that is, to clarify this one last time, Western Christendom) judged and named itself, it *reincarnated* itself as secular." Anidjar, "Secularism," 60. Robert Wuthnow, like many other scholars and policymakers, has focused on Christian organizations and structures in his discussion of "faith-based organizations." See Wuthnow, *Saving America?*

10. http://www.faithtrustinstitute.org/about-us/history.

11. See the FaithTrust Institute store where interested parties can buy DVDs, books, and brochures in several languages. The store allows the user to search by issue, for example, domestic violence, sexual violence, child abuse, etc., and also by religious tradition. Some materials are general enough to use in different communities, although it is here that Christian terminology such as "clergy" for religious leaders betrays the origins and Christian assumptions of the organization. http://similarwww.faithtrustinstitute.org/store. There are two films, notable as precursors to *Garments*, namely, *Broken Vows: Religious Perspectives on Domestic Violence* (1994) and *To Save a Life: Ending Domestic Violence in Jewish Families* (2009).

12. There are, of course, far more feminist religious engagements with questions of domestic and sexual abuse and power dynamics as well as marriage and gender roles than can be fully attended to here. Such feminist works and approaches, very much like in Muslim contexts, are not sufficiently utilized in religious advocacy work against DV, for reasons that I suspect are similar as well: fear of being seen as radical and marginal, rejection of religious feminisms, or a commitment to some version of religiously framed protective patriarchy. See, for example, Sharma and Young, *Feminism and World Religions*; and Gross, *Feminism & Religion*. A volume

more specifically focused on violence against women is Maguire and Shaikh, *Violence against Women in Contemporary World Religions*.

13. Back cover of Twerski, *The Shame Borne in Silence*.

14. Now housed at Taylor & Francis Online, the journal was initially produced by Haworth Press, a publisher itself founded in 1978 and acquired by Taylor & Francis/Routledge in 2007, only a year before the journal ceased production.

15. Alkhateeb, "Ending Domestic Violence in Muslim Families."

16. Fortune and Marshall, *Forgiveness and Abuse*.

17. Fortune, "From the Editor's Desk."

18. Fortune, "From the Editor's Keyboard: A Farewell."

19. Both Amina Wadud and Aysha Hidayatullah have reflected on this dynamic within religious feminist circles. See Wadud, *Inside the Gender Jihad*, 55–86; Hidayatullah, "Inspiration and Struggle"; and Hidayatullah, "Muslim Feminist Birthdays."

20. This was a two-part workshop titled "Lethality Assessment for Faith Leaders." The first part was led by an elder in the United Methodist Church and the second by a rabbi.

21. Wadud's book *Inside the Gender Jihad* immediately comes to mind.

22. For a discussion of the longer history of this exclusion, through racist frameworks and rejection of the religious other, see GhaneaBassiri, "Islamophobia and American History"; see also my discussion of Edward Curtis and Sylvester Johnson later in the chapter.

23. Buzawa, Buzawa, and Stark, *Responding to Domestic Violence*.

24. Buzawa, Buzawa, and Stark, *Responding to Domestic Violence*, especially chap. 3.

25. FaithTrust Institute, *To Save a Life*.

26. Finigan, "Intimate Violence, Foreign Solutions," 142.

27. See Buel, "Fifty Obstacles to Leaving"; and Gordon, Burton, and Porter, "Predicting the Intentions of Women."

28. The conference as a whole contained very few presentations that related to the role of religion in social work, and Rabia's contribution was the only one that addressed Muslims specifically.

29. See the discussion in chapter 6. This list was linked on the websites of many Muslim DV organizations and in numerous information brochures. The organization no longer maintains that list but it can still be found here, even though dated to 2009: https://www.peacefulfamilies .org/uploads/1/1/0/5/110506531/apiidvdirectory.pdf.

30. http://www.api-gbv.org/violence/culture.php. These short paragraphs are only a glimpse of the resources posted at this link, which discuss issues of defining culture much more deeply.

31. Cainkar, *Assessing the Need, Addressing the Problem*; Cainkar and del Toro, *An Investigation*.

32. cooke, "Multiple Critique"; Terman, "Islamophobia, Feminism, and the Politics of Critique."

33. Shaikh, "A *Tafsir* of Praxis," 85–86.

34. This approach to Q 4:34 as an ethical test from God is developed further by Laury Silvers in her "'In the Book We Have Left Nothing Out'": "Because of the comprehensive nature of the Trust, we bear the burden of full responsibility for our choices. We consider the weight of this burden carefully. Muhammad is reported to have said about the Last Day: 'If you knew

what I knew you would laugh less and cry more.' I read this to mean that we would be terrified if we knew the extraordinary extent of our responsibility in being human" (178).

35. Faizi, "Domestic Violence," 211.

36. Faizi, "Domestic Violence," 230.

37. See many resources from this literature listed in this public syllabus titled "Islamo-phobia Is Racism," which can be found here: https://islamophobiaisracism.wordpress.com/. I participated in the creation of this syllabus, together with Su'ad Abdul Khabeer, Arshad Ali, Evelyn Alsultany, Sohail Daulatzai, Lara Deeb, Carol Fadda, Zareena Grewal, Nadine Naber, and Junaid Rana.

38. Hammer, "Gendering Islamophobia"; Hammer, "Center Stage"; and most recently, Hammer, "Muslim Women, Anti-Muslim Hostility."

39. Johnson, *African American Religions*, especially 377–400; Curtis, "The Black Muslim Scare."

40. Curtis, "The Black Muslim Scare," 75.

41. Curtis, "The Black Muslim Scare," 99.

42. See, for example, Abu Lughod, *Do Muslim Women Need Saving?*

43. See Mahmood and Hirschkind, "Feminism, the Taliban, and Politics of Counter-Insurgency"; and Mahmood, "Feminism, Democracy, and Empire."

44. See the discussion in chapter 5.

45. Rudrappa, "Radical Caring"; Supriya, "Evocation of and Enactment in *Apna Ghar*"; Abraham, *Speaking the Unspeakable*, 188–91.

Chapter 8. Looking Back and the Road Ahead: Gender-Based Violence, Activism, and Critique

1. http://taleefcollective.org/.

2. See Bill Donahue, "An Unlikely Messenger Becomes a Guiding Spirit to Young Muslims," *Washington Post*, January 19, 2017, https://www.washingtonpost.com/lifestyle/magazine/an-unlikely-messenger-becomes-a-guiding-spirit-to-young-muslims/2017/01/18/.

3. See the important work of Kecia Ali and Scott Kugle on same-sex intimacy and consent-based sexual ethics for Muslims. Ali, *Sexual Ethics and Islam*; Kugle, *Homosexuality in Islam*; Kugle, *Living Out Islam*.

4. See http://www.hhri.org/thematic/gender_based_violence.html for some history.

5. See the description of the program here: https://www.dhs.gov/countering-violent-extremism. CVE offered grants to researchers and community organizations and focused rather clearly on Muslim communities. This paragraph is instructive: "Here in the United States, acts perpetrated by violent extremists can have far-reaching consequences. Countering violent extremism (CVE) has therefore become a key focus of DHS's work to secure the homeland. CVE aims to address the root causes of violent extremism by providing resources to communities to build and sustain local prevention efforts and promote the use of counter-narratives to confront violent extremist messaging online. Building relationships based on trust with communities is essential to this effort."

6. Aziz, "Losing the 'War of Ideas,' " 257.

7. In the early days of the Trump presidency, in 2017, the CVE program suspended its disbursement of grant money and there were discussions about revamping and renaming it "Countering Islamic Extremism."

8. Shaikh, *Sufi Narratives of Intimacy*, 21–22.

9. Ritchie, *Arrested Justice*, 65.

10. Ritchie, *Arrested Justice*, 67.

11. See Ritchie, *Arrested Justice*, 114.

12. Esack, *Qur'an, Liberation and Pluralism*, 104.

13. Wadud, *Inside the Gender Jihad*, 10.

14. Jackson, *Islam and the Problem of Black Suffering*, 4.

15. Ali, *Sexual Ethics and Islam*, 187–88.

Appendix. Understanding Domestic Violence

1. US Code, Title 42, Chapter 136, Subchapter III, Section 13925(a)(6); see also https://www.gpo.gov/fdsys/pkg/BILLS-109hr3402enr/pdf/BILLS-109hr3402enr.pdf.

2. https://www.cdc.gov/violenceprevention/intimatepartnerviolence/definitions.html.

3. From a training manual for DV service providers, written by Anne Ganley, a psychologist in Seattle. The manual is widely used and posted on the websites of many organizations, such as the Alaska Network on Domestic Violence and Sexual Assault: www.andvsa.org/wp-content/uploads/2009/12/60-ganely-general-dv-article.pdf.

4. See the "About" section of DAIP here, https://www.theduluthmodel.org/about-us/. A Muslim power and control wheel was developed by Sharifa Alkhateeb and can be found here: https://www.familyjusticecenter.org/wp-content/uploads/2017/10/Muslim-Power-_-Control-Wheel-Sharifa-Alkhateeb.pdf. An LGBTQ-specific wheel can be found here: http://tcfv.org/pdf/Updated_wheels/LGBT.pdf; and one focusing on DV in the military can be found here: https://www.familyjusticecenter.org/resources/military-power-control-wheel/.

5. https://www.theduluthmodel.org/wp-content/uploads/2017/03/PowerandControl.pdf.

6. Adapted from a website, described as a public service at the bottom of the main page, by Creative Communications Group; see http://domesticviolence.org/cycle-of-violence/.

BIBLIOGRAPHY

Abou-Bakr, Omaima. "The Interpretive Legacy of Qiwamah as an Exegetical Construct." In *Men in Charge? Rethinking Authority in the Muslim Legal Tradition*, ed. Ziba Mir-Hosseini, Mulki Al-Sharmani, and Jana Rumminger, 44–64. Oxford: Oneworld, 2015.

Abraham, Margaret. "Sexual Abuse in South Asian Immigrant Marriages." *Violence Against Women* 5:6 (1999): 591–618.

———. "Isolation as a Form of Marital Violence: The South Asian Immigrant Experience." *Journal of Social Distress and the Homeless* 9:3 (2000): 221–36.

———. *Speaking the Unspeakable: Marital Violence among South Asian Immigrants in the United States.* New Brunswick: Rutgers University Press, 2000.

Abu Lughod, Lila. "Do Muslim Women Really Need Saving?" *American Anthropologist* 104:3 (September 2002): 783–90.

———. *Do Muslim Women Need Saving?* Cambridge, MA: Harvard University Press, 2015.

Abu Lughod, Lila, and Maya Mikdashi. "Tradition and the Anti-Politics Machine: DAM Seduced by the 'Honor Crime.'" *Jadaliyya*, November 23, 2012. http://jadaliyya2.koeinbeta .com/Details/27467/Tradition-and-the-Anti-Politics-Machine-DAM-Seduced-by-the -%E2%80%9CHonor-Crime%E2%80%9D.

———. "Honoring Solidarity during Contentious Debates." *Jadaliyya*, December 26, 2012. http://jadaliyya2.koeinbeta.com/Details/27700/Honoring-Solidarity-During-Conten tious-Debates-A-Letter-to-DAM-From-Lila-Abu-Lughod-and-Maya-Mikdashi.

Abugideiri, Hibba. "Hagar: A Historical Model for Gender Jihad." In *Daughters of Abraham: Feminist Thought in Judaism, Christianity, and Islam*, ed. Y. Haddad and J. Esposito, 81–107. Gainesville: University of Florida Press, 2001.

———. "A Tribute to Sharifa Alkhateeb: Carrying the Mantle." *Hawwa* 3:1 (2005): 1–8.

Abugideiri, Salma. *Garments for One Another: Ending Domestic Violence in Muslim Families, Study Guide for Facilitators.* Seattle: FaithTrust Institute, 2007.

———. "Domestic Violence: Muslim Communities: United States of America." In *Encyclopedia of Women & Islamic Cultures*, ed. Suad Joseph. Brill Online, 2010. https://referenceworks .brillonline.com/entries/encyclopedia-of-women-and-islamic-cultures/domestic-vio lence-muslim-communities-united-states-of-america-EWICCOM_0690.

———. "Domestic Violence." In *Counseling Muslims: Handbook of Mental Health Issues and Interventions*, ed. Sameera Ahmed and Mona Amer, 309–28. New York: Routledge, 2012.

Abugideiri, Salma, and Zainab Alwani. *What Islam Says about Domestic Violence: A Guide for Helping Muslim Families*, 2nd ed. Herndon, VA: FAITH, 2003.

Abu-Odeh, Lama. "Honor Killings and the Construction of Gender in Arab Societies." *American Journal of Comparative Law* 58:4 (2010): 911–52.

Abu-Ras, Wahiba. "Cultural Beliefs and Service Utilization by Battered Arab Immigrant Women." *Violence Against Women* 13:10 (2007): 1002–28.

Abu-Ras, Wahiba, Ali Gheith, and Francine Cournos. "The Imam's Role in Mental Health Promotion: A Study of 22 Mosques in New York City's Muslim Community." *Journal of Muslim Mental Health* 3:2 (September 2008): 155–76.

Adam, Najma, and Paul Schewe. "A Multilevel Framework Exploring Domestic Violence against Immigrant Indian and Pakistani Women in the United States." *Journal of Muslim Mental Health* 2:2 (2007): 5–20.

Adams, Richard, Joseph Boscarino, and Charles Figley. "Compassion Fatigue and Psychological Distress among Social Workers: A Validation Study." *American Journal of Orthopsychiatry* 76:1 (2006): 103–8.

Ahmed, Leila. *Women and Gender in Islam: Historical Roots of a Modern Debate*. New Haven: Yale University Press, 1992.

Ahmed, Sameera, and Mona Amer, eds. *Counseling Muslims: Handbook of Mental Health Issues and Interventions*. New York: Routledge, 2012.

Albarus, Carmeta. *The Making of Lee Boyd Malvo: The D.C. Sniper*. New York: Columbia University Press, 2012.

Ali, Ayaan Hirsi. *The Caged Virgin*. New York: Atria Books, 2008.

———. *Heretic: Why Islam Needs a Reformation Now*. San Francisco: Harper, 2016.

Ali, Kecia. " 'The Best of You Will Not Strike': Al-Shafi'i on Qur'an, Sunnah, and Wife-Beating." *Comparative Islamic Studies* 2:2 (2006): 143–55.

———. "Timeless Texts and Modern Morals: Challenges in Islamic Sexual Ethics." In *New Directions in Islamic Thought*, ed. Kari Vogt, Lena Larsen, and Christian Moe, 89–100. London: I. B. Tauris, 2009.

———. *Marriage and Slavery in Early Islam*. Cambridge, MA: Harvard University Press, 2013.

———. *Sexual Ethics and Islam: Feminist Reflections on Qur'an, Hadith, and Jurisprudence*. 2nd rev. ed. Oxford: Oneworld, 2016.

Ali, Wajahat, Eli Clifton, Matthew Duss, Lee Fang, Scott Keyes, and Faiz Shakir. "Fear Inc.: The Roots of the Islamophobia Network in America." 2011. https://www.americanprogress .org/issues/religion/reports/2011/08/26/10165/fear-inc/.

Alkhateeb, Maha, and Salma Abugideiri, eds. *Change from Within: Diverse Perspectives on Domestic Violence in Muslim Communities*. Herndon, VA: Peaceful Families Project, 2007.

Alkhateeb, Sharifa. "Ending Domestic Violence in Muslim Families." *Journal of Religion and Abuse* 44:1 (1999): 49–59.

Almeida, Rhea, and Ken Dolan-Delvecchio. "Addressing Culture in Batterers Intervention: The Asian Indian Community as an Illustrative Example." *Violence Against Women* 5:6 (1999): 654–83.

Ammar, Nawal. "Wife Battery in Islam: A Comprehensive Understanding of Interpretations." *Violence Against Women* 13:5 (2007): 516–26.

Anidjar, Gil. "Secularism." *Critical Inquiry* 33:1 (2006): 52–77.

Anitha, Sundari. "Legislating Gender Inequalities: The Nature and Patterns of Domestic Violence Experienced by South Asian Women with Insecure Immigration Status in the United Kingdom." *Violence Against Women* 17:10 (2011): 1260–85.

Araji, Sharon, and John Carlson. "Family Violence Including Crimes of Honor in Jordan." *Violence Against Women* 7:5 (2001): 586–621.

Assaf, Shireen, and Stephanie Chaban. "Domestic Violence against Single, Never-Married Women in the Occupied Palestinian Territory." *Violence Against Women* 19:3 (2013): 422–41.

Aydin, Cemil. *The Idea of the Muslim World: A Global Intellectual History*. Cambridge, MA: Harvard University Press, 2017.

Ayyub, R. "Domestic Violence in the South Asian Muslim Immigrant Population in the United States." *Journal of Social Distress and the Homeless* 9:3 (2000): 237–48.

Azam, Hina. *Sexual Violation in Islamic Law: Substance, Evidence, and Procedure*. New York: Cambridge University Press, 2015.

Aziz, Sahar. "Losing the 'War of Ideas': A Critique of Countering Violent Extremism Programs." *Texas International Law Journal* 52:2 (2017): 256–80.

Baker, Nancy, Peter Gregware, and Margery Cassidy. "Family Killing Fields: Honor Rationales in the Murder of Women." *Violence Against Women* 5:2 (1999): 164–84.

Barazangi, Nimat. *Women's Identity and the Qur'an*. Gainesville: University Press of Florida, 2004.

Barlas, Asma. *"Believing Women in Islam": Unreading Patriarchal Interpretation of the Qur'an*. Austin: University of Texas Press, 2002.

Bauer, Karen. " 'Traditional' Exegeses of Qur'an 4:34." *Comparative Islamic Studies* 2:2 (2006): 129–42.

Bent-Goodley, Tricia, and Dawnovise Fowler. "Spiritual and Religious Abuse: Expanding What Is Known about Domestic Violence." *Affilia* 21:3 (2006): 282–95.

Boba, Rachel, and David Lilley. "Violence Against Women Act (VAWA) Funding: A Nationwide Assessment of Its Effects on Rape and Assault." *Violence Against Women* 15 (2009): 168–85.

Boy, Angie, and Andrzej Kulczycki. "What We Know about Intimate Partner Violence in the Middle East and North Africa." *Violence Against Women* 14:1 (2008): 53–70.

Brunson, Rod. " 'Police Don't Like Black People': African-American Young Men's Accumulated Police Experiences." *Criminology & Public Policy* 6:1 (2007): 71–101.

Buel, Sarah. "Fifty Obstacles to Leaving, a.k.a. Why Abuse Victims Stay." *Colorado Lawyer* 28:10 (1999): 19–28.

Bukhari, Zahid, Sulayman Nyang, Mumtaz Ahmad, and John Esposito, eds. *Muslims' Place in the American Public Square*. Walnut Creek, CA: Altamira Press, 2004.

Bumiller, Kristin. "The Nexus of Domestic Violence Reform and Social Science: From Instrument of Social Change to Institutionalized Surveillance." *Annual Review of Law and Social Science* 6 (2010): 173–93.

Buzawa, Eve, and Carl Buzawa. *Domestic Violence: The Criminal Justice Response*. 3rd ed. Thousand Oaks, CA: Sage, 2003.

Buzawa, Eve, Carl Buzawa, and Evan Stark. *Responding to Domestic Violence: The Integration of Criminal Justice and Human Services*. Los Angeles: Sage, 2012.

Cainkar, Louise. "Assessing the Need, Addressing the Problem: Working with Disadvantaged Muslim Immigrant Families and Communities." Anne E. Casey Foundation, 2003. In author's possession.

Cainkar, Louise, and Sandra del Toro. "An Investigation into the Social Context of Domestic Violence in the Arab/Muslim American Community: Identifying Best Practices for

Successful Prevention and Intervention." Arab American Action Network, 2010. In author's possession.

Cannon, Angie. 23 *Days of Terror: The Compelling Story of the Hunt and Capture of the Beltway Snipers.* New York: Pocket Books, 2003.

Censer, Jack. *On the Trail of the DC Sniper: Fear and the Media.* Charlottesville: University of Virginia Press, 2010.

Chaudhry, Ayesha. "The Problems of Conscience and Hermeneutics: A Few Contemporary Approaches." *Comparative Islamic Studies* 2:2 (2006): 157–70.

———. " 'I Wanted One Thing and God Wanted Another ...': The Dilemma of the Prophetic Example and the Qur'anic Injunction on Wife-Beating." *Journal of Religious Ethics* 39:3 (2011): 416–39.

———. *Domestic Violence and the Islamic Tradition.* New York: Oxford University Press, 2014.

Conrad, David, and Yvonne Kellar-Guenther. "Compassion Fatigue, Burnout, and Compassion Satisfaction among Colorado Child Protection Workers." *Child Abuse & Neglect* 30:10 (2006): 1071–80.

Cook, Phillip. *Abused Men: The Hidden Side of Domestic Violence.* New York: Praeger, 2004.

Cook-Masaud, Carema, and Marsha Wiggins. "Counseling Muslim Women: Navigating Cultural and Religious Challenges." *Counseling and Values* 55 (2011): 247–56.

cooke, miriam. "Multiple Critique: Islamic Feminist Rhetorical Strategies." *Nepantla: Views from the South* 1:1 (2000): 91–110.

Coy, Maddy, Liz Kelly, and Joanne Foord. "Map of Gaps: The Postcode Lottery of Violence against Women Support Services in the UK." London: End Violence Against Women Coalition, 2007, 2009.

Coy, Maddy, Liz Kelly, Joanne Foord, and Janet Bowstead. "Roads to Nowhere? Mapping Violence against Women Services." *Violence Against Women* 17:3 (2011): 404–25.

Crenshaw, Kimberlé. "Mapping the Margins: Intersectionality, Identity Politics, and Violence against Women of Color." *Stanford Law Review* 43 (1993): 1242–99.

Critelli, Filomena. "Voices of Resistance: Seeking Shelter Services in Pakistan." *Violence Against Women* 18:4 (2012): 437–58.

Curtis, Edward. "The Black Muslim Scare of the Twentieth Century: The History of State Islamophobia and Its Post-9/11 Variations." In *Islamophobia in America: The Anatomy of Intolerance,* ed. Carl Ernst, 75–106. New York: Palgrave, 2013.

Daniels, Cynthia, ed. *Feminists Negotiate the State: The Politics of Domestic Violence.* Lanham, MD: University Press of America, 1997.

Dasgupta, Shamita Das. "A Framework for Understanding Women's Use of Nonlethal Violence in Intimate Heterosexual Relationships." *Violence Against Women* 8:11 (2002): 1364–89.

———, ed. *Body Evidence: Intimate Violence against South Asian Women in America.* New Brunswick: Rutgers University Press, 2007.

Dragiewicz, Molly. "Patriarchy Reasserted: Fathers' Rights and Anti-VAWA Activism." *Feminist Criminology* 8:2 (2008): 121–44.

———. *Equality with a Vengeance: Men's Rights Groups, Battered Women, and Antifeminist Backlash.* Boston: Northeastern University Press, 2011.

Dressler, Joshua. "Battered Women and Sleeping Abusers." *Ohio State Journal of Criminal Law* 3 (2006): 457–85.

Dube, Shanta, et al. "Exposure to Abuse, Neglect, and Household Dysfunction among Adults Who Witnessed Intimate Partner Violence as Children: Implications for Health and Social Services." *Violence & Victims* 17:1 (2002): 3–17.

Duss, Matthew, Yasmine Taeb, Ken Gude, and Ken Sofer. "Fear Inc. 2.0: The Islamophobia Network's Efforts to Manufacture Hate in America." February 2015. https://cdn.american progress.org/wp-content/uploads/2015/02/FearInc-report2.11.pdf.

Ellison, Christopher, and Kristin Anderson. "Religious Involvement and Domestic Violence among U.S. Couples." *Journal for the Scientific Study of Religion* 40:2 (June 2001): 269–86.

Elsaidi, Murad. "Human Rights and Islamic Law: A Legal Analysis Challenging the Husband's Authority to Punish 'Rebellious Wives.'" *Muslim World Journal of Human Rights* 7:2 (2011): 1–25.

Enger, Cindy, and Diane Gardsbane, eds. *Domestic Abuse and the Jewish Community: Perspectives from the First International Conference.* New York: Haworth, 2004.

Ernst, Carl, ed. *Islamophobia in America: The Anatomy of Intolerance.* New York: Palgrave, 2013.

Esack, Farid. *Qur'an, Liberation and Pluralism: An Islamic Perspective of Interreligious Solidarity against Oppression.* Oxford: Oneworld, 1996.

———. "Islam and Gender Justice: Beyond Simplistic Apologia." In *What Men Owe to Women: Men's Voices from World Religions,* ed. John Raines and Daniel Maguire, 187–210. Albany: SUNY Press, 2001.

FaithTrust Institute. *Broken Vows: Religious Perspectives on Domestic Violence.* DVD. Seattle: FaithTrust Institute, 1994.

———. *Garments for One Another: Ending Domestic Violence in Muslim Families.* DVD. Seattle: FaithTrust Institute, 2007.

———. *To Save a Life: Ending Domestic Violence in Jewish Families.* DVD and brochure. Seattle: FaithTrust Institute, 2009.

Faizi, Noora. "Domestic Violence in the Muslim Community." *Texas Journal of Women and the Law* 10:2 (2001): 209–33.

Fikree, Fariyal, Junaid Razzak, and Jill Durocher. "Attitudes of Pakistani Men to Domestic Violence: A Study from Karachi, Pakistan." *Journal of Men's Health & Gender* 2:1 (2005): 49–58.

Fineman, Martha Albertson, and Roxanne Mykitiuk, eds. *The Public Nature of Private Violence: The Discovery of Domestic Abuse.* New York: Routledge, 1994.

Finigan, Maura. "Intimate Violence, Foreign Solutions: Domestic Violence Policy and Muslim-American Women." *Duke Forum for Law & Social Change* 2:141 (2010): 141–53.

Fortune, Marie. *Keeping the Faith: Guidance for Christian Women Facing Abuse.* New York: HarperCollins, 1987.

———. "From the Editor's Desk." *Journal of Religion and Abuse* 1:1 (1999): 1–6.

———. "From the Editor's Keyboard: A Farewell." *Journal of Religion and Abuse* 8:4 (2008): 1–6.

Fortune, Marie, and Joretta Marshall, eds. *Forgiveness and Abuse: Jewish and Christian Reflections.* New York: Haworth Press, 2002.

Foucault, Michel. *Power/Knowledge: Selected Interviews and Other Writings, 1972–77.* Ed. Colin Gordon. London: Pantheon Books, 1980.

Fowler, Dawnovise, Monica Faulkner, Joy Learman, and Ratonia Runnels. "The Influence of Spirituality on Service Utilization and Satisfaction for Women Residing in Domestic Violence Shelters." *Violence Against Women* 17:10 (2011): 1244–59.

GhaneaBassiri, Kambiz. "Islamophobia and American History: Religious Stereotyping and Out-Grouping of Muslims in the United States." In *Islamophobia in America*, ed. Carl Ernst, 53–74. New York: Palgrave, 2013.

Gill, Aisha. "Voicing the Silent Fear: South Asian Women's Experiences of Domestic Violence." *Howard Journal of Criminal Justice* 43:5 (2004): 465–83.

———. "Reconfiguring 'Honour'-Based Violence as a Form of Gendered Violence." In *Honour, Violence, Women and Islam*, ed. Mohamad Idriss and Tahir Abbas, 218–31. Abingdon: Routledge, 2011.

Goodman Kaufman, Carol. *Sins of Omission: The Jewish Community's Reaction to Domestic Violence—What Needs to Be Done.* Boulder, CO: Westview, 2003.

Goodmark, Leigh. "Autonomy Feminism: An Anti-Essentialist Critique of Mandatory Interventions in Domestic Violence Cases." *Florida State University Law Review* 37:1 (2009–10): 1–48.

Gordon, Kristina, Shacunda Burton, and Laura Porter. "Predicting the Intentions of Women in Domestic Violence Shelters to Return to Partners: Does Forgiveness Play a Role?" *Journal of Family Psychology* 18:2 (2004): 331–38.

Gracia, Enrique. "Unreported Cases of Domestic Violence against Women: Towards an Epidemiology of Social Silence, Tolerance and Inhibition." *Journal of Epidemiology and Community Health* 58 (2004): 536–37.

Graetz, Naomi. *Silence Is Deadly: Judaism Confronts Wifebeating.* Northvale, NJ: Jason Aronson Inc., 1998.

Gray, John. *Men Are from Mars, Women Are from Venus: A Practical Guide for Improving Communication and Getting What You Want in Your Relationship.* San Francisco: Harper, 1993.

Grewal, Zareena. "Death by Culture: How Not to Talk about Islam and Domestic Violence." Institute for Social Policy and Understanding, July 2009. https://www.ispu.org/wp-content /uploads/2017/07/2009_Death-by-Culture.pdf.

———. *Islam Is a Foreign Country.* New York: New York University Press, 2014.

Gross, Rita. *Feminism & Religion: An Introduction.* Boston: Beacon Press, 1996.

Guardi, Jolanda. "Women Reading the Qur'an: Religious Discourse and Islam." *Hawwa* 2:3 (2004): 301–15.

Gubkin, Liora. "'I Will Espouse You with Righteousness and Justice': Domestic Violence and Judaism." In *Violence against Women in Contemporary World Religions: Roots and Cures*, ed. Daniel Maguire and Sa'diyya Shaikh, 193–205. Cleveland: Pilgrim Press, 2007.

Haaken, Janice, and Nan Yragui. "'Going Underground': Conflicting Perspectives on Domestic Violence Shelter Practices." *Feminism & Psychology* 13:1 (2003): 49–71.

Haj-Yahia, Muhammad. "Beliefs about Wife Beating among Palestinian Women: The Influence of Their Patriarchal Ideology." *Violence Against Women* 4:4 (1998): 533–58.

———. "Attitudes of Palestinian Physicians toward Wife Abuse." *Violence Against Women* 19:3 (2013): 376–99.

Hammer, Juliane. *American Muslim Women, Religious Authority, and Activism: More than a Prayer.* Austin: University of Texas Press, 2012.

———. "Gendering Islamophobia: (Muslim) Women's Bodies and American Politics." *Bulletin for the Study of Religion* 42:1 (February 2013): 29–36.

———. "Center Stage: Muslim Women and Islamophobia." In *Islamophobia in America*, ed. Carl Ernst, 107–44. New York: Palgrave, 2013.

———. "Men Are the Protectors of Women: American Muslim Negotiations of Domestic Violence, Marriage, and Feminism." In *Feminism, Law, and Religion*, ed. Marie Failinger, Lisa Schiltz, and Susan Stabile, 237–56. London: Ashgate, 2013.

———. "Marriage in American Muslim Communities." *Religion Compass* 9:2 (2015): 35–44.

———. "To Work for Change: Normativity, Feminism, and Islam." *Journal of the American Academy of Religion* 84:1 (March 2016): 98–112.

———. "Gender Matters: Normativity, Positionality, and the Politics of Islamic Studies." *Muslim World* 106 (October 2016): 655–70.

———. "Muslim Women, Anti-Muslim Hostility, and the State in the Age of Terror." In *Muslims and Contemporary US Politics*, ed. Mohammad Khalil. Cambridge, MA: Harvard University Press, 2019.

Hassouneh-Phillips, Dena. "American Muslim Women's Experiences of Leaving Abusive Relationships." *Health Care for Women International* 22 (2001): 415–32.

———. " 'Marriage Is Half of Your Faith and the Rest Is Fear of Allah': Marriage and Spousal Abuse among American Muslims." *Violence Against Women* 7:8 (2001): 927–46.

———. "Polygamy and Wife Abuse: A Qualitative Study of Muslim Women in America." *Health Care for Women International* 22 (2001): 735–48.

———. "Strength and Vulnerability: Spirituality in Abused American Muslim Women's Lives." *Issues in Mental Health Nursing* 24:6–7 (2003): 681–94.

Hegland, Mary. "Wife Abuse and the Political System: A Middle Eastern Case Study." In *Sanctions and Sanctuary: Cultural Perspectives on the Beating of Wives*, ed. Dorothy Ayers Counts, Judith Brown, and Jacquelyn Campbell, 203–18. Boulder, CO: Westview Press, 1992.

Helba, Cynthia, Matthew Bernstein, Mariel Leonard, and Erin Bauer. "Report on Exploratory Study into Honor Violence (2015) Produced for the US Department of Justice." https://www.ncjrs.gov/pdffiles1/bjs/grants/248879.pdf.

Hibri, Azizah Al-. "An Islamic Perspective on Domestic Violence." *Fordham International Law Journal* 27:1 (2003): 195–219.

Hidayatullah, Aysha. "Inspiration and Struggle: Muslim Feminist Theology and the Work of Elizabeth Schuessler-Fiorenza." *Journal of Feminist Studies in Religion* 25:1 (2009): 162–70.

———. "Muslim Feminist Birthdays." *Journal of Feminist Studies in Religion* 27:1 (2011): 119–22.

———. *Feminist Edges of the Qur'an*. Oxford: Oxford University Press, 2014.

Higginbotham, Evelyn. *Righteous Discontent: The Women's Movement in the Black Baptist Church, 1880–1920*. Cambridge, MA: Harvard University Press, 1994.

Holt, Maria. "Violence against Women in the Context of War: Experiences of Shi'i Women and Palestinian Refugee Women in Lebanon." *Violence Against Women* 19:3 (2013): 316–37.

Holt, Stephanie, Helen Buckley, and Sadhbh Whelan. "The Impact of Exposure to Domestic Violence on Children and Young People: A Review of the Literature." *Child Abuse & Neglect* 32:8 (2008): 796–810.

Hope, Merjanne. "Broken Wings No More." In *Change from Within: Diverse Perspectives on Domestic Violence in Muslim Communities*, ed. Maha Alkhateeb and Salma Abugideiri, 171–82. Herndon, VA: Peaceful Families Project, 2007.

Ibrahim, Nada, and Mohamed Abdalla. "A Critical Examination of Qur'an 4:34 and Its Rele-
vance to Intimate Partner Violence in Muslim Families." *Journal of Muslim Mental Health*
5:3 (2011): 327–49.

Idriss, Mohammad, and Tahir Abbas, eds. *Honour, Violence, Women and Islam*. Abingdon: Routledge, 2011.

Iyengar, Radha. "Does the Certainty of Arrest Reduce Domestic Violence? Evidence from Mandatory and Recommended Arrest Laws." *Journal of Public Economics* 93:1–2 (2009): 85–98.

Jackson, Sherman. *Islam and the Blackamerican: Looking towards the Third Resurrection*. New
York: Oxford University Press, 2005.

———. *Islam and the Problem of Black Suffering*. New York: Oxford University Press, 2009.

Johnson, Michael. "Domestic Violence: It's Not about Gender—Or Is It?" *Journal of Marriage
and Family* 67:5 (2005): 1126–30.

———. *A Typology of Domestic Violence*. Boston: Northeastern University Press, 2008.

Johnson, Sylvester. *African American Religions, 1500–2000: Colonialism, Democracy, and Freedom*.
New York: Cambridge University Press, 2015.

Kahera, Akel. *Deconstructing the American Mosque*. Austin: University of Texas Press, 2002.

Kahf, Mohja. "The Muslim in the Mirror." In *Living Islam Out Loud: American Muslim Women
Speak*, ed. Saleemah Abdul Ghafur, 130–38. Boston: Beacon Press, 2006.

Kalam, Siraha. "My Story." In *Change from Within: Diverse Perspectives on Domestic Violence in
Muslim Communities*, ed. Maha Alkhateeb and Salma Abugideiri, 157–58. Herndon, VA:
Peaceful Families Project, 2007.

Kandiyoti, Deniz. "Bargaining with Patriarchy." *Gender and Society* 2:3 (1988): 274–90.

———. "Gender, Power, and Contestation: Rethinking Bargaining with Patriarchy." In *Feminist Visions of Development: Gender Analysis and Policy*, ed. Cecile Jackson and Ruth Pear-
son, 135–51. London: Routledge, 1998.

———. "Feminist Therapy: Its Use and Implications in South Asian Immigrant Survivors of
Domestic Violence." *Women & Therapy* 30:3–4 (2007): 109–27.

Karim, Jamillah. *American Muslim Women: Negotiating Race, Class, and Gender within the
Ummah*. New York: New York University Press, 2009.

Kausar, Sadia, Sjaad Hussain, and Mohammad Idriss. "Does the Qur'an Condone Domestic
Violence?" In *Honour, Violence, Women and Islam*, ed. Mohammad Idriss and Tahir Abbas,
96–113. Abingdon: Routledge, 2011.

Kiely-Froude, Cameron, and Samira Abdul-Karim. "Providing Culturally Conscious Mental
Health Treatment for African American Muslim Women Living with Spousal Abuse." *Journal of Muslim Mental Health* 4:2 (2009): 175–86.

Kobeisy, Ahmed. *Counseling American Muslims: Understanding the Faith and Helping the People*.
Westport, CT: Praeger, 2004.

———. "Faith-Based Practice: An Introduction." *Journal of Muslim Mental Health* 1:1 (2006):
57–63.

Kort, Alexis. "Dar al-Cyper Islam: Women, Domestic Violence and the Islamic Reformation
on the World Wide Web." *Journal of Muslim Minority Affairs* 25:3 (2005): 363–83.

Koyama, Emi. "Disloyal to Feminism: Abuse of Survivors with the Domestic Violence Shelter System." In *Color of Violence: The INCITE! Anthology*, ed. INCITE! Women of Color
Against Violence, 208–22. Cambridge, MA: South End Press, 2006.

Krause, Joan. "Distorted Reflections of Battered Women Who Kill: A Response to Professor Dressler." *Ohio State Journal of Criminal Law* 4 (2006–7): 555–74.

Kroeger, Catherine Clark, and Nancy Nason-Clark. *No Place for Abuse: Biblical & Practical Resources to Counteract Domestic Violence.* Downers Grove, IL: Intervarsity, 2001.

Kugle, Scott. *Homosexuality in Islam: Critical Reflections on Gay, Lesbian, and Transgender Muslims.* Oxford: Oneworld, 2010.

———. *Living Out Islam: Voices of Gay, Lesbian, and Transgender Muslims.* New York: New York University Press, 2014.

Kulczycki, Andrzej, and Sarah Windle. "Honor Killings in the Middle East and North Africa: A Systematic Review of the Literature." *Violence Against Women* 17:11 (2011): 1442–64.

Kulwicki, Anahid, and June Miller. "Domestic Violence in the Arab American Population: Transforming Environmental Conditions through Community Education." *Issues in Mental Health Nursing* 20:3 (1999): 199–215.

Landesman, Toby. *You Are Not Alone: Solace and Inspiration for Domestic Violence Survivors, Based on Jewish Wisdom.* Seattle: FaithTrust Institute, 2004.

Lasson, Kenneth. "Bloodstains on a 'Code of Honor': The Murderous Marginalization of Women in the Islamic World." *Women's Rights Law Reporter* 30:3–4 (2009): 407–41.

Lawless, Elaine. *Women Escaping Violence: Empowerment through Narrative.* Columbia: University of Missouri Press, 2001.

Lean, Nathan. *The Islamophobia Industry: How the Right Manufactures Fear of Muslims.* London: Pluto Press, 2012.

Lev, Rachel. *Shine the Light: Sexual Abuse and Healing in the Jewish Community.* Boston: Northeastern University Press, 2003.

Levitt, Heidi, and Kimberly Ware. "'Anything with Two Heads Is a Monster': Religious Leaders' Perspectives on Marital Equality and Domestic Violence." *Violence Against Women* 12:12 (2006): 1169–90.

Lockhart, Lettie, and Fran Davis, eds. *Domestic Violence: Intersectional and Culturally Competent Practice.* New York: Columbia University Press, 2010.

Loseke, Doileen, Richard Gelles, and Mary Cavanaugh, eds. *Current Controversies on Family Violence.* London: Sage, 2005.

Love, Erik. *Islamophobia and Racism in America.* New York: New York University Press, 2017.

MacFarlane, Julie. *Islamic Divorce in North America.* New York: Oxford University Press, 2012.

Maguire, Daniel, and Sa'diyya Shaikh, eds. *Violence against Women in Contemporary World Religions: Roots and Cures.* Cleveland: Pilgrim Press, 2007.

Mahmood, Saba. *Politics of Piety.* Princeton: Princeton University Press, 2005.

———. "Feminism, Democracy, and Empire: Islam and the War on Terror." In *Women's Studies on the Edge,* ed. Joan Scott, 81–114. Durham: Duke University Press, 2008.

Mahmood, Saba, and Charles Hirschkind. "Feminism, the Taliban, and Politics of Counter-Insurgency." *Anthropological Quarterly* 75 (2002): 339–54.

Mahmoud, Mohamed. "To Beat or Not to Beat: On the Exegetical Dilemma over Qur'an, 4:34." *Respect* 8 (July 2008): 1–16.

Mahoney, Martha. "Legal Images of Battered Women: Redefining the Issue of Separation." *Michigan Law Review* 90:1 (1991): 1–94.

Majeed, Debra. *Polygyny: What It Means When African American Muslim Women Share Their Husbands.* Gainesville: University Press of Florida, 2015.

Mamdani, Mahmood. *Good Muslim, Bad Muslim: America, the Cold War, and the Roots of Terror.* New York: Three Leaves Press, 2004.

Mann, Ruth. "Emotionality and Social Activism: A Case Study of a Community Development Effort to Establish a Shelter for Women in Ontario." *Journal of Contemporary Ethnography* 31:3 (June 2002): 251–84.

Marin, Manuela. "Disciplining Wives: A Historical Reading of Qur'an 4:34." *Studia Islamica* 97 (2003): 5–40.

Masuzawa, Tomoko. *The Invention of World Religions.* Chicago: University of Chicago Press, 2005.

Mattson, Ingrid. *Story of the Qur'an: Its History and Place in Muslim Life.* Oxford: Blackwell, 2008.

McGoldrick, Monica, Joe Giordano, and Nydia Garcia-Preto, eds. *Ethnicity & Family Therapy.* 3rd ed. New York: Guilford Press, 2005.

Mir-Hosseini, Ziba. "Muslim Women's Quest for Equality: Between Islamic Law and Feminism." *Critical Inquiry* 32:4 (2006): 629–45.

Mir-Hosseini, Ziba, Mulki Al-Sharmani, and Jana Rumminger, eds. *Men in Charge? Rethinking Authority in Muslim Legal Tradition.* Oxford: Oneworld, 2015.

Moe, Angela. "Silenced Voices and Structured Survival: Battered Women's Help Seeking." *Violence Against Women* 13:7 (2007): 676–99.

Mohamed, Jennifer. "A Survivor's Story." In *Change from Within: Diverse Perspectives on Domestic Violence in Muslim Communities,* ed. Maha Alkhateeb and Salma Abugideiri, 183–84. Herndon, VA: Peaceful Families Project, 2007.

Muftic, Lisa, and Jennifer Cruze. "The Laws Have Changed, but What about the Police?: Policing Domestic Violence in Bosnia and Herzegovina." *Violence Against Women* 20:6 (2014): 695–715.

Musawah. *Women's Stories, Women's Lives: Male Authority in Muslim Contexts.* Rabat: Musawah, 2016. http://www.musawah.org/sites/default/files/MusawahGPL2016.pdf.

Nafar, Tamer, Suhell Nafar, and Mahmood Jrery (DAM). "DAM Responds." *Jadaliyya,* December 26, 2012. http://jadaliyya2.koeinbeta.com/Details/27683/DAM-Responds-On-Tradition-and-the-Anti-Politics-of-the-Machine.

Narayan, Uma. *Dislocating Cultures: Identities, Traditions, and Third-World Feminism.* New York: Routledge, 1997.

Nash, Shondrah Tarrezz, and Latonya Hesterberg. "Biblical Framings of and Responses to Spousal Violence in the Narratives of Abused Christian Women." *Violence Against Women* 15:3 (2009): 340–61.

Nason-Clark, Nancy. "When Terror Strikes at Home: The Interface between Religion and Domestic Violence." *Journal for the Scientific Study of Religion* 43:3 (2004): 303–10.

Nelson, Kristina. *The Art of Reciting the Qur'an.* Cairo: AUC Press, 2001.

Nguyen, Tuyen D., ed. *Domestic Violence in Asian American Communities: A Cultural Overview.* Lanham, MD: Lexington Books, 2005.

Nilan, Pam, Argyo Demartoto, Alex Broom, and John Germov. "Indonesian Men's Perceptions of Violence against Women." *Violence Against Women* 20:7 (2014): 869–88.

Obeid, Nadine, Doris Chang, and Jeremy Ginges. "Beliefs about Wife Beating: An Exploratory Study with Lebanese Students." *Violence Against Women* 16:6 (2010): 691–712.

Oliver, William. "Preventing Domestic Violence in the African American Community: The Rationale for Popular Culture Interventions." *Violence Against Women* 6:5 (May 2000): 533–49.

Parthasarathy, Remla. "Identifying and Depicting Culture in Intimate Partner Violence Cases." *Buffalo Journal of Gender, Law & Social Policy* 22 (2013–14): 71–104.

Pinnewala, Parvani. "Good Women, Martyrs, and Survivors: A Theoretical Framework for South Asian Women's Responses to Partner Violence." *Violence Against Women* 15:1 (2009): 81–105.

Pleck, Elizabeth. *Domestic Tyranny: The Making of American Social Policy against Family Violence from Colonial Times to the Present.* Urbana: University of Illinois Press, 1987.

Plesset, Sonja. *Sheltering Women: Negotiating Gender and Violence in Northern Italy.* Stanford: Stanford University Press, 2006.

Potter, Hillary. "Battered Black Women's Use of Religious Services and Spirituality for Assistance in Leaving Abusive Relationships." *Violence Against Women* 13:3 (2007): 262–84.

Profitt, Norma Jean. *Women Survivors, Psychological Trauma, and the Politics of Resistance.* New York: Routledge, 2000.

Puar, Jasbir. *Terrorist Assemblages: Homonationalism in Queer Times.* Durham: Duke University Press, 2007.

Rahim, Habibeh. "Virtue, Gender, and the Family: Reflections on Religious Texts in Islam and Hinduism." *Journal of Social Distress and the Homeless* 9:3 (2000): 187–99.

Raj, Anita, and Jan Silverman. "Violence against Immigrant Women: The Roles of Culture, Context, and Legal Immigrant Status on Intimate Partner Violence." *Violence Against Women* 8:3 (2002): 367–98.

Razack, Sherene. "Domestic Violence and Gender Persecution: Policing the Borders of Nation, Race, and Gender." *Canadian Journal of Women and Law* 8 (1995): 45–65.

———. "A Violent Culture or Culturalized Violence? Feminist Narratives of Sexual Violence against South Asian Women." *Studies in Practical Philosophy* 3:1 (2003): 81–104.

Ritchie, Beth. *Arrested Justice: Black Women, Violence, and America's Prison Nation.* New York: New York University Press, 2012.

———. *Compelled to Crime: The Gender Entrapment of Battered, Black Women.* London: Routledge, 1995.

Rojas Durazo, Ana Clarissa. "Medical Violence against People of Color and the Medicalization of Domestic Violence." In *Color of Violence: The INCITE! Anthology,* ed. INCITE! Women of Color Against Violence, 179–88. Cambridge, MA: South End Press, 2006.

Rudrappa, Sharmila. "Radical Caring in an Ethnic Shelter: South Asian American Women Workers at Apna Ghar, Chicago." *Gender & Society* 18:5 (2004): 588–609.

Ruttenberg, Miriam. "A Feminist Critique of Mandatory Arrest: An Analysis of Gender and Race in Domestic Violence Policy." *American University Journal of Gender & Law* 2 (1994): 171–87.

Sack, Emily. "Battered Women and the State: The Struggle for the Future of Domestic Violence Policy." *Wisconsin Law Review* (2004): 1657–1739.

Said, Edward. *Orientalism.* New York: Pantheon Book, 1978.

Schuler, Sidney. "Women's Rights, Domestic Violence, and Recourse Seeking in Rural Bangladesh." *Violence Against Women* 14:3 (2008): 326–45.

Scott, Rachel. "A Contextual Approach to Women's Rights in the Qur'an: Readings of 4:34." *Muslim World* 99 (January 2009): 60–85.

Seedat, Fatima. "Islam, Feminism, and Islamic Feminism: Between Inadequacy and Inevitability." *Feminist Studies in Religion* 29:2 (Fall 2013): 25–45.

———. "When Islam and Feminism Converge." *Muslim World* 103:3 (2013): 404–20.

Sev'er, Aysan, and Gökçeçiçek Yurdakul. "Culture of Honor, Culture of Change: A Feminist Analysis of Honor Killings in Rural Turkey." *Violence Against Women* 7:9 (2001): 964–98.

Shaikh, Sa'diyya. "A *Tafsir* of Praxis: Gender, Marital Violence, and Resistance in a South African Muslim Community." In *Violence against Women in Contemporary World Religions: Roots and Cures*, ed. Daniel Maguire and Sa'diyya Shaikh, 66–90. Cleveland: Pilgrim Press, 2007.

———. *Sufi Narratives of Intimacy: Ibn 'Arabi, Gender, and Sexuality*. Chapel Hill: University of North Carolina Press, 2012.

Shalhoub-Kevorkian, Nadera, and Suhad Daher-Nashif. "Femicide and Colonization: Between the Politics of Exclusion and the Culture of Control." *Violence Against Women* 19:3 (2013): 295–315.

Sharma, Anita. "Healing the Wounds of Domestic Abuse: Improving the Effectiveness of Feminist Therapeutic Interventions with Immigrant and Racially Visible Women Who Have Been Abused." *Violence Against Women* 7:12 (2001): 1405–28.

Sharma, Arvind, and Katherine Young, eds. *Feminism and World Religions*. Albany: SUNY Press, 1999.

Sharp, Shane. "Resisting Religious Coercive Control." *Violence Against Women* 20:12 (2014): 1407–27.

Silvers, Laury. "'In the Book We Have Left Nothing Out': The Ethical Problem of the Existence of Verse 4:34 in the Qur'an." *Comparative Islamic Studies* 2:2 (2006): 171–80.

Singh, Anneliese, Danica Hays, Barry Chung, and Laurel Watson. "South Asian Immigrant Women Who Have Survived Child Sexual Abuse: Resilience and Healing." *Violence Against Women* 16:4 (2010): 444–58.

Sisters in Islam and Yasmine Masidi. *Are Men Allowed to Beat Their Wives?* Selangor: Sisters in Islam, 2009.

Slezic, Lana. *Forsaken: Afghan Women*. New York: Powerhouse Books, 2007.

Smith, Andrea, Beth Richie, Julia Sudbury, Janelle White, and the INCITE! Anthology co-editors. "The Color of Violence: Introduction." In *Color of Violence: The INCITE! Anthology*, ed. INCITE! Women of Color Against Violence, 1–10. Cambridge, MA: South End Press, 2006.

Sokoloff, Natalie, ed. *Domestic Violence at the Margins: Readings on Race, Class, Gender, and Culture*. New Brunswick: Rutgers University Press, 2005.

Sokoloff, Natalie, and Ida Dupont. "Domestic Violence at the Intersection of Race, Class, and Gender: Challenges and Contributions to Understanding Violence against Marginalized Women in Diverse Communities." *Violence Against Women* 11:1 (2005): 38–64.

Sontag, Susan. *Regarding the Pain of Others*. New York: Picador, 2003.

Spivak, Gayatri. "Criticism, Feminism, and the Institution." Interview with Elizabeth Grosz. *Thesis Eleven* 10–11:1 (February 1985): 175–87.

————. "An Interview with Gayatri Spivak, by Sara Danius and Stefan Jonsson." *Boundary 2* 20:2 (Summer 1993): 24–50.

Sullivan, Courtney, and Courtney Martin, eds. *Click: When We Knew We Were Feminists*. Berkeley: Seal Press, 2010.

Supriya, K. E. "Evocation of and Enactment in *Apna Ghar*: Performing Ethnographic Self-Reflexivity." *Text and Performance Quarterly* 21:4 (2001): 225–46.

Terman, Rochelle. "Islamophobia, Feminism, and the Politics of Critique." *Theory, Culture & Society* 1 (2015): 1–26.

Ting, Laura, and Subadra Panchanadeswaran. "Barriers to Help-Seeking among Immigrant African Women Survivors of Partner Abuse: Listening to Women's Own Voices." *Journal of Aggression, Maltreatment, and Trauma* 18 (2009): 817–38.

Tizro, Zahra. *Domestic Violence in Iran: Women, Marriage, and Islam*. New York: Routledge, 2012.

Twerski, Abraham. *The Shame Borne in Silence: Spouse Abuse in the Jewish Community*. Pittsburgh: Mirkov, 1996.

Volpp, Leti. "Feminism versus Multiculturalism." *Columbia Law Review* 101:5 (2001): 1181–1218.

————. "On Culture, Difference, and Domestic Violence." *American University Journal of Gender, Policy & the Law* 11:1 (2002): 393–99.

————. "Disappearing Acts: On Gendered Violence, Pathological Cultures, and Civil Society." *PMLA* 121:5 (2006): 1631–38.

Wachholz, Sandra, and Baukje Miedema. "Risk, Fear, Harm: Immigrant Women's Perceptions of the 'Policing' Solution to Women Abuse." *Crime, Law and Social Change* 34 (2000): 301–17.

Wadud, Amina. *Qur'an and Woman: Rereading the Sacred Text from a Woman's Perspective*. New York: Oxford University Press, 1999.

————. *Inside the Gender Jihad: Women's Reform in Islam*. Oxford: Oneworld, 2006.

Ware, Kimberly, Heidi Levitt, and Gary Bauer. "May God Help You: Faith Leaders' Perspectives of Intimate Partner Violence within Their Communities." *Violence Against Women* 5:2 (2004): 55–81.

Ware, Rudolph. *The Walking Qur'an*. Chapel Hill: University of North Carolina Press, 2014.

Watlington, Christina, and Christopher Murphy. "The Roles of Religion and Spirituality among African American Survivors of Domestic Violence." *Journal of Clinical Psychology* 62:7 (2006): 837–57.

Weatherholt, Anne. *Breaking the Silence: The Church Responds to Domestic Violence*. Harrisburg, PA: Morehouse, 2008.

Weber, Beverly. *Violence and Gender in the "New" Europe: Islam in German Culture*. New York: Palgrave, 2013.

Weitzman, Susan. *"Not to People Like Us": Hidden Abuse in Upscale Marriages*. New York: Basic Books, 2000.

Welchman, Lynn, and Sara Hossain. *"Honour": Crimes, Paradigms, and Violence against Women*. London: Zed Books, 2005.

White, Evelyn. *Chain, Chain, Change: For Black Women in Abusive Relationships*. Emeryville, CA: Seal Press, 1994.

Williams, Suzan. "Toasted Cheese Sandwiches." In *Change from Within: Diverse Perspectives on Domestic Violence in Muslim Communities*, ed. Maha Alkhateeb and Salma Abugideiri, 159–70. Herndon, VA: Peaceful Families Project, 2007.

Wuthnow, Robert. *Saving America?: Faith-Based Services and the Future of Civil Society*. Princeton: Princeton University Press, 2004.

Yoshioka, Marianne, and Deborah Choi. "Culture and Interpersonal Violence Research: Paradigm Shifts to Create a Full Continuum of Domestic Violence Services." *Journal of Interpersonal Violence* 30:4 (April 2005): 513–19.

Zakar, Rubeena, Muhammad Zakar, and Alexander Kraemer. "Men's Beliefs and Attitudes toward Intimate Partner Violence against Women in Pakistan." *Violence Against Women* 19:2 (2013): 246–68.

INDEX

Abid, Zerqa, 62, 97

Abraham, Margaret, 163, 164, 169–70, 216

Abu Lughod, Lila, 22–23, 245n28

Abugideiri, Hibba, 59, 129–30, 280n6

Abugideiri, Salma, 32, 59–60, 88, 105–8, 108–11, 167

abuse: cycle of, 240–42; recognition of, 89–94

abuse victims/survivors: advising to call police, 128; challenged to finding help, 159–60; communal shaming of, 251n29; not believing, 143–44; providing services to, 21, 152–87; punishing for not protecting children, 251n17, 259n10; reasons for not leaving abusive relationships, 259n9; statistics on, 157–58; stories of, 96–97; who kill abusers, 256–57n29. *See also* battered women

Abused Persons Program, 156

abusers: outing, 145; possibility of reforming, 132, 144, 211–12; women who kill, 256–57n29

abusive relationships: challenges of leaving, 65; children endangered in, 70; danger of murder in, 72, 241; need for support in, 210–11; power and control dynamic in, 205; remaining in, 255n6, 259n9; typical pattern in, 241–42

academic critique: as activism, 21–24; deconstruction and, 22

accountability: of abuser, 145, 184; human, 133–34; individual and collective, 170, 216; of service organizations, 103–4

activism: academic critique and, 21–24; scholarship and, 21–23, 116–51, 232–33

ADAMS (All Dulles Area Muslim Society), 35, 81, 116; FAITH and, 165–66, 168

African American Muslims: dealing with domestic abuse, 121–23; invisibility of, 18–19, 41–44, 73; state surveillance of, 128, 221; as threat to state, 43, 221

After the Trauma, 39, 191

AHA Foundation, 45–46

Ahmed, Ambreen, 252–53n4

Alaska Network on Domestic Violence and Sexual Assault, 265n3

Albarus, Carmeta, 41

Alexander, Marissa, 259n10

Ali, Abdullah Yusuf, 251n20

Ali, Arshad, 264n37

Ali, Ayaan Hirsi, 45

Ali, Kecia, 12, 13, 14, 238, 258n40, 264n3

Ali, Wajahat, 36

Alkhateeb, Maha, 59–60

Alkhateeb, Sharifa, 199; activism of, 58–60; as IFCADV conference Theme Speaker, 200; as new Muslim woman leader, 280n6

al Maghrib Institute, 116–17

Alsultany, Evelyn, 264n37

Alwani, Zainab, 88, 105–8, 147, 167, 257n3

analysis: as critique, 22–24, 233–35; Muslim feminist, 15–19; of texts and sources, 4

Anidjar, Gil, 262n9

anti–domestic violence advocates: burnout in, 4, 57, 104, 154–55, 182, 229; generational differences in, 229–30;

A NOTE ON THE TYPE

This book has been composed in Arno, an Old-style serif typeface in the classic Venetian tradition, designed by Robert Slimbach at Adobe.